You Can Trust
a Skinny Cook

Allison Fishman

You Can Trust a Skinny Cook

WILEY

JOHN WILEY & SONS, INC.

PHOTOGRAPHY BY LUCY SCHAEFFER

Food styling by Simon Andrews

Prop styling by Deborah Williams

Graphic Design by idesign, inc.

Library of Congress Cataloging-in-Publication Data:

Fishman, Allison, 1972-

    You can trust a skinny cook / Allison Fishman.

        p. cm.

Includes index.

ISBN 978-0-470-87635-0 (cloth); ISBN 978-0-0470-94559-9 (ebk); ISBN 978-0-470-94560-5 (ebk); ISBN 978-0-470-94561-2 (ebk)

 1. Reducing diets--Recipes. I. Title.

 RM222.2.F515 2011

 641.5'63--dc22

                           2010023282

Printed in China

10 9 8 7 6 5 4 3 2 1

For Mom, who writes in the margins of her cookbooks. For Dad, who clips the recipes from the paper. You showed me that cooking is a conversation.

contents

acknowledgments

A good cookbook, which I hope this has turned out to be, is a nod to old-fashioned craftsmanship. Craftsmanship never comes easy, and along the way I relied on (and am indebted to) the following guides for their grace, humor, and insight:

Steve Goldberg, who read and improved every page, and Sue Park, who tested each recipe. Food and word friends Harry Eastwood, Andrew Burman, Tamar Haspel, Nikki Elkins, and Michelle Duda.

The Institute for Culinary Education, the NYU Food Studies program, and Tim Harper's graduate journalism classes.

Those of you who gave me a chance to try it for the first time: Martha Stewart, Susan Sugarman, Susan Spongen, Lucinda Scala Quinn, Sarah Carey, John Barricelli, Bob Altman, Heidi Diamond, Linda Corradino, Sara Kozak, Diane Hensley, James Peterson, Francine Segan, Einav Gefen, Melanie Underwood Karmazin, Jennifer Clair, Olivia Buehl, Michael Bernstein, Marge Perry, David

Bonom, Mindy Fox, Mark Ferri, Ben Fink, Ellie Krieger, Kathryn Corro, Bernice Mast, Ellen Jackson, Tia Cannon, Deb Richman, Karen Affinito Greco, Scott Mowbray, Ann Taylor Pittman, Mark Turner, Tracy Weiss, Samantha Paladini, and Christine Connor.

My divine editor, Justin Schwartz. Natalie Chapman, Suzanne Sunwoo, Amy Zarkos, Joline Rivera, Jana Norstrand, David Greenberg, Chandni Patel, Lucy Schaeffer, Simon Andrews, and Deborah Williams, who made sure this book flew first class, nonstop.

The best kind of literary agent, one who knows when the time is right: Stacey Glick.

Aaron Task, who will always try a bite.

And most importantly, all the cooking students who trusted me to guide them from cutting board to skillet, and every friend who shared a recipe.

you can trust a skinny cook

I am a cook, not a nutritionist. There are nutritionists who can tell you what to eat, but this isn't that kind of book. I'm going to show you how to make food that tastes good and is low in calories.

For almost a decade, I was a corporate executive, running around, eating food that was cooked by other people. I was overweight. When I ate at home, it was to everyone's benefit that I didn't cook. I was a disaster in the kitchen.

I left the corporate world and went to culinary school. I wanted to help people who had never learned how to cook (like me) make good food and gain confidence in the kitchen.

And then, something crazy happened. I cooked all morning at school, practiced what I learned at home in the afternoon, ate a lot, and lost 20 pounds. I knew that cooking for myself was the healthiest way to eat for a variety of reasons, but how could a person eat so much and lose weight?

I ATE MORE, BUT IN A DIFFERENT WAY. HERE'S HOW I DID IT.

1. **I nibbled and snacked throughout the day.** Cooks taste their dishes constantly to determine what they need. In school, I was tasting all the time, and as a result, I was never ravenous. I ate small bites all day long instead of three big meals.

2. **I was surrounded by delicious food and said "yes" to everything.** For six months, I was surrounded by perfectly seared steaks, homemade bread, and just-churned ice cream. I did not lose 20 pounds eating rice cakes while lusting after brioche. I ate a little bit of everything and never felt deprived.

3. **I ate what I cooked.** Here's a funny secret that most home cooks already know. If you take the time to prepare a meal, you're in the kitchen with caramelizing onions, sizzling steak, maybe licking the beaters while the cake is baking. What's the cumulative effect of hearing, smelling, watching, touching, and—yes—tasting delicious food as you make it? You're not as hungry when mealtime comes. **Cooking helps you eat less.**

4. **I cooked what I ate.** During my pastry courses at culinary school, I consumed half a day's worth of calories before lunch. At home, I chose to improvise lighter cooking since I was already full of butter, eggs, cream, and sugar. Instead of adding half-and-half to the mashed potatoes, I went with whole milk (see page 160). Instead of a savory breakfast of bacon and eggs, I started making Mexican-style scrambled eggs with salsa (see page 36). When you're in charge of the kitchen, you decide what to eat and how to cook it. This book will equip you with the skills to make intelligent—and tasty—choices.

5. **I moved around a lot.** Cooking is good exercise. When you cook, you're standing, reaching, lifting, bending, and walking. At the end of the day, you've earned your seat. Cooking is a physical activity; when you cook, you're burning calories.

I've kept a healthy weight ever since I graduated from culinary school. And believe me, it's not like I deprive myself. I eat a lot. When I'm not cooking, I'm eating out, learning about new foods and flavor combinations. The more I learn, the more I want to eat.

For some people, it's music. For others, it's art. For me, it's food. I plan to live a long, healthy life eating delicious food every day.

introduction

"**The only time to eat diet food**
IS WHILE YOU'RE WAITING FOR THE STEAK
to cook."

—JULIA CHILD

When it comes to healthy eating, why do we deprive ourselves? We eat egg white omelets, fat-free creams, and sugarless sweeteners. Enjoying in moderation seems like indulging in confusion. For those who live to eat and eat to live, life is a balancing act between pleasure, moderation, and modification. We can't deprive ourselves and expect to be happy or healthy. The sweet spot is in the middle.

This book is designed to help you get to that sweet spot. And to do so, let's agree to the following:

> You Don't Have to Go Hungry to Be Skinny
> Nobody Wants to Be Fat
> Cooking Has to Be Learned (but It's Not Calculus)
> "Skinny" Cooking Is About Balance

YOU DON'T HAVE TO GO HUNGRY TO BE SKINNY

When I say "skinny", I don't mean skin and bones; I mean lean and happy. I'm 5 foot 6 inches and 135 pounds; I pack a lot in there. I'm a size 6 on top and 8 on the bottom, and I like my curves, which is good because with my genes, there's no getting rid of 'em. I can rock a shift dress or a wrap (skip the pencil skirts), and if you see me in pants, I'm wearing heels to give myself a little length.

I could be thinner, but I wouldn't be as healthy. I'll take healthy and happy over scrawny and cranky any day.

Skinny is strong—your best you.

NOBODY WANTS TO BE FAT

I enjoy cooking and eating so much that I've made it my livelihood, but you know what? I don't want to be fat.

No one wants to be overweight. Of course not, it's not healthy. You want to feel energetic while enjoying life, which includes cooking and eating delicious food. You don't want to carry around a backpack filled with brick, and you don't want to carry around unnecessary weight.

But that doesn't mean you need to be afraid of delicious food. One of the biggest obstacles I face when teaching home cooking is my students' fear of calories—whether she's a lean marathoner or a mom trying to lose her baby weight. They're afraid to cook tasty food because they are afraid they'll like it too much.

So what's the alternative? Cook mediocre food? That's no way to live.

COOKING HAS TO BE LEARNED (BUT IT'S NOT CALCULUS)

Home cooking is the best way I know to eat well.

For a recipe to make it into this book, it had to taste great and needed to be simple. I wanted to make sure that even first-time cooks would have success in the kitchen. And so, each recipe had to pass these tests:

1. Are the ingredients natural (something grandma would recognize) and easy to find?
2. Is the recipe easy to make?
3. Will you have fun when you make this?
4. Will you be proud of what you made? Does it pass the friends and family "mmmmm" test?
5. Does it taste good? *Really good?*

Although this is a skinny cookbook, as you can see, calories aren't my first priority. I want to help you cook good-tasting food and enjoy the process. If you don't enjoy making it and it doesn't taste terrific, then who cares if it's lower in calories? Unsatisfying food will have you back in the kitchen, hunting around for something that tastes good. To lose weight and keep it off, you have to eat food that satisfies.

When you follow these recipes, you'll learn how to cook. After you make Garlicky Sautéed Spinach (page 139), Seared Duck Breast with Ginger Bok Choy (page 198), or Pot of Mussels (page 211) a couple of times, you'll know how to do it. You'll start improvising variations on your own. Soon you won't be following recipes. You'll be cooking.

You can do this; we can do this together.

"SKINNY" COOKING IS ABOUT BALANCE

Like it or not, calories count. Picture a seesaw with "calories in" on one side and "calories out" on the other. If you want to lose weight, tip it one way. To gain, tip it the other. To maintain a healthy weight, you need balance.

Calories are an effective tool for keeping track of what you consume. When I was the co-host of *Cook Yourself Thin*, we used a simple equation to figure out how many calories our guests could eat in a day to get to their goal weight:

Take your desired weight and add a zero to it; this is the number of calories you can consume in a day. If you weigh 170 pounds and you (and your doctor) want you to be 140 pounds, consume 1,400 calories a day. At a minimum.

I say "minimum" because that number presumes you lay in bed all day, and we both know you don't. You exercise, of course—it's not possible to be your healthy best without getting that heart rate up, whether it's a long walk around the neighborhood, a hike in the woods, a swim in the ocean, or dancing in front of the mirror. *You've got to shake your groove thang.* Of course you exercise; it's part of a balanced life.

In *So Easy*, my colleague Ellie Krieger recommends the following when allocating a 2,000-calorie diet (the recommendation for moderately active women at a healthy weight):

BREAKFAST: 250–400 CALORIES
LUNCH: 350–500 CALORIES
DINNER: 450–550 CALORIES

Ellie is a nutritionist, and my recipes are in line with her recommendations. You'll notice the calories count above total less than 2,000 calories per day, so you'll have room for snacks and dessert or a drink and still be in the sweet spot. I've included nutritional information for every recipe so you can supplement Weight Watchers, South Beach, Atkins, or any other plan that requires calorie, protein, fat, fiber, or carb counts.

IS THIS BOOK FOR YOU?

This book is for the women and men who put dinner on the table most nights of the week. It is for those who cook and eat at home and seek dependable, delicious recipes.

This book is for a neighbor who tells me she's a great cook but laments: *"I cook everything. I braise, I stew, I grill. . . . You should taste my desserts. My family is lucky. But I hate it. I make these delicious meals for them, and what do I do? I microwave a diet meal every night while they eat my food. Do you know how depressing that is?"*

It is for a generation of college-educated working men and women who never learned to cook and want to gain kitchen confidence.

This book is for food lovers who want a rich macaroni and cheese one night, a skinny scampi the next, and want to enjoy both, guiltlessly.

This book is a gift for a bride-to-be who loves cooking for her fiancée and wants to look her best on her wedding day. It is for young mothers seeking lose-the-baby-fat casseroles (especially now that their kids are in school) and want to prepare simple, tasty dinners.

This book is for dads who will use the book for inspiration, techniques, and tips and will quote calories like it's the score of the big game.

This book is for retirees who are back in the kitchen, with more time to enjoy cooking together. They are newly focused on healthy cooking; they want to run around with their grandchildren for years to come!

This book is for my family, parents, aunts, siblings, cousins, and grandparents, who love to eat. It's in our genes to love food maybe a little too much. It's time to love the food that loves us back.

This book is for home cooks who want to enjoy honest, healthy recipes enhanced by relatable, let's-not-take-it-all-so-seriously tips and sidebars.

Above all, this is for everyone who wants to cook and eat delicious homemade meals.

10 COMMANDMENTS FOR YOUR BEST BODY

1. Be kind to yourself. You're looking for *your* best body, not someone else's. Figure out what that looks like, and let that be your goal.

2. Eat 10 times your desired weight in calories when you're trying to lose weight. To maintain your goal weight, increase that amount. Add more calories if you're exercising or if you're hungry. *Never go hungry.*

3. Exercise. Everyone has something they enjoy doing that gets the heart rate up. Figure out what your thing is and do it.

4. Get enough sleep.

5. Take five. Stress sends your body into "keep the calories" mode; avoid it.

6. Drink water. Fizzy water, flat water, water with mint, orange slice, or cucumber. Make lots of tea. But don't drink your calories. Sure, enjoy that glass of wine, but avoid drinking more than 10 percent of your calories.

7. Fill half your plate with vegetables (and not the starchy ones).

8. Have breakfast and make it at least 250 calories

9. Snack between meals (at least two snacks per day) and have smaller portions at mealtime.

10. Enjoy what you eat. If you don't like it, don't put it in your mouth.

good morning:
breakfast & brunch

i've always liked the

word "breakfast" because it says what it means. You're literally breaking a fast, poor thing! You haven't eaten for ten, maybe twelve hours. Let's get you back on track.

Many dieters think breakfast is a chance to start over. They think they can make amends for last night's steak-and-cheesecake fiasco with a chaste 90-calorie cup of fat-free yogurt. But that's actually going to set you up for a battle with a cheeseburger later.

Too few calories in the morning and you'll be hungry all day. I'm a protein person, so my breakfast needs to have a good amount of it, or I'll have a rumbling tummy midmorning. That's not a happy place for me (or anyone in close proximity to me).

But when I do breakfast right, I'm bright, bouncy, and full of energy. When I don't, I end up with an energy deficit. All day long I'm searching for the calories I should have had earlier.

If you don't feel hungry for a big meal first thing in the morning, have one after you've woken up a bit. A few years ago, I visited a Shaker village in upstate New York, and they described how there would be two breakfasts every day: one small breakfast first thing in the morning to get the Shakers shaking, and a second hot breakfast once the fires were lit to keep them working in the fields until lunch. You can do that too; just let your substantial breakfast switch places with your midmorning snack.

For busy weekday mornings, try the Mexican Breakfast Tortillas (page 36) or the Crisp Bread with Egg and Avocado (page 29), which take less than ten minutes to prepare. If you want a grab-and-go breakfast that you can make ahead, try Banana-Blueberry Bread (page 22) or Sunrise Muffins (page 27).

To make brunch for a crowd, try Beach House Breakfast Casserole (page 30), Spinach and Feta Frittata (page 33), or Breakfast Bread Pudding with Peaches and Blueberries (page 28). Savory breakfast lovers will adore Sweet Potato Hash (page 34). If you've got a sweet tooth, try the Crepes with Sautéed Apples (page 23), which also doubles as dessert.

A good breakfast sets you up for the day. You know you need to eat it; these recipes are so simple that you'll want to make it.

banana-blueberry bread

PREP TIME: 15 minutes TOTAL TIME: 2 hours, including cooking and cooling time MAKES 8 servings SERVING SIZE: Two ½-inch slices

This is the same banana bread recipe I've been making since I was a kid; it's dense with bananas and easy to make. When I taught nursery school, I used to make this recipe with the class. Kids love to cook, and making banana bread is tactile and unfussy, the perfect way to introduce kids to the kitchen.

If you'd rather not act like a kid, feel free to use beaters instead of rolling up your sleeves and getting messy (step 3). You'll end up in the same happy banana bread place, with a bit less banana goo on your hands.

1. Preheat the oven to 350°F.

2. In a medium bowl, whisk together the flour, baking soda, and salt. Put the blueberries in a separate medium bowl and toss with 1 tablespoon of the flour mixture.

3. In a large bowl, combine the sugar, butter, eggs, and bananas and roll up your sleeves. Mash the banana mixture with a potato masher or your hands. Sprinkle the flour mixture on top of the banana mixture and stir with those sticky hands or a wooden spoon until just combined; don't over-mash. Add the floured blueberries and stir gently to incorporate.

4. Coat an 8x4-inch loaf pan with cooking spray and pour the batter into the pan. Bake until the top bounces back when gently pressed, about 1 hour. If you see the edges of the bread browning before the top, cover the loaf with aluminum foil and continue cooking. Transfer the loaf pan to a cooling rack until it's cool enough to handle.

5. Remove the bread from the pan and let the bread finish cooling on the rack for about 1 hour. When cool, slice with a serrated knife and serve.

NUTRITION INFORMATION
(PER SERVING):

CALORIES 301, CARBS 56G, FIBER 2G, PROTEIN 5G, TOTAL FAT 7G, SATURATED FAT 4G

1½ cups all-purpose flour
1 teaspoon baking soda
½ teaspoon kosher salt
1 cup fresh blueberries
1 cup sugar
4 tablespoons (½ stick) unsalted butter, at room temperature
2 large eggs
3 seriously ripe bananas (about 1½ cups mashed)
   Cooking spray

 SKINNY TIP § Smackdown: Blueberries vs. Chocolate Chips If you love chocolate, you can add ½ cup chocolate chips for an additional 50 calories per serving. Seems like a lot, right? Let's compare: Chocolate chips have more than 800 calories per cup while blueberries

have 84 per cup. That's ten times the calories! Yowza.

 SKINNY TIP § Sensible Slices If this is the banana bread I've been making since the 70's, what makes this recipe skinny? Slicing. Instead of serving one honkin'

gone-before-you-know-it piece, I use a serrated knife to cut thin slices after the bread has cooled. That way you get two slices for the caloric price of one. Twice the banana bread means there's more to enjoy.

crepes with sautéed apples

PREP TIME: 40 minutes   TOTAL TIME: 45 minutes   MAKES 4 servings   SERVING SIZE: Three 5½-inch crepes with apples, yogurt, & honey

This simple recipe for crepe batter can be made in a blender in about 2 minutes. After your mad success with this recipe, you'll want to make crepes all the time, so experiment with fillings like jam and fresh berries, lemon curd (page 251), Nutella and banana, walnuts and honey, toasted marshmallows or fresh lemon juice and a dusting of powdered sugar. Each crepe has only 45 calories, so fill at will.

1. Melt 1 tablespoon of the butter in a large skillet over medium-high heat. Add the apples, sprinkle with 1 tablespoon of the sugar and the cinnamon, and cook, turning the slices occasionally, until golden, about 6 minutes. Add the lemon juice, toss to combine, and remove from the heat.

2. Melt the remaining tablespoon of butter in the microwave or a skillet. In a blender, combine the milk, flour, eggs, remaining tablespoon sugar, salt, and melted butter. Blend until smooth.

3. Coat a small nonstick skillet with cooking spray and place over medium-high heat. When the skillet is warm, pour 3 tablespoons of the batter into the pan and quickly swirl to coat the bottom. Cook until the crepe begins to set and turns opaque, 30 seconds to 1 minute. Use a spatula to gently pull the crepe edge from the pan and flip. Cook until lightly browned on the second side, about 30 seconds.

4. Transfer the crepes to a plate and repeat with the remaining batter. Line apples in the center of the crepes and fold the sides toward the center. Repeat with remaining crepes. Serve 3 crepes per person, seam side down, with a dollop of yogurt and a drizzle of honey.

NUTRITION INFORMATION
(PER SERVING):

CALORIES 350, CARBS 57G, FIBER 3G, PROTEIN 12G, TOTAL FAT 10G, SATURATED FAT 5G

- 2 tablespoons unsalted butter
- 4 medium Golden Delicious or other sweet cooking apples, peeled, cored, and cut into ¼-inch slices
- 2 tablespoons sugar
  Big pinch of ground cinnamon
  Juice of ½ lemon
- ¾ cup skim milk
- ½ cup all-purpose flour
- 2 large eggs
  Pinch of kosher salt
  Cooking spray
- 1⅓ cups 2% Greek yogurt
- 3 tablespoons honey

KITCHEN TIP § How Chefs Do It
Measuring 3 tablespoons of batter quickly can get a little tedious. What you want to do is just cover the bottom of the pan with batter. Swirl in what you need, and if you've got too much, pour the excess back into the blender. Yes, this gives your crepe an odd little tail, so you'll probably figure out a way to eyeball it in a hurry.

KITCHEN TIP § A Stitch in Time
Want to make this recipe without cooking for the better part of an hour? Make the crepes in advance. They'll keep in a sealed bag in the fridge for 5 days, and will keep frozen for 1 month. Or, sauté the apples in advance, up to 3 days ahead. To make crepe-making more efficient, you can use two skillets at the same time, a larger skillet to make bigger crepes, or my personal favorite: Find an eager sous chef to help out.

"enjoy what you eat.

IF YOU DON'T LIKE IT,
DON'T PUT IT IN YOUR MOUTH."

sunrise muffins

PREP TIME: 15 minutes TOTAL TIME: 40 minutes MAKES 12 servings SERVING SIZE: 1 muffin

My mother introduced me to these muffins. She's a very good cook, though her priority is an easy clean up. If she sees more than two bowls in a recipe, it's not happening.

I adore this muffin recipe for two reasons (in addition to their tastiness): One, you make the batter in a blender—how fun is that? Two, it calls for a whole orange, skin and all. This recipe is proof that you can be cleanup conscious and a good cook.

This recipe is adapted from Claire Porterfield's version in the *Tea to Greens* cookbook. As for the name, it's a tip-off to the color. The muffins are bright orange, sans food coloring, with flecks of red.

1. Preheat the oven to 375°F. Coat a standard-size 12-cup muffin tin with cooking spray.

2. Put the orange wedges, orange juice, egg, and oil into a blender and blend until smooth.

3. In a medium bowl, whisk together the flour, sugar, baking powder, baking soda, and salt; whisk to incorporate. Make a well in the center of the dry ingredients; pour the orange mixture into it and stir to make a thick batter. Stir in the cranberries.

4. Divide the mixture among the muffin tins, filling the tins about ¾ full, and bake until the muffins are golden and push back when gently pressed, 20 to 25 minutes. Let cool on a rack and enjoy warm or toasted.

NUTRITION INFORMATION (PER SERVING):

CALORIES 175, CARBS 31G, FIBER 1G, PROTEIN 2G, TOTAL FAT 5G, SATURATED FAT 0G

  Cooking spray
1 navel orange, cut into eighths
½ cup orange juice
1 large egg
¼ cup vegetable oil
1½ cups all-purpose flour
¾ cup sugar
1 teaspoon baking powder
1 teaspoon baking soda
1 teaspoon kosher salt
½ cup dried cranberries, chopped

 SKINNY TIP § Grab a Partner! The calorie count for these muffins is so low that you might want to have two for breakfast. Or, enjoy your muffin toasted and spread with a teaspoon of butter and a cup of cold skim milk and the calorie total comes to 291.

 KITCHEN TIP § Muffins Chillin' Out One of the pastry chefs I worked with taught me to turn muffins on their side as soon as you can touch them, about 5 minutes after they come from the oven. When you tilt the muffins in their nooks, they release steam and cool more efficiently.

 KITCHEN TIP § Muffin Tops These muffins come out different every time I make them as a result of the orange I choose. Pithy oranges (more white stuff) make flatter muffins, while less pithy ones tend to make muffins with a dome. Though they look different, they taste exactly the same.

breakfast bread pudding with peaches and blueberries

PREP TIME: 30 minutes   TOTAL TIME: 2 hours   MAKES 8 servings   SERVING SIZE: 4½ by 3-inch piece

If we can have muffins, pancakes, and waffles for breakfast, why not a little bread pudding? Typically, I don't have the kind of sweet tooth that has me leaning toward the sugary stuff, but when you start adding custard, plus my favorite fruit combo of peaches and blueberries, I'm in!

1. Coat a 9x13-inch baking dish with cooking spray, and put the bread cubes in the dish. Add the peaches and blueberries to the bread cubes, sprinkle with the cinnamon, and toss to combine.

2. Meanwhile, whisk the eggs together in a medium bowl. Add the milk, half-and-half, sugar, vanilla, and salt and whisk to blend.

3. Pour the egg mixture over the bread. Press the solids gently to ensure that the bread is submerged. Let sit until the bread is soaked at room temperature for 30 minutes, or in the refrigerator, covered, overnight.

4. Meanwhile, preheat the oven to 350°F.

5. Place baking dish in the oven and bake until the top is golden and springs back when pushed gently, about 45 minutes to 1 hour. Cool until set, cut into portions, and serve warm or at room temperature.

NUTRITION INFORMATION (PER SERVING):
CALORIES 344, CARBS 49G, FIBER 2G, PROTEIN 10G, TOTAL FAT 9G, SATURATED FAT 4G

Cooking spray
1   8-ounce loaf stale Italian bread, cubed, (about 8 cups; see tip below)
1   1-pound bag frozen sliced peaches, defrosted, or 3 fresh peaches, cut into wedges
1   pint fresh blueberries, or 2 cups frozen blueberries, defrosted and drained of liquid
¼   teaspoon ground cinnamon
6   large eggs
2   cups whole milk
1   cup half-and-half
¾   cup sugar
1   teaspoon vanilla extract
Large pinch of kosher salt

SKINNY TIP § How'd You Get That Calorie Count So Low? **Bread puddings are often made with challah, brioche, or other rich, dense, eggy breads. For this bread pudding, we use an 8-ounce loaf of Italian bread, which has only 600 calories in the whole loaf. That gives us room to use the tasty stuff, like whole eggs and half-and-half. Enjoy the indulgence!**

KITCHEN TIP § Why Stale Bread? **When Italian bread goes stale, it's because the moisture inside the bread has evaporated. This is a good thing for bread pudding because you can replace that moisture with custard (eggs, milk, half-and-half) by letting the stale bread soak before baking. If you have fresh bread, facilitate the evaporation by putting your bread cubes in a 325°F oven until the bread gets firm, 15 to 20 minutes.**

crisp bread with egg and avocado

PREP TIME: 10 minutes TOTAL TIME: 10 minutes MAKES 1 serving SERVING SIZE: 2 topped crackers

Crisp bread rules. Here's why: In this time of 500-calorie bagels and 150-calorie slices of bread, crisp bread offers an alternative: You can get the crunch, flavor, and open-face sandwich experience for only 45 calories. There's nothing I can put on toast or a bagel that I wouldn't put on crisp bread, plus I can eat more of it. And eating more, guiltlessly, is my goal (for more topping ideas, see tip on page 209).

Crisp breads can be found in the cracker aisle or near the deli counter. Look for brands like Wasa and RyKrisp.

1. Put the avocado in a bowl with the lime juice and salt. Mash with a fork until creamy-chunky.

2. Divide the mashed avocado between slices of crisp bread, and spread to cover. Top the avocado with the chopped egg. Season the egg with salt and a few grinds of pepper. Sprinkle the cilantro leaves (if desired) and sunflower seeds on top.

NUTRITION INFORMATION
(PER SERVING):

CALORIES 300, CARBS 28G, FIBER 9G, PROTEIN 12G, TOTAL FAT 17, SATURATED FAT 3G

- ½ ripe Hass avocado
- 1 tablespoon fresh lime juice
  Kosher salt
- 2 pieces multigrain crisp bread
- 1 hard-boiled egg (see Deviled Eggs, page 102), peeled and chopped
  Freshly ground black pepper
  8 to 10 cilantro leaves (optional)
- 1 teaspoon roasted salted sunflower seeds

KITCHEN TIP § Egg Slicer? Grandpa Was Right Remember those old-fashioned egg slicers—the kind that looked like teeny banjos with metal strings? At first I dismissed this tool. After all, what could be more of a unitasker than an egg slicer?

And then I realized it's the perfect tool for slicing any fragile ingredient, like goat cheese, roasted beets, or button mushrooms. It might be called an egg slicer, but in actual fact it's a fragile ingredient slicer.

When you thinly slice fragile ingredients, you can enjoy the flavors for many more bites. For this recipe, if you have an egg slicer, forgo the mashing and chopping. Simply slice the egg and avocado and layer, alternating, on crisp bread.

beach house breakfast casserole

PREP TIME: 30 minutes TOTAL TIME: 2 hours 15 minutes or overnight MAKES 8 servings SERVING SIZE: 4½ by 3-inch piece

To feed a crowd that wants a long and lazy brunch instead of breakfast and lunch, you need something hearty. This breakfast casserole will have you out in the sun and surf, taking long bike rides, and burning tons of calories without thinking about it. Plus, a casserole is a lot less labor-intensive than flipping pancakes for a crowd, and you can make it the night before.

1. Heat the oil in a medium skillet over medium-high heat. Add the sausage and cook, breaking it up with a wooden spoon, until the sausage is warmed through, about 5 minutes. Remove the skillet from the heat.

2. Coat a 9x13-inch baking dish with cooking spray and put the bread cubes in the dish. Layer the spinach, cheese, and cooked sausage on top of the bread.

3. In a medium bowl, whisk together the eggs, milk, salt, Worcestershire sauce, and hot sauce (if desired). Pour over the sausage mixture and press solids gently to be sure that the bread is submerged. Cover and let the casserole sit at room temperature for 30 minutes or in the refrigerator, covered, overnight. I know, it looks a little flat. Don't worry, it will soufflé (puff) as it cooks.

4. Preheat the oven to 350°F.

5. Put the casserole in the oven and cook until set, about 45 minutes. If the casserole is coming straight from the refrigerator, let it come to room temperature before cooking, or cook for an additional 10 to 15 minutes. Let cool for 5 minutes, slice, and serve warm.

NUTRITION INFORMATION
(PER SERVING):

CALORIES 365, CARBS 21G, FIBER 2G, PROTEIN 22G, TOTAL FAT 22G, SATURATED FAT 8G

- 1 tablespoon vegetable oil
- 12 ounces turkey or chicken breakfast sausage, removed from casing
  Cooking spray
- 10 slices sandwich bread, cubed (about 6 cups; see tip right)
- 1 10-ounce package frozen spinach, defrosted and drained
- 1½ cups shredded sharp cheddar cheese (about 6 ounces)
- 6 large eggs
- 2 cups skim milk
- 1 teaspoon salt
- ½ teaspoon Worcestershire sauce
  A few shakes hot sauce (optional, plus to serve at the table)

SKINNY TIP § *Love Me, Love My Sausage* I adore pork products like bacon and sausage. I recommend chicken or turkey sausage for this recipe because most brands have 70 percent less fat than pork sausage, which means you're saving a lot of calories. Because it has less fat, chicken or turkey sausage might not break apart as easily as pork sausage when you cook it, so you might need to give it a rough chop prior to cooking. Experiment to find your favorite brand; there are some terrific sausages out there.

 KITCHEN TIP § *Do You Like It Squidgy?* If you choose to use bread slices straight out of the package, you'll end up with a slightly squidgy casserole, almost like a soufflé. If you like that, proceed. If you want a firmer casserole, dry the bread slices by popping them in a 375°F oven for 6 to 8 minutes, or leave them on a cooling rack at room temperature for 4 hours or overnight. Most cooks prefer using stale bread, as it's an opportunity to replace flavorless water moisture with custard (see Breakfast Bread Pudding tip, page 28). Cook's choice!

SKINNY TIP § *Best Bread?* The bread aisle gives you lots of options, from white to whole wheat and oatmeal to multigrain, and the per-slice calorie count really runs the gamut. I made this recipe with a basic slice of bread, which weighs in at about 70 calories. Use your favorite, and if you're using a bigger slice, adjust the recipe accordingly so that you have about 6 cups of bread cubes.

"Unsatisfying food will have you back in the kitchen, hunting for something that tastes good."

spinach and feta frittata

PREP TIME: 15 minutes TOTAL TIME: 30 minutes MAKES 6 servings SERVING SIZE: 1 large wedge

Though they sound fancy, frittatas are really just one-skillet egg casseroles with stuff in them. Think of them as a crustless quiche, except that instead of baking the quiche (and making a crust), you cook the frittata on the stovetop, with heat cooking the eggs from the bottom, then pop it under the broiler to finish cooking from the top.

And as good as it is for breakfast, I love frittata as a light dinner with a salad or as a savory snack. Serve it warm or at room temperature; this dish improves as it sits.

1. Place an oven rack 5 inches from the broiler element and turn the broiler on.

2. Heat a large oven-safe nonstick skillet over medium heat and add the olive oil. When warm, add the spinach, basil, and ½ teaspoon salt and cook, turning with coated tongs, until wilted, 2 to 3 minutes. Remove the spinach from the pan with tongs and transfer to a plate.

3. Add the onion to the olive oil in the same pan and cook, stirring, until softened, 3 to 5 minutes. Gently crush the oregano with your fingers (releasing fragrance— mmm!), and add to the skillet. Return the wilted spinach to the pan; add the roasted peppers, olives, and red pepper flakes, and heat through.

4. Gently beat the eggs in a medium bowl with the remaining ½ teaspoon salt. Add the egg mixture and feta to the skillet. Cook the eggs gently, pushing the cooked eggs from the bottom of the pan with a spatula for the first minute or two. When the eggs are almost set, after 5 to 7 minutes, place the skillet under the broiler and cook until puffed, lightly browned, and set, 3 to 5 minutes.

5. Let the frittata cool for 2 to 3 minutes, then run a flexible spatula around the edge of the skillet to loosen the frittata. Continue to run the spatula under the frittata to be sure it is loose. Slide the frittata out of the platter, or invert the frittata onto a serving skillet or a large cutting board, cut into wedges, and serve. If removing the frittata from the skillet seems a little intimidating, bring the skillet to the table and serve family style. Remember, the skillet is hot, so use a trivet and warn those at the table with curious hands.

NUTRITION INFORMATION
(PER SERVING):
CALORIES 219, CARBS 4G, FIBER 1G, PROTEIN 16G, TOTAL FAT 16G, SATURATED FAT 5G

- 1 tablespoon olive oil
- 6 ounces baby spinach (or frozen, defrosted, and drained)
- ½ cup gently packed torn fresh basil leaves
- 1 teaspoon kosher salt
- 1 small red onion, chopped
- ½ teaspoon dried oregano
- ¼ cup drained and thinly sliced roasted red peppers
- ⅓ cup pitted kalamata olives, roughly chopped
- Pinch of red pepper flakes
- 12 large eggs
- 2 ounces feta cheese, crumbled (about ½ cup)

KITCHEN TIP § This Frittata Is Just a Framework Frittatas are a great way to use up leftover side dishes like Crispy Roast Broccoli (page 138) or Garlicky Sautéed Spinach (page 139). When filling, be sure to cook all the excess liquid out of the vegetables (see step 2), because too much liquid will prevent the egg from setting.

SKINNY TIP § More Calories, Please? This flavorful frittata is almost too light in calories. Serve it with a side of toast, or better yet, Roasted Baby Potatoes with Caramelized Garlic (page 180) or the roasted potato combo that's the first step of Sweet Potato Hash (page 34), which has fewer than 120 calories for a ⅔-cup serving.

sweet potato hash

PREP TIME: 20 minutes TOTAL TIME: 1 hour MAKES 4 servings SERVING SIZE: ¾ cup hash with 1 egg

Do you love a savory breakfast? Steak and eggs, leftover pizza, or even cold moo shu pork (out of the container)? Ain't no shame in that game, and I'm right beside you, reaching for the hot sauce. In this recipe, you can rework a favorite—hash—by substituting some sweet potatoes for the starchy and savory condiments for the pork products. And, yes, you still get that drippy poached egg on top.

1. Preheat the oven to 425°F.

2. Place the sweet and red potato cubes in a roasting pan and toss with 1 tablespoon of the oil and the salt. Be sure that the potatoes are spread in one layer. Put the pan in the oven and cook until the potatoes are soft and golden, about 30 minutes. Let cool for 5 minutes before removing so that they release from pan.

3. Heat the remaining tablespoon oil in a large nonstick or cast-iron skillet over medium-high heat. Add the onion and jalapeño to the pan and season with salt. Cook, stirring, until golden, about 5 minutes.

4. Add the cooked potatoes, ketchup, and Worcestershire sauce to the skillet. Season with salt and press the mixture into the skillet, smashing the potatoes. Reduce the heat to medium and cook until a golden crust forms, about 5 minutes. (If you made the potatoes in advance and they're coming straight out of the fridge, you may need to cook them a bit longer.)

5. Meanwhile, add enough water to a medium saucepan so that it measures 2 inches high from the bottom of the pot (eyeball it—it's about the length of your thumb). Add the vinegar and bring to a gentle simmer. Crack an egg into a small cup and slide it into the simmering water. Poach until the white is set and the yolk is still runny, 3 to 3½ minutes.. Remove the egg from the water with a slotted spoon and drain on paper towels. Repeat until all the eggs are used.

6. Serve the hash topped with poached eggs and garnished with parsley. Don't forget to serve with hot sauce for the masochists.

NUTRITION INFORMATION
(PER SERVING):

CALORIES 316, CARBS 43G, FIBER 5G, PROTEIN 11G, TOTAL FAT 12G, SATURATED FAT 2G

2 large sweet potatoes, peeled and cut into ½-inch cubes
1 large red-skinned or baking potato, peeled and cut into ½-inch cubes
2 tablespoons vegetable oil
1 teaspoon kosher salt, plus more to taste
1 medium red onion, chopped
1 jalapeño, chopped (with seeds if you like heat)
¼ cup ketchup
1½ tablespoons Worcestershire sauce
1 tablespoon white wine vinegar
4 large eggs
2 tablespoons chopped fresh parsley
   Hot sauce, for serving

KITCHEN TIP § *Yesterday's Dinner Is Today's Shortcut* Rumor has it that hash was born when a frontier cook needed a way to finish last night's leftover corned beef and mashed potatoes. Follow his lead. Roast the potatoes in advance and this recipe takes almost no time at all. Make the potatoes as a side dish for dinner, and your breakfast hash the next day is more than halfway done.

KITCHEN TIP § *No Vinegar?* If you don't have white wine vinegar, any acidic liquid will do the trick: cider vinegar, lemon juice, or even 2 tablespoons of white wine. The acid keeps the egg tight and together and prevents it from flowing all over the pan. Gently simmering water helps too; boiling water will break the egg apart, and you'll end up with something that resembles egg drop soup!

KITCHEN TIP § *Cast-Iron Is the Original Nonstick* Nonstick skillets have a special coating that prevents food from sticking to them. Unfortunately, this coating also keeps these skillets from getting as hot as their uncoated cousins.

Cast-iron skillets get very hot and are able to retain their heat. That's part of the reason many home cooks choose cast iron for deep-frying; the hot oil is more likely to remain at a stable temperature.

If you want to make hash with a crispy edge, reach for a well seasoned cast-iron skillet, and smash the hash down into it. Don't fuss with it; just let it cook, as the crisp edge will develop only when the potato is in contact with the hot skillet.

mexican breakfast tortillas

PREP TIME: 10 minutes   TOTAL TIME: 10 minutes   MAKES 1 serving   SERVING SIZE: 2 tortillas with eggs

If you want eggs for breakfast but don't want to commit to a knife-and-fork meal, this is the breakfast to choose. It's fast and makes use of pantry ingredients like pickled jalapeños and salsa that will wake you up. Grab it and go.

1. Warm the tortillas according to the package directions.

2. Heat the oil in a small nonstick skillet over medium heat. Add the scallion and cook, stirring, until softened, about 1 minute. Turn the heat down to medium-low, crack the eggs into the skillet, scramble with your spatula, and season with salt; the eggs should cook in about 30 seconds. Remove from the heat while still slightly loose; they will continue to cook.

3. Lay the warmed tortillas on a plate (or a grab-and-go paper towel), and layer the eggs, salsa, cilantro, and jalapeños (if desired) on the tortillas. Fold and enjoy warm.

NUTRITION INFORMATION
(PER SERVING):
CALORIES 302, CARBS 25G, FIBER 4G, PROTEIN 16G, TOTAL FAT 16G, SATURATED FAT 4G

2   small corn tortillas
1   teaspoon vegetable oil
1   scallion, green and white parts, chopped
2   large eggs
    Pinch of kosher salt
2   tablespoons salsa
A   few sprigs cilantro
A   few pickled jalapeños (optional)

KITCHEN TIP § Kiss of Fire Tortilla packages generally tell you to heat the tortillas in a dry skillet or the microwave. This will make them warm and pliable, but if you like the flavor of a charred tortilla (and have a gas stovetop), here's how to do it: Turn the flame to medium and place the tortillas directly on the burner until they begin to char, about 30 seconds per side. Use tongs to flip the tortilla. Remove from the flame and keep warm under a towel. Keep an eye on these as they cook because you are playing with fire, after all.

salad days:

crisp salads & homemade dressings

"salad days" is a phrase

from Shakespeare's *Antony and Cleopatra*. Cleopatra uses the term when describing her romance with Caesar, back in the "salad days" of her youth. She is regretting the Caesar romance and a time when she was young and not yet a woman of the world, a time when she didn't think about consequence. Sorta like when you were a teenager playing three sports and could plow through a box of Chips Ahoy without gaining a pound.

But I digress. Point is, this chapter takes a have-your-Caesar-and-croutons-too approach to salad. These salads are high in flavor and low in calories (most have fewer than 160 calories per serving). They are designed to put you back in the days when you didn't have to think about consequences.

They all offer something crunchy and delicious, like Maple-Glazed Pecans (page 53), Garlic and Herb Croutons (page 56), or toasted walnuts. I've included a thick homemade Caesar dressing (page 56) that you'll soon be bottling for your friends and a Carrot-Ginger Dressing (page 61), exactly like the one you've enjoyed at Japanese restaurants (but can't find in the grocery store). There are two salads with bacon. Real bacon. And one of them has a gooey poached egg sitting right on top, just like they do it in French bistros.

In addition, you've got the classics, like an Iceberg Wedge with Creamy Blue Cheese Dressing (page 58), Greek Salad (page 47), plus a steakhouse-style Spinach Salad (page 54). And, because vegetables change with the calendar, I include a few seasonal winners, like Asparagus Tangle with Parmesan Vinaigrette (page 49), Marinated Tomatoes (page 43), and Roasted Beet Salad with Goat Cheese and Walnuts (page 45).

So turn the page and let's get started. These are *your* salad days.

arugula salad with parmesan and truffle oil

PREP TIME: 5 minutes TOTAL TIME: 5 minutes MAKES 6 servings SERVING SIZE: 2 cups

This is the salad I make when someone shows up for dinner unexpectedly. It calls for five ingredients I like to keep around: sunflower seeds (freezer), Parmesan cheese (fridge), white truffle oil (pantry), a container of pre-washed baby arugula (fridge), and some sort of acid, either vinegar or lemon juice (arm's reach). It's so simple that you can throw it together in 3 minutes. Between this salad and an omelet (page 233), you'll have one happy, well-fed unexpected guest.

1. In a large bowl, combine the arugula, sunflower seeds, and Parmesan cheese. Drizzle with the truffle oil and a squeeze of lemon juice (or the sherry vinegar); toss to combine. Taste and season with salt and pepper as needed.

NUTRITION INFORMATION
(PER SERVING):

CALORIES 89, CARBS 2G, FIBER 1G, PROTEIN 3G, TOTAL FAT 8G, SATURATED FAT 2G

- 1 5-ounce box baby arugula
- ¼ cup roasted salted sunflower seeds
- ¼ cup grated Parmesan cheese
- 1½ tablespoons white truffle oil
  Squeeze of ½ lemon, or 2 teaspoons sherry vinegar
  Kosher salt and coarsely ground black pepper

KITCHEN TIP § Truffle Oil Fresh truffles are expensive. White truffle oil is a less expensive option, though it's not exactly cheap. A 2-ounce bottle can be found online for under $12. As always, you'll be rewarded for a volume purchase: An 8½-ounce bottle is under $30. Truffle oil is a finishing oil, which means you don't want to cook with it, but you do want to drizzle it . . . on risotto, an omelet, or roasted vegetables after they've come from the oven. Truffle oil is flavorful, so a little goes a long way. In this recipe, 1½ tablespoons is all that's needed to dress a salad for six. Consider it instead of a bottle of wine next time you're invited to a dinner party. It's a unique gift and will be enjoyed long after the wine is gone.

KITCHEN TIP § Shaved Parmesan You know those long, thin pieces of Parmesan that accompany salads in posh restaurants? They're easy to make at home. Just take a vegetable peeler and a wedge of Parmesan, and shave strips from the wedge (start with a corner for better leverage). It's simple and the kind of thing you can't buy; you have to make it.

marinated tomatoes

PREP TIME: 15 minutes TOTAL TIME: 45 minutes MAKES 4 servings SERVING SIZE: ¾ cup

My mom made a version of this recipe for me a few months after I graduated from culinary school. When she told me it had two kinds of dried herbs and garlic powder, I turned my nose up at it; after all, I was now a culinary professional and committed to fresh herbs. Garlic powder? *Puh-lease!*

Wrong, wrong, wrong. The flavor wouldn't be the same (nor would the salad last as long) with fresh parsley, oregano, and garlic. Today I use a lot of dried parsley, especially when making coatings for chicken cutlets (page 190) or croutons (page 56), and I almost exclusively use dried oregano. Dried herbs keep their color and stick to a coating far better than fresh. Plus, they're much less expensive and keep for months.

Special thanks to Mom's friend Kay Teagardner, who grew up on a family farm in Ohio. This was one of her aunt's favorite recipes. When it comes to making homegrown food taste good, farmers trump food snobs every time.

NUTRITION INFORMATION
(PER SERVING):

CALORIES 148, CARBS 6G, FIBER 2G, PROTEIN 1G, TOTAL FAT 14G, SATURATED FAT 2G

- 1 pound ripe tomatoes, cut into wedges
- ¼ cup olive oil
- 3 tablespoons red wine vinegar
- 1½ tablespoons dried parsley
  Greens of 1 scallion, chopped
- ½ teaspoon dried oregano
- 1 teaspoon kosher salt
- ½ teaspoon sugar
- ½ teaspoon garlic powder
- ¼ teaspoon coarsely ground black pepper

1. Place the tomatoes in a resealable container. In a small bowl, whisk together olive oil, vinegar, parsley flakes, scallion greens, oregano, salt, sugar, garlic powder, and black pepper. Pour the marinade over the tomatoes. Cover and marinate at room temperature for at least 30 minutes or refrigerate for up to 5 days.

2. Allow the tomatoes to come to room temperature before eating.

 KITCHEN TIP § Shake It Up Since you've put the tomatoes in a resealable container, flip them every so often so they can soak evenly in the juice of the marinade

 SKINNY TIP § Tomato Liquid Gold If you let these tomatoes sit overnight, you might be surprised by how much liquid is in the container the next morning. The salt in the marinade pulls a lot of liquid from the tomatoes. Bonus! Let's use that tasty liquid. Brush a nice thick piece of

bread with olive oil, toast it in a skillet or grill it, top it with the tomatoes, and drench it in the liquid. Yum. Or, use it for dunking yesterday's bread. Or, tweak the recipe a bit and turn it into a pasta sauce. Assemble your ingredients but don't combine them; sauté the tomatoes in 2 tablespoons of oil and add the remainder of the vinaigrette to the skillet once the tomatoes burst. Toss the sauce with spaghetti or capellini, and finish with torn fresh basil. Then invite me over, 'kay?

 KITCHEN TIP § But What Kind of Tomatoes? Whatever kind is best where and when you're buying them. Out of season, I like baby and grape tomatoes. In season, anything will do. Beefsteaks are terrific raw, or you can play with heirloom varieties. Personally, I'm a sucker for homegrown and, yes, here in Brooklyn you do get little tomato plants growing out of the sidewalks in front of restaurants in the summer. If you grow your own, please share! The marinade is on me.

roasted beet salad with goat cheese and walnuts

PREP TIME: 30 minutes TOTAL TIME: 1 hour 15 minutes MAKES 6 servings SERVING SIZE: 1 cup

Beets, goat cheese, and walnuts are classic partners; they're often featured together in salads, pastas, and even soups. But sometimes, someone puts these ingredients together in a way that's fresh, that makes you see them differently.

One snowy night last winter, the kind when no one leaves their apartment, my friend Dennis invited me to dinner at Minetta Tavern in Manhattan and recommended their version of this combo. It was stunning, with deep red beets, bright white goat cheese, and fresh herbs scattered about. The next day I needed to have it again, so I made this version. It is my favorite snowed-in salad.

1. Preheat the oven to 425°F.

2. Scrub the beets and place on a large piece of aluminum foil. Toss with 1 tablespoon of the olive oil and a generous pinch of salt and pepper. Fold the foil to create a packet for the beets and place the packet on a baking sheet. Place in the oven and cook for 45 minutes to 1 hour, until the tip of a paring knife slides easily into the beets. When cool enough to handle, trim, peel, and cut into wedges.

3. While the beets are cooking, place the walnuts on a baking sheet and toast in the oven until fragrant, 8 to 10 minutes. Remove from the oven, let cool for 5 minutes, and roughly chop.

4. In a small bowl, combine the goat cheese, milk, and chives. Stir with a fork to make a thick sauce. Season to taste with salt and pepper.

5. To assemble, spoon the goat cheese sauce on each plate. Top the sauce with beets, toasted walnuts, and parsley. Season the beets with salt and pepper and drizzle with the remaining 1½ tablespoons of oil.

NUTRITION INFORMATION (PER SERVING):

CALORIES 158, CARBS 9G, FIBER 3G, PROTEIN 6G, TOTAL FAT 12G, SATURATED FAT 4G

- 1 pound beets, without greens (see tip below)
- 2½ tablespoons olive oil Kosher salt and freshly ground black pepper
- ⅓ cup chopped walnuts
- 4 ounces fresh goat cheese, at room temperature
- ¼ cup skim milk
- 1 teaspoon chopped fresh chives
- ¼ cup chopped fresh parsley

 KITCHEN TIP § Alternatives to Roasting? If you don't want to roast your beets, you can boil them. Put medium beets (about 2½ inches in diameter) in a pot of salted water, bring it to a simmer, and let them cook for about 25 minutes. If your beets are larger or smaller, adjust the cooking time accordingly. Poke them with a paring knife before you drain the cooking water to be sure they're cooked through.

 KITCHEN TIP § Peeling Beets Peeling beets is fun. After they have cooked and cooled, you can push the skin with your fingers, and it slips right off. But be forewarned: Beets will stain whatever they come in contact with, so protect your hands with plastic gloves, or wash your hands with soap immediately after peeling the beets.

 KITCHEN TIP § Beet Greens If you can purchase beets with the greens still attached, do. Beet greens are delicious sautéed on their own as a side vegetable or tossed with pasta. Separate the greens from the beets and keep them wrapped in a plastic bag in the vegetable bin for up to 3 to 5 days. If you've never had 'em, you're in for a treat (see recipe for Beet Greens with Pine Nuts, page 149).

bistro salad with warm bacon vinaigrette

PREP TIME: 15 minutes TOTAL TIME: 15 minutes MAKES 4 servings SERVING SIZE: 1½ cups

This recipe is decadent, and exactly the kind of thing you won't find in diet cookbooks. Bacon? Poached eggs? On a salad?

Yes, that's exactly where I want them. We're not having a three-egg omelet with cheddar and ¼ pound of bacon on the side; we're making salad for four, using 1 slice of bacon. It's crunchy. It's smoky. It's just a little.

And because we sauté those shallots in bacon fat, the smoky bacon flavor travels far. Remember, a tablespoon of bacon fat is just as caloric as other fats. Yes, it has more saturated fat than olive oil, which is why we're going easy on it. Going easy, not going without.

1. Add enough water to a medium pot so that it comes at least 2 inches from the bottom. Add the white wine vinegar and bring to a gentle simmer. Crack an egg into a small cup and slide it into simmering water. Repeat until all the eggs are used. Poach the eggs until the whites are set and the yolks are still runny, 3½ to 4 minutes. Using a slotted spoon, remove the eggs one at a time and drain on paper towels.

2. Heat the olive oil in a medium skillet over medium heat and add the bacon. Cook until it begins to crisp, about 3 minutes. Add the shallot and cook until it softens and begins to brown, 3 minutes. You may need to tilt the pan to keep bacon and shallot submerged. Add the red wine vinegar to the skillet, and use a wooden spoon to scrape up the browned bits from the bottom. Remove the skillet from the heat, whisk in the mustard, and add the frisée to the pan. Coat the frisée with the dressing and season to taste with salt and pepper. Divide the salad among plates and top with a poached egg.

NUTRITION INFORMATION
(PER SERVING):

CALORIES 154, CARBS 4G, FIBER 2G, PROTEIN 8G, TOTAL FAT 12G, SATURATED FAT 3G

- 1 tablespoon white wine vinegar
- 4 large eggs
- 1 tablespoon olive oil
- 1 strip bacon, cut into ½-inch-wide pieces
- 1 shallot, minced
- 2 tablespoons red wine vinegar
- ½ teaspoon Dijon mustard
- 2 medium heads frisée lettuce torn into bite-size pieces (about 8 cups)
  Kosher salt and freshly ground black pepper

KITCHEN TIP § Frisée? Frisée is a kind of chicory. It's in the same family as endive and escarole. It looks like a bulb of endive that was put into an electrical outlet and got shocked. Frisée is frizzy. Curly, wacky lettuce. Strength and attitude are what makes frisée perfect for this salad. Other lettuces, like baby spinach or arugula, could not stand up to the warm vinaigrette. Chicory, like frisée, is on the bitter side, which contrasts with the smoky bacon and sweet shallot. Plus, it has that curly shape and will stay fresh and perky in your mouth.

greek salad

PREP TIME: 25 minutes TOTAL TIME: 25 minutes MAKES 6 servings SERVING SIZE: 1⅓ cups

As a teenager, I spent a good deal of my allowance eating at the Golden Reef Diner in Rockville Centre, Long Island. Most of the time I would order gravy fries or cheese fries, though if I had made some extra babysitting bucks that week I'd go for it and have cheese fries with gravy. I loved it. But in a teenage girl-ish way. At the diners in college, I moved on to Greek salads. It was the dressing that got me, with tangy feta, lemon, and oregano. A sophomore love.

My own Greek salad dressing adds a few additional flavors, and instead of the lettuce, I'm dressing tomatoes, cucumbers, peppers, and onions. As I've grown more comfortable with commitment, this dressing has become a constant in my fridge. Whether I'm tossing it with shredded iceberg lettuce or cut-up vegetables, it still makes me weak in the knees.

1. In a bowl, whisk together the feta, dill, olive oil, vinegar, lemon juice, oregano, salt, and pepper. In a serving bowl, combine the cucumber, green pepper, tomatoes, red onion, olives, and pepperoncini. Toss the vegetables with the dressing before serving.

NUTRITION INFORMATION
(PER SERVING):
CALORIES 142, CARBS 8G, FIBER 2G, PROTEIN 3G, TOTAL FAT 12G, SATURATED FAT 3G

- ½ cup crumbled feta cheese (about 2 ounces)
- ¼ cup chopped fresh dill
- ¼ cup olive oil
- 2 tablespoons red wine vinegar Juice of 1 lemon
- 1½ teaspoons dried oregano
- 1 teaspoon kosher salt, plus more to taste
- ¼ teaspoon freshly ground black pepper, plus more to taste
- 1 cucumber, halved lengthwise and cut into half-moons
- 1 large green bell pepper, cut into 1-inch squares
- 1 pint grape or cherry tomatoes, halved
- 1 small red onion, halved and thinly sliced, soaked in ice water for 15 minutes and drained (optional)
- ⅓ cup pitted kalamata olives (about 12)
- 12 pepperoncini (optional)

KITCHEN TIP § Raw Onions Without the Sting I'm not a raw onion kinda gal. Nor do I like smooching raw onion kinda guys. With one exception: If you soak a purple onion in ice water for 15 minutes before eating it, you can actually remove the "sting", that unpleasant reminder that stays with you long after the thrill of the onion is gone. That way, I can enjoy the taste when I want it and not when I don't.

KITCHEN TIP § Pepperoncinis Are Perky Pickled Peppers When I order a Greek Salad, and it comes out with a couple of pepperoncinis on the side, I start to salivate. In fact, I can salivate just thinking about them. These days you can also find pepperoncinis at salad bars and make-your-own sandwich places. They are light green, crispy, slightly spicy, and about 2 inches long; they are often in Greek and Italian dishes. If you love 'em, you love 'em, and if you don't, there's someone at the table who has been eyeing your pepperoncini since your plate was put in front of you. Plus, according to the nutritional information on the jar, 3 pepperoncini have 0 calories. *'Nuff said.*

asparagus tangle with parmesan vinaigrette

PREP TIME: 20 minutes **TOTAL TIME:** 20 minutes **MAKES** 6 servings **SERVING SIZE:** 1 cup

It's amazing what you can do with a vegetable peeler. By peeling stalks of asparagus into long shavings instead of using them whole, you get this visually compelling salad. If you have access to good purple or white asparagus, try a tricolor tangle. And since purple asparagus loses color when it is cooked, the only way to enjoy that color on a plate is to have it raw.

1. Lay the asparagus on a cutting board and shave with a vegetable peeler, starting an inch or two below the end of the stalk. Continue until all the asparagus has been shaved into thin strips; discard the thick ends after shaving.

2. In a large bowl, whisk together the olive oil, lemon juice, Parmesan cheese, and anchovy paste. Toss the asparagus with the vinaigrette and season with salt and pepper.

NUTRITION INFORMATION
(PER SERVING):
CALORIES 103, CARBS 3G, FIBER 1G, PROTEIN 2G, TOTAL FAT 10G, SATURATED FAT 2G

1 pound thick asparagus
¼ cup olive oil
1 tablespoon fresh lemon juice
3 tablespoons grated Parmesan cheese
1 teaspoon anchovy paste
 Kosher salt and freshly ground black pepper

 KITCHEN TIP § Don't Trim the Asparagus Though you usually want to trim the woody end from the asparagus before you cook it, for this recipe, don't. When you're shaving the asparagus, use the woody end as a handle and discard it at the end, when you're down to that last thin strip of asparagus.

 KITCHEN TIP § Thicker Is Better For this recipe, choose thick asparagus. Those little baby ones are delicate and great for eating whole. But here, thicker stalks mean fewer stalks per pound, which means fewer stalks to shave and less work for you. Think about it.

 SKINNY TIP § Secret Ingredient: Grated Parm Parmesan cheese is an ingredient that delivers vivid flavor in a small amount. It'll run you only 20 calories per tablespoon. You'll be surprised how far that goes. On top of pasta, a teaspoon of grated Parm seems generous. Total calories: 7.

"it's time to love the food

THAT LOVES US BACK."

mixed greens, apples, cheddar, and maple pecans in honey-dijon vinaigrette

PREP TIME: 15 minutes **TOTAL TIME:** 15 minutes **MAKES** 4 servings **SERVING SIZE:** 2 cups salad with pecans

This is a fall salad. If you've ever spent a day apple picking and wanted to do something delicious with your haul, yet were too zonked from all reaching, stooping, and nippy fresh air to start with an apple pie, this is your salad. I prefer sweet Gala apples in this salad, but feel free to use your favorite red-skinned eating apple, as the red contrasts beautifully with the greens.

1. In a large bowl, whisk together the honey, mustard, and oil. When the sauce is cohesive, whisk in the cheddar. Add the greens and chopped apple, and toss with your hands to coat with the vinaigrette. Top the salad with the pecans and serve.

NUTRITION INFORMATION
(PER SERVING):

CALORIES 172, CARBS 16G, FIBER 3G, PROTEIN 3G, TOTAL FAT 12G, SATURATED FAT 3G

- 1 tablespoon honey
- 1 tablespoon Dijon mustard
- 1 tablespoon vegetable oil
- ⅓ cup grated cheddar cheese (about 1½ ounces)
- 8 cups mixed baby greens
- 1 large apple, chopped
- ¼ cup Maple-Glazed Pecans (recipe follows)

 KITCHEN TIP § Flavor to the Fifth Power Apples and cheddar cheese is a popular pairing. So is cheddar and Dijon. Honey mustard is a favorite dressing, and many folks adore apples drizzled with honey in the fall. Pecans partner well with apples, especially in a crumble (page 238). In this salad, you'll find each of these partnerships, which makes it like flavor to the fifth power.

 KITCHEN TIP § A Simple Honey Mustard Dressing If you aren't ready for that mind-blowing math, start easy with the honey mustard vinaigrette. It is the simplest dressing in this book. To enjoy it, all you need is a bag of prewashed greens, honey, mustard, oil, and a whisk.

 SKINNY TIP § Skip the Cheddar If you skip the cheddar, you'll save 34 calories per serving, 3 grams of fat, and 2 grams of saturated fat. Your choice!

maple-glazed pecans

PREP TIME: 5 minutes **TOTAL TIME:** 30 minutes **MAKES** 8 servings **SERVING SIZE:** 1 tablespoon

If this were a "how-to-gain-weight" book, I'd recommend making bowls of Maple-Glazed Pecans, especially during the holidays, so that you and your guests could fill up on hundreds of calories before you sat down to dinner. But this isn't that book. Instead, enjoy these nuts in place of croutons on a salad, so that you can have terrific flavor and a waistline, too.

1. Preheat a toaster oven to 375°F, and line a small baking sheet with aluminum foil.
2. In a small bowl, stir together the nuts, syrup, cayenne, thyme, and salt. Spread the nut mixture on the prepared sheet. Cook until the nuts are fragrant, about 12 minutes.

3. Remove the nuts from the oven, let cool for 5 minutes on the baking sheet, and separate the nuts using two forks. Let cool fully before using, another 10 minutes.

NUTRITION INFORMATION (PER SERVING):

CALORIES 54, CARBS 3G, FIBER 1G, PROTEIN 1G, TOTAL FAT 5G, SATURATED FAT 0G

½ cup chopped pecans
1 tablespoon maple syrup
   Pinch of cayenne
¼ teaspoon dried thyme
¼ teaspoon kosher salt

 KITCHEN TIP § What If I Can't Find Chopped Pecans? In most grocery stores, chopped pecans are less expensive than pecan halves, kind of like those "irregulars" you find at a discount clothes store. It's still a perfectly good shirt but somewhere, something is not quite symmetrical . . . bummer for the retailer but good for you! If your store doesn't sell chopped pecans, buy them whole and chop before using. When you use coarsely chopped pecans instead of whole, the maple mixture will coat the surfaces of the nuts; you'll end up with a better syrup-to-nut ratio.

spinach salad with sautéed mushrooms, pickled red onions, blue cheese, and bacon

PREP TIME: 25 minutes **TOTAL TIME:** 25 minutes **MAKES** 6 servings **SERVING SIZE:** 2 cups

I love a good steakhouse. Ribeye steaks are bliss, and a classic steakhouse spinach salad with crisp bacon, mushrooms, red onions, and blue cheese is the right way to get the party started.

And when the kitchen goes to the extra effort to sauté the mushrooms and pickle the red onions, nothing can keep me away. This is that version.

1. Put the onion in a small bowl and cover with the red wine vinegar. Let the onion marinate until soft and tangy, at least 10 minutes. Drain before using, reserving the vinegar.

2. Put the bacon in a medium skillet and cook over medium heat until soft-crisp, about 5 minutes. Drain the bacon on a paper towel–lined plate; chop when cool enough to handle.

3. Place the mushrooms in the same skillet with the bacon fat and season with ½ teaspoon salt. Cook until golden, about 5 minutes. Add 2 tablespoons of the red wine vinegar from the onion mixture to the skillet with the mushrooms and scrape up any browned bits from the bottom of the pan with a wooden spoon.

4. Put the spinach in a large bowl; drizzle with the olive oil, 1 teaspoon of the red wine vinegar from the onion mixture, the remaining ½ teaspoon salt, and the pepper. Toss to coat the spinach.

5. To serve, divide the spinach among serving plates and top with the drained pickled onions, mushrooms, bacon, and blue cheese.

NUTRITION INFORMATION (PER SERVING):

CALORIES 98, CARBS 3G, FIBER 1G, PROTEIN 4G, TOTAL FAT 8G, SATURATED FAT 3G

- ⅓ cup thinly sliced red onion
- ½ cup red wine vinegar
- 2 strips bacon
- 6 ounces white mushrooms, sliced
- 1 teaspoon kosher salt
- 1 6-ounce bag baby spinach
- 1 tablespoon olive oil
- ¼ teaspoon freshly ground black pepper
- ¼ cup crumbled blue cheese (about 1 ounce)

SKINNY TIP § Composed Salad
What's up with step 5, where you're placing all the components of the salad on the greens? Why not simply toss this salad? There is a reason for it. Since you eat with your eyes first, when you lay the elements of the salad on top of the greens, you get maximum visual impact. If I can see all those mushrooms and all that blue cheese, versus having those treats hiding under the lettuce, I feel I'm getting a lot more, even though I'm not.

Skinny eating is sometimes just about rearranging the elements that are already there. A composed salad is like a push-up bra; it shows off what you've got.

KITCHEN TIP § Mandoline: The Kitchen Guillotine A mandoline is a kitchen tool that helps you slice ingredients paper-thin. Everything you can do with a mandoline can be done with a knife, presuming you've got excellent knife skills. Remember that scene from *Goodfellas*, where Paulie is using a razor to slice garlic so thin you can see through it? That's the kind of thin I'm talking about.

There are two kinds of mandolines on the market: the Japanese kind that looks like a flat board with a sharp razor in the center, typically running about $20; and the French kind that's big, scary, and usually at least $150. Go with the simple Japanese-style mandoline (branded Benriner). The big bad expensive mandoline will help you julienne, make waffle fries, and more, so it's really helpful if you're starting a bistro, but my bet is that you just want to get a good meal on the table. Proceed carefully, as you would with the sharpest knife. Trust me on this.

"A composed salad is like a push-up bra; it shows off what you've got."

caesar salad with garlic and herb croutons

PREP TIME: 25 minutes **TOTAL TIME:** 25 minutes **MAKES** 6 servings **SERVING SIZE:** 1½ cups

You may not know it yet, but in your hands you hold a super-delicious recipe for Caesar dressing. This little recipe will cement your reputation as a gifted cook. Make big jars of the stuff and give them away as holiday gifts. (Just keep them refrigerated.) You think I'm kidding, but that's just because you haven't tried the recipe yet.

In fact, the only thing better than this dressing is the homemade croutons that go with it. They'll keep for a week sealed in an airtight container at room temperature.

1. For the croutons: Melt the butter in a large nonstick skillet over medium-high heat. Add the bread cubes and sprinkle with garlic powder. Stir to coat the bread cubes with butter. Cook about 4 minutes, stirring occasionally, until the bread cubes are golden and toasted. Sprinkle with the parsley and ¼ teaspoon of the salt and toss to coat. Remove the skillet from the heat and set aside.

2. For the salad: In a large bowl, mash the garlic, anchovy, and ¼ teaspoon of the salt with the back of a fork. Add the mayonnaise, Parmesan, and lemon juice and whisk to combine. Add the lettuce to a bowl and toss to coat with the dressing. Season with the remaining ¼ teaspoon salt and the pepper and toss again.

3. Divide the salad among plates, top with the croutons, and serve. Garnish with Parmesan shavings, if desired.

NUTRITION INFORMATION
(PER SERVING):

CALORIES 178, CARBS 14G, FIBER 4G, PROTEIN 5G, TOTAL FAT 13G, SATURATED FAT 4G

- 2 tablespoons unsalted butter
- 8 inch piece of Italian bread, cut or torn into ¾-inch cubes (about 3 cups)
- ¼ teaspoon garlic powder
- 1 teaspoon dried parsley
- ¾ teaspoon kosher salt
- 1 small garlic clove, minced
- 1 teaspoon anchovy paste, or 1 anchovy, chopped
- ¼ cup mayonnaise
- 2 tablespoons grated Parmesan cheese
- 1 tablespoon fresh lemon juice
- 1 large head romaine lettuce, cut into ½-inch ribbons (about 10 cups)
- ¼ teaspoon freshly ground black pepper
  Parmesan shavings (optional garnish; see tip page 42)

KITCHEN TIP § Smile, You're Using Full-Fat Mayo I tested this recipe almost too many times to count before perfecting the version that made it into the book. At first, I made a real Caesar with raw egg yolks, but then I realized that lots of folks don't dig raw egg yolks and all the pregnant ladies would be left out. I couldn't have that. So I went to low-fat mayo because it had 55 fewer calories per tablespoon.

It seemed like a good idea at the time. Let's just say I went through a lot of romaine before I realized what was wrong with my weak, watery dressing. It was the mayo! As soon as I returned to full-fat mayo, I was rewarded with a vivid and tangy dressing. I always say to keep the real stuff whenever you're going to taste it, and in this situation,

I'm reminded why! In this recipe, the fatty stuff is an extra 37 calories per serving. Is it worth it? Heck, yeah! The light mayo dressing tasted fine until I tossed it with the lettuce. Then it was as if I hadn't dressed the greens at all. If what you eat doesn't taste great, you'll be unsatisfied. Your satisfaction is my priority. For this dressing, use full-fat mayo.

iceberg wedge with creamy blue cheese dressing

PREP TIME: 15 minutes **TOTAL TIME:** 15 minutes **MAKES** 8 servings **SERVING SIZE:** 1 wedge with 2 tablespoons dressing

I know it's out of vogue these days (low nutritional value, blah, blah, blah), but I've got a soft spot for iceberg lettuce; I grew up on the stuff. And so maybe it doesn't have all the vitamins of darker leaf lettuces, but it's not like you're eating a candy bar.

Plus, it's fun to take a knife to a whole head of lettuce and chop it. I can't help but channel my inner Miss Piggy as I pick up the knife, and squeal, *"Take that, lettuce! Haaaay-ya!"*

1. In a medium bowl, combine the blue cheese, olive oil, vegetable oil, red wine vinegar, and Dijon mustard; whisk together until emulsified. Whisk in the water and pepper.

2. Drizzle 2 tablespoons dressing over each wedge. Serve cold.

NUTRITION INFORMATION (PER SERVING):
CALORIES 155, CARBS 3G, FIBER 1G, PROTEIN 4G, TOTAL FAT 14G, SATURATED FAT 4G

- 4 ounces Danish or Maytag blue cheese, crumbled (about ½ cup)
- 3 tablespoons extra-virgin olive oil
- 3 tablespoons vegetable oil
- 2 tablespoons red wine vinegar
- 2 teaspoons Dijon mustard
- ¼ cup water
- ¼ teaspoon coarsely ground black pepper
- 1 large head iceberg lettuce, cut into 8 wedges

 SKINNY TIP § Maximizing Flavor Let's discuss this dressing. Of course it's delicious. And based on the ingredient list, it's pretty obvious that nothing is spared. Two kinds of oil, blue cheese: good stuff but not the lightest. Per food writer, thinker, and all-around super-smart dude Michael Pollan, "Don't eat anything your great-great-grandmother wouldn't recognize as food."

I avoid the dreaded zone of low-cal fake foods because I turned the bottle of "zero calorie" blue cheese dressing around and didn't recognize half the ingredients I saw. I want to eat real foods, the good stuff, and look good doing it. I use Maytag or Danish blue cheese in this recipe because they're assertive. A strong cheese means you can use a smaller amount, as a little intense flavor goes a long way. More flavor, real food, fewer calories. Amen!

shaved salad with miso dressing

PREP TIME: 15 minutes **TOTAL TIME:** 15 minutes **MAKES** 6 servings **SERVING SIZE:** 1½ cups salad with dressing

This salad has two unusual ingredients that are common in Asian cooking: mung bean sprouts and radishes. Bean sprouts can be found in the grocery store near other refrigerated vegetables, sometimes in a bag. Radishes are spicy, and the contrast between their red skin and bright white interior is pretty against arugula.

1. Combine the arugula, carrots, radishes, and mung bean sprouts in a bowl. Add the dressing and toss to coat the salad.

 KITCHEN TIP § How to Shave a Carrot After you've peeled your carrot to remove the outer skin, keep on peeling. Those long, thin strips of carrot are what give this salad its charm.

NUTRITION INFORMATION
(PER SERVING):

CALORIES 71, CARBS 6G, FIBER 1G, PROTEIN 2G, TOTAL FAT 5G, SATURATED FAT 1G

- 5 cups baby arugula
- 2 carrots, peeled into long, thin strips (see tip left)
- 4 radishes, trimmed and cut into wedges
- 1 cup mung bean sprouts
- ¼ cup Sweet Miso Dressing (recipe follows)

sweet miso dressing

PREP TIME: 8 minutes **TOTAL TIME:** 8 minutes **MAKES** 16 servings **SERVING SIZE:** 1 tablespoon

This simple dressing is a "dump and stir." Every ingredient is in your pantry or refrigerator; no knife needed. Make a big batch (this recipe makes 1 cup), and toss it with bagged lettuce for a quick salad. This dressing will keep in an airtight container in the refrigerator for up to 2 weeks.

1. Put all the ingredients in a bowl and whisk together until combined.

 KITCHEN TIP § Immersion Blender If the ingredients aren't coalescing when you whisk them together, they might be too cold (are they coming straight from the fridge?). For a 10-second fix, use an immersion blender (also called a stick blender). It does what a blender does without requiring all that apparatus; you just stick the blade in a container, turn it on, and—*buzz*—you're dressing is done.

NUTRITION INFORMATION
(PER SERVING):

CALORIES 70, CARBS 3G, FIBER 0G, PROTEIN 1G, TOTAL FAT 7G, SATURATED FAT 1G

¼ cup miso paste
½ cup vegetable oil
¼ cup rice vinegar
1 tablespoon soy sauce
2 tablespoons brown sugar
1 teaspoon toasted sesame oil

creamy fresh herb dressing

PREP TIME: 15 minutes **TOTAL TIME:** 15 minutes **MAKES** 8 servings **SERVING SIZE:** 1 tablespoon

When I asked my friend Josh to taste this dressing, he took a bite and was instantly transported to the wood-paneled basement of his childhood, sneaking bites from a crudité platter that his mom made for soon-to-arrive guests. When he came back from the herb dip time machine, he said, "Hang on a second; is this Green Goddess dressing?"

Old food memories die hard. I designed this to be a riff on that 70's classic (which has anchovies and sour cream; this has neither). It is so good that you might think you've taken *The Love Boat* to *Fantasy Island*.

1. Combine the mayonnaise, yogurt, basil, parsley, tarragon, garlic, lemon juice, and salt in a food processor and blend until you have a thick, creamy green sauce.

2. This will keep in a sealed container in the refrigerator for up to 2 weeks.

NUTRITION INFORMATION
(PER SERVING):
CALORIES 64, CARBS 1G, FIBER 0G, PROTEIN 1G, TOTAL FAT 6G, SATURATED FAT 1G

- ¼ cup mayonnaise
- ½ cup 2% Greek yogurt
- 1 cup gently packed fresh basil leaves
- ¼ cup gently packed fresh parsley leaves
- 1 tablespoon chopped fresh tarragon leaves
- 1 small garlic clove, peeled
- 2 tablespoons fresh lemon juice
- 1 teaspoon kosher salt

SKINNY TIP § Take a Dip
Like other delicious thick and creamy dressings, this one can also be used as a dip. And can you believe: ¼ cup of this rich-tasting dip has fewer than 60 calories! I didn't believe it either, which is why I checked the calorie count at least five times. It's true.

carrot-ginger dressing

PREP TIME: 25 minutes TOTAL TIME: 25 minutes MAKES 10 servings SERVING SIZE: 2 tablespoons

I have loved this dressing ever since I was a kid. Carrot-Ginger dressing, which almost always accompanies a green salad in Japanese restaurants, has a sweet and tangy flavor combination that everyone seems to love. But it was only recently that I learned the two secrets to this dressing. One: You have to cook the carrots ever so slightly to soften them and bring out their sweetness. Two: The secret ingredient that makes the dressing "pop" is neither carrot nor ginger. It's shallot.

1. Bring a medium pot of salted water to a boil. Add the carrots, return the water to a boil, and cook the carrots for 2 minutes. Remove the carrots from the water and place in a food processor.

2. Add the shallot and ginger to the food processor with the carrots. Pulse until finely chopped. Add the oil, vinegar, and soy sauce and pulse to incorporate. Add the water to thin the dressing and pulse again.

3. This dressing will keep in a sealed container in the refrigerator for up to 2 weeks.

NUTRITION INFORMATION
(PER SERVING):

CALORIES 53, CARBS 3G, FIBER 0G, PROTEIN 1G, TOTAL FAT 4G, SATURATED FAT 0G

- 2 medium carrots, peeled and cut into ½-inch pieces (1 cup)
- 1 large shallot, chopped (¼ cup)
- 1 2-inch piece fresh ginger, peeled and chopped (3 tablespoons)
- 3 tablespoons vegetable oil
- 2 tablespoons seasoned rice vinegar
- 1½ tablespoons soy sauce
- ¼ cup water

 SKINNY TIP § Seasoned Rice Vinegar Seasoned rice vinegar is simply sweetened rice vinegar. If you have unseasoned rice vinegar and want to use it for this recipe, add a teaspoon of sugar for every tablespoon of rice vinegar; it will have the same flavor and calorie count.

SKINNY TIP § Boxed and Bagged Lettuces I am a fan of prewashed lettuce. Every week, I pick up a new mix at the grocery store, and I eat my way through it during the week. Prewashed lettuce mixes make salad eating almost too easy; all you need is a terrific dressing, and this book gives you recipes for quite a few.

slurp!
soups & stews

here's a confession:

Only recently did I "get" soup. To me, soups were what you had to eat when your jaw was wired shut or when you only had time to open a can. Soups weren't special.

And then I ate some really good homemade soups.

On the skinny side, soup is filling. They need to be enjoyed slowly. You can't rush a soup. As any dietician (or mom) will tell you, this is a healthy way to eat. Plus, soups can warm you up or cool you down. There is a reason they are enjoyed by every culture around the world.

Soup is social. It is meant to be shared, and that goes for the making as well as the slurping. Next time you make soup, invite friends over and make it together. Get a lot of containers, masking tape, and a Sharpie pen so that you can label and freeze your soups.

Before the days when everyone had his or her own kitchen, the women (and it was the women) would gather, make a fire, cook together, and divvy up the grub. They didn't have Tupperware, but they did have fun gossiping about the new hottie spotted down by the well.

Plus, unlike other dishes, when you make soup your objective is to make more than you need. Enough so that you can give some of it away or freeze it for another time. This strategy works especially well for chicken soup because, when it's needed most, it's needed *right away*. Some of the soups in the following pages can feed an army, like the Chicken and Andouille Gumbo (page 88), the Soulful Chicken Soup (page 78), and the Moroccan Saffron Chickpea Soup (page 84). And in case you are feeling nervous about the time commitment, note that some of these soups take as little as 15 minutes to make, like the Gazpacho (page 66) and the Chilled Cucumber-Dill Soup (page 67).

Though none of these recipes have cream, the Roasted Tomato Soup (page 74), New England Clam Chowder (page 80), and Parsnip-Apple Soup (page 73) sure taste like they do. With skinny cooking techniques, like rouxs, panadas, and starch purees, you'll see how to thicken your soups without adding unnecessary calories.

They're *cream-y* without cream.

Most of the soups in this chapter are served by the cupful as a starter, a mid-afternoon snack, or something to have with half a sandwich or salad for lunch. Or, double the portions and enjoy them for dinner. Serve the stews at the end of the chapter over rice for a filling meal. Soups are flexible.

And so I stand corrected. Soups are liquid happiness for your body, your friends, and your freezer.

gazpacho

PREP TIME: 5 minutes **TOTAL TIME:** 15 minutes **MAKES** 4 servings **SERVING SIZE:** 1⅛ cups

Want a 15-minute soup that can be made in a blender? This is it. Gazpacho is a cold tomato soup that you can make quickly.

Gazpacho is traditionally made with ripe summer tomatoes and a piece of bread that binds the liquid so you have soup, not tomato juice. But my favorite gazpachos have lots of olive oil. So I dropped the bread in favor of the oil, turning this soup from a pleasant tomato-and-bread soup to a "What's *in* this?" experience.

Plus, by using canned tomatoes, you can enjoy this quick soup year-round.

1. Put the tomatoes and tomato puree, cucumber, olive oil, vinegar, and salt in a blender and blend on low speed until you have puree, about 20 seconds. Add the basil, jalapeño, and onion and pulse on high speed until incorporated, about 15 seconds.

- 1 28-ounce can whole peeled tomatoes, with puree
- 1 Kirby or small cucumber (about 5 inches long), peeled and coarsely chopped
- ¼ cup extra-virgin olive oil
- 1 teaspoon red wine vinegar
- 2 teaspoons kosher salt
- 1 handful basil leaves, plus more for garnish
- ½ jalapeño, stem removed, halved lengthwise, with seeds
- ½ small red onion, peeled and quartered

 SKINNY TIP § Croutons I like to serve this soup with a large crouton. You can either pour the soup over the crouton or serve it with the soup. To make these croutons (which are the same as crostini, page 96), use a serrated knife to cut a baguette into ⅓-inch-thick slices. Bake at 375°F until crisp—about 10 minutes. If you serve the soup over this crouton; at first it crackles, then it soaks in the soup. Terrific texture for about 20 calories per crouton.

KITCHEN TIP § Some Like It Hot Keep the jalapeño veins and seeds for a spicier soup; remove them if you want a milder one. Some people say the seeds are where the heat is, and others contend it's the veins. As far as I'm concerned, they're kissing cousins, and the heat of one rubs off on the other. Remove both or neither, depending on the level of heat you seek.

chilled cucumber-dill soup

PREP TIME: 15 minutes **TOTAL TIME:** 15 minutes **MAKES** 4 servings **SERVING SIZE:** 1 cup

One summer, I taught a class for a cooking student who gave me this challenge: He wanted a delicious summer meal made with only raw ingredients. Not because he was a raw foods fan, no; it was because he was a New Yorker who had permanently turned off his oven so that it could be used it for storage. *And you thought that was just an urban legend!*

This was one of the dishes I developed for his class. It's refreshing and perfect for the summer when you want to avoid the heat of the oven, or if you have an oven full of shoes, overdue library books, or a vintage collection of *Welcome Back, Kotter* lunch boxes.

1. In a blender, combine the sour cream, cucumbers, dill, salt, horseradish, and Worcestershire sauce. You may need to do this in batches. Process until pureed. Serve cold, garnished with dill.

NUTRITION INFORMATION
(PER SERVING):
CALORIES 136, CARBS 8G, FIBER 1G, PROTEIN 2G, TOTAL FAT 12G, SATURATED FAT 7G

1 cup sour cream
2 English cucumbers, chopped
½ cup loosely packed fresh dill leaves, plus more for garnish
2 teaspoons kosher salt
1 teaspoon prepared horseradish
½ teaspoon Worcestershire sauce

SKINNY TIP § Full-Fat Sour Cream? That's right, we're using full-fat sour cream in this recipe. Why? Because it tastes good. Plus, cucumbers are so low in calories, this soup can afford to splurge. Sour cream is lower in calories than actual cream—just 30 calories per tablespoon.

KITCHEN TIP § Go English I've tested this recipe with regular cucumbers and with English cucumbers; English won hands down. Here's why: The skin of an English cucumber is thinner and less bitter than a regular cuke, which means you can toss the cuke, skin and all, right into the blender. No peeling means less work for you.

Also, English cucumbers are considered "seedless." Anyone who has sliced an English cucumber in half knows that is not technically true, but they have fewer seeds, and the seeds they do have are smaller. So they could be more accurately be called "less prominently seedy," but that sounds like a description a real estate agent might give to an up-and-coming neighborhood.

Anyway, because the seeds are less prominent, they make a more full-bodied soup. Of course, you can use regular cucumbers, but be sure to peel them and remove the seeds first. To do this, cut the cucumbers in half lengthwise, and run the inside tip of a spoon down the center, right along the seed line. Use 4 medium cucumbers, enough to make 6 cups chopped.

carrot-ginger soup

PREP TIME: 5 minutes **TOTAL TIME:** 35 minutes **MAKES** 4 servings **SERVING SIZE:** Generous 1 cup

As I write this, it's snowing outside. Soups are wonderful on cold days and even better on snowy ones, and this soup is particularly so. The carrots make it bright orange and the ginger makes it spicy: a smiling bowl of warm sunshine on a snowy day.

1. Melt the butter in a medium skillet over medium heat. Add the carrots, onion, ginger, thyme, and salt and cook, stirring, until the vegetables begin to soften, about 6 minutes.

2. Add the chicken broth to vegetables, raise the heat to medium-high, and bring to a simmer. Reduce the heat and simmer until the vegetables are completely tender, 12 to 15 minutes.

3. Add the vegetable mixture to a blender. Before you puree, be sure to remove the clear plastic disk in the center of the lid and cover with a kitchen towel. If you leave the lid on, the pressure from the blender will build and pop a sealed top (and give your walls and ceiling a splatter paint treatment—really). Puree the soup. Serve warm, garnished with the chopped chives or parsley.

NUTRITION INFORMATION (PER SERVING):

CALORIES 131, CARBS 15G, FIBER 4G, PROTEIN 5G, TOTAL FAT 6G, SATURATED FAT 4G

- 2 tablespoons unsalted butter
- 1 pound carrots, peeled and chopped into ½-inch pieces (about 3 cups)
- 1 large onion, peeled and chopped into ½-inch pieces
- 1 2-inch piece fresh ginger, peeled and chopped into ½-inch pieces
- ½ teaspoon fresh thyme leaves, or ¼ teaspoon dried thyme
- ½ teaspoon kosher salt
- 3 cups lower-sodium chicken broth
- 1 tablespoon chopped fresh chives or parsley, for garnish

KITCHEN TIP § *Smaller* Is Better?
As long as we're talkin' carrots, yes ma'am. Smaller, thinner carrots tend to be sweeter. Big carrots are sometimes called horse carrots because they can be tough and fibrous, fit for a horse to chomp on but not as tasty for a person. I know, it's a bit more work to peel the small ones, but it's worth it.

SKINNY TIP § Rick's Corn Relish
My friend Rick Field owns a pickle and condiment company called Rick's Picks. His products cost $8 to $12 a jar, a pretty penny for a puckery pickle. But boy are they good. If you use his condiments slowly, as I do, they'll last a long time and are well worth the splurge. I love garnishing Carrot-Ginger Soup with his corn relish (he calls it "Handy Corn", 'cause it's sweet like candy corn). Dollop 2 tablespoons of the stuff in the center of your soup bowl; it will run you an extra 30 calories and adds amazing flavor. If they don't carry his products at your grocery store, you can find them online at www.rickspicksnyc.com. If you know someone else who makes good local corn relish, by all means use it!

potato-leek soup

PREP TIME: 15 minutes **TOTAL TIME:** 45 minutes **MAKES** 5 servings **SERVING SIZE:** 1 cup

This is potato-leek soup minus the cream. And yes, though cream carries flavor in a most delicious way, when you make this recipe, you're not going to miss it. In fact, you can treat yourself to a little dish of ice cream for dessert and still have the same calorie count as you would have had you used cream. And if two kinds of creaminess in the same meal aren't better than one, what is?

1. Melt the butter in a medium pot over medium-high heat. Add the leeks and salt, and turn the heat down to medium-low. Cook, covered and stirring occasionally, until translucent and soft, about 10 minutes.
2. Remove the cover, raise the heat to medium-high, and add the wine. Cook until the liquid is reduced by half, about 2 minutes. Add the potatoes, broth, milk, and thyme to the pot and bring to a sim- mer. Simmer until the potatoes are cooked through, about 15 minutes.

3. Add the potato mixture to the blender. Before you puree, be sure to remove the clear plastic disk in the center of the lid and cover with a kitchen towel. (If you leave the lid on, the pressure from the blender will build and pop the sealed top.) Puree the soup. Serve warm, gar- nished with chives.

NUTRITION INFORMATION
(PER SERVING):

CALORIES 189, CARBS 26G, FIBER 2G, PROTEIN 8G, TOTAL FAT 5G, SATU- RATED FAT 3G

- 2 tablespoons unsalted butter
- 1 bunch leeks (3 large or 4 medium), halved lengthwise and sliced into 1-inch pieces, white and light green parts only
- 1 teaspoon kosher salt
- ½ cup dry white wine
- 1 pound russet potatoes, peeled and cut into 1-inch cubes
- 3 cups lower-sodium chicken broth
- 1 cup skim milk
- ½ teaspoon fresh thyme leaves, or ¼ teaspoon dried thyme
- 1½ tablespoons chopped fresh chives, for garnish

 KITCHEN TIP § *You Say You Are Potato Leek? Impostor! You Are Vichyssoise!* That's right, this is vichyssoise. And it's Potato Leek. They're the same soup, one hot, one not. If you choose to serve this soup cold, be sure to add another ½ teaspoon or so of salt, as cold temperatures inhibit flavor and require an extra boost.

 KITCHEN TIP § *Cleaning Leeks* Leeks are sandy. To clean, submerge them in a bowl of cold water. Give the leeks a good swish, and all that sand that gets stuck in between the layers will fall to the bottom of the bowl. If you slice the leeks first, the sand will tumble out more easily. Lift the leeks out of the water, leaving the sand behind, and proceed with your recipe.

black bean soup like you mean it

PREP TIME: 20 minutes **TOTAL TIME:** 30 minutes **MAKES** 6 servings **SERVING SIZE:** 1 cup

Beans are a terrific skinny ingredient. Loaded with fiber and protein, they make you feel full longer.

Hang on—that's not a very sexy way to sell a recipe, so let me try again: This is a spicy soup that will transport you to another place. A hotter place. A place by the ocean with the person of your dreams. *There. That's better.*

As soon as the cumin and chili powder hit the pan, you get this intense, south of the border aromatherapy. Then you puree and get that *body*. The finished soup brings it all home with cilantro, scallion, and a squeeze of lime. Take a bite, close your eyes, and you're on a beach in Puerto Rico. That good body in your bowl translates to a great body in a bikini. *Ay, mami chula!*

1. Heat the oil in a large pot over medium heat. Add the onion, garlic, and ½ teaspoon of the salt and cook, stirring occasionally, until the onion is soft and golden, 8 to 10 minutes. Add the cumin and chili powder, and cook until you can smell them, about 30 seconds.
2. While the onion is cooking, puree half the beans in a food processor with ½ cup of the chicken broth. Add the bean puree to the soup with remaining whole black beans, the remaining 1½ cups chicken broth, the tomatoes, and the remaining teaspoon salt. Bring to a simmer and cook for 5 minutes.
3. Serve the soup warm, garnished with cilantro, scallions, and lime wedges.

NUTRITION INFORMATION
(PER SERVING):
CALORIES 180, CARBS 30G, FIBER 10G, PROTEIN 10G, TOTAL FAT 2G, SATURATED FAT 0G

- 2 tablespoons vegetable oil
- 1 large onion, chopped
- 4 garlic cloves, sliced
- 1½ teaspoons kosher salt
- 1½ teaspoons ground cumin
- 1 teaspoon chili powder
- 2 15½-ounce cans black beans, rinsed and drained
- 2 cups lower-sodium chicken broth
- 1 14½-ounce can diced tomatoes
- ⅓ cup chopped fresh cilantro
  Greens from 3 scallions, chopped
- 1 lime, cut into wedges

 KITCHEN TIP § DIY Black Beans
If you've made the black beans on page 175, then you already know how good the flavor can be when you make them yourself. Imagine the possibilities in this already powerful soup! If you want to use homemade black beans instead of canned, figure there are 1¾ cups of beans in a can, for a total of 3½ cups of (rehydrated) beans in the recipe.

 SKINNY TIP § Garnishes:
Accessorize Your Food I've chosen some calorically modest yet flavorful garnishes for this soup. If you want to amp it up with guacamole or sour cream, go right ahead. Surprisingly, you're looking at only 227 calories for a whole Hass avocado (about 38 calories per serving if it serves 6) and about 30 calories for a tablespoon of sour cream. So you can uber-garnish a bowl of this flavor-packed soup for under 70 calories—good options, calorically speaking, so the choice is yours. If you have 'em both, your cup of soup is still only 220 calories. Make it a double-portion bowl of soup instead of a cup, and you just created a delicious meal for under 500 calories.

parsnip-apple soup with pumpernickel croutons

PREP TIME: 25 minutes **TOTAL TIME:** 1 hour **MAKES** 6 servings **SERVING SIZE:** 1 cup with a scant ¼ cup croutons

At first, this creamy off-white soup looks like potato-leek, so it might fool your friends. But then all these unexpected flavors start to reveal themselves. First, there is sweet apple, then something herby—*is that celery*? Then, back to something sweet, then something nutty, and finally there's a buttery, salty, crunchy crouton. Perplexing. Exciting. And ultimately, delicious.

My recommendation? Serve this at the table and don't tell people what's in it; let them speculate. Their guesses will be a riot and might give you ideas for a magical mystery soup for next time.

1. Preheat oven to 400°F. Place the parsnips and apples in aluminum foil and drizzle with the olive oil and ½ teaspoon of the salt. Fold the foil to form a packet and place on a baking sheet. Bake the parsnips and apples in the oven for 30 to 45 minutes, until the parsnips are soft.

2. Melt 1 tablespoon of the butter in a medium saucepan over medium heat. Add the shallots and celery, and cook, stirring occasionally, until soft, about 4 minutes. Add the cooked parsnip mixture and the broth. Bring to a boil, reduce the heat to a simmer, and cook until very soft, about 10 minutes. Remove from the heat and stir in the vinegar and thyme.

3. While the parsnip mixture is simmering, melt the remaining tablespoon of butter in a large skillet over medium heat and add the bread cubes. Cook, stirring occasionally, until croutons are crisp, about 5 minutes. Season with ¼ teaspoon of the salt and set aside.

4. Add the parsnip mixture and broth to blender in batches; do not fill the blender more than ⅔ full. Before you puree, be sure to remove the clear plastic disk in the center of the lid and cover with a kitchen towel. (If you leave the lid on, the pressure from the blender will build and pop the sealed top.) Puree the soup. Season with the remaining ¼ teaspoon salt. Serve warm, garnished with croutons and celery leaves.

NUTRITION INFORMATION
(PER SERVING):
CALORIES 194, CARBS 30G, FIBER 5G, PROTEIN 6G, TOTAL FAT 7G, SATURATED FAT 3G

- 1 pound parsnips, peeled and chopped into ½-inch rounds
- 2 Golden Delicious apples, peeled, cored, and cut into ½-inch wedges
- 1 tablespoon olive oil
- 1 teaspoon kosher salt
- 2 tablespoons unsalted butter
- 2 large shallots, chopped
- 2 celery stalks, chopped plus ¼ cup pale inner celery leaves, for garnish
- 4 cups lower-sodium chicken broth
- 1 tablespoon cider vinegar
- 1 teaspoon fresh thyme leaves, or ⅓ teaspoon dried thyme
- 2 slices pumpernickel bread, cut or torn into ½-inch cubes

 KITCHEN TIP § Fresh Thyme Is on Your Side As you know, your wallet is important to me (let's keep *that* fat), so I don't typically include a fresh ingredient like an herb unless the recipe uses a lot of it. However, fresh thyme (unlike cilantro and parsley) will keep for about a month in the refrigerator, which is a good thing, since thyme is in a number of recipes in this book.

Here is another good thing about thyme. Soups usually simmer for a while and because of that, they have a rich intensity. A fresh herb is a welcomed flavor pop, whether it's parsley, fresh chives, or thyme—it's a bright contrast. But, unlike parsley and fresh chives, thyme is best enjoyed cooked. Cilantro or tarragon will wilt in the heat, but thyme can take it and comes out ahead.

roasted tomato soup

PREP TIME: 30 minutes **TOTAL TIME:** 45 minutes **MAKES** 6 servings **SERVING SIZE:** 1 cup

When I make this soup for friends, there are three layers to their experience. There's the first sip with the expected *mmmm*. Then they swallow and there's an *ooooh*. Then, they look up, as if to say, I've had tomato soup before but not like this.

So how does one make a tomato soup that rivals Campbell's? You incorporate two *mmmm*- and *oooh*-generating cooking techniques—roasting and caramelizing—into one preparation. Together, they intensify the flavors that are already present and cost you nothing, calorically speaking.

1. Preheat the oven to 425°F. Cover a baking sheet with parchment paper.

2. Remove the whole tomatoes from the puree and squish them a bit so they leave their inside liquid and seeds with the rest of the puree. Set the puree aside and place the tomatoes on the parchment paper–lined baking sheet. Cook the tomatoes in the oven until they begin to char, about 20 minutes. If you can't see the char on top and the parchment is browning, that means the heat in your oven comes from the bottom, and your tomatoes are probably browning on the underside. If there isn't any color after 20 minutes, pop them under the broiler for 3 to 5 minutes; you'll get your color.

3. Melt the butter in a large pot over medium heat and add the onion, garlic, and 1 teaspoon of the salt. Cook, stirring occasionally, until the onion has softened, 6 to 8 minutes. Add tomato puree to the onion and cook, stirring occasionally, until

you have a thick paste, about 10 minutes. Raise the heat to medium-high and cook, stirring regularly but not constantly, until the paste begins to stick to the bottom of the pan and caramelize, about 3 minutes. Remember, the tomato paste needs to be in contact with the bottom of the pan in order to caramelize.

4. Add the cooked tomatoes, broth, thyme, and remaining ½ teaspoon salt to the pot. Simmer for 10 minutes to blend the flavors. If you want to enjoy the soup chunky, break up the tomatoes with a wooden spoon, add the milk, and enjoy. For a puree, add the milk, put the soup in a blender, and puree in batches. Before you puree, be sure to remove the clear plastic disk in the center of the lid and cover with a kitchen towel. (If you leave the lid on, the pressure from the blender will build and pop the sealed top.) Blend the soup until smooth.

NUTRITION INFORMATION (PER SERVING):
CALORIES 139, CARBS 15G, FIBER 2G, PROTEIN 8G, TOTAL FAT 6G, SATURATED FAT 3G

- 1 28-ounce can whole peeled tomatoes, with puree
- 1½ tablespoons unsalted butter
- 1 large onion, sliced
- 4 garlic cloves, peeled and smashed
- 1½ teaspoons kosher salt
- 4 cups lower-sodium chicken broth
- 1 teaspoon fresh thyme leaves, or ⅓ teaspoon dried thyme
- 2 cups whole milk

"You incorporate two *mmmm-* and *oooh*-generating cooking techniques—roasting and caramelizing—into one preparation."

 KITCHEN TIP § Roasting and Caramelizing While you roast the tomatoes in the oven, you're also caramelizing the tomato puree on the stovetop. In both techniques, we're removing the water and toasting the sugars. But, then we add the water moisture back in the form of broth. Why?

It is only after removing the water that the heat can access the sugars in the tomato and tomato sauce to caramelize them. Remove the liquid, cook the sugars, and add a more flavorful liquid in place of the water. This technique enhances flavor with minimal additional calories.

SKINNY TIP § Whole Milk? I tried this recipe with skim, with 2 percent, with whole milk, and even without dairy, and there was no contest. It had to be whole milk. Quite frankly, this is a decision that is as much about relationships as food. Here is what I mean: Have you ever had a friend who was a little difficult, and then he or she found an incredible partner who could just calm the person down? *That's what the whole milk does.* Tomatoes are acidic (it's not their fault; it's their nature) and need a partner who helps them relax. Whole milk (3¼ percent milk fat) calms those tomatoes in a way that skim milk can't. This is one of those perfect couples where 1+1=3; the whole is greater than the sum of the parts.

SKINNY TIP § But Where's My Grilled Cheese? You think I'd forget about something as important to tomato soup as a melty, gooey grilled cheese? *Never.* Here's how you do it: Preheat your oven to 375°F. Now make those croutons by cutting a baguette into ⅓-inch slices with a serrated knife (the kind you make with Gazpacho, page 66). Grate some sharp cheddar (⅓ cup works well for 6 croutons). Mound the cheese on the croutons and cook in the oven for 10 minutes, about 45 calories per crispy, melty crouton.

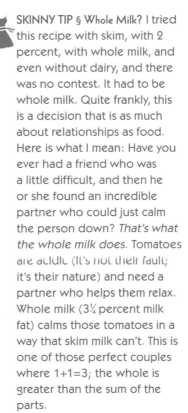

asparagus soup with toasted almonds

PREP TIME: 10 minutes **TOTAL TIME:** 25 minutes **MAKES** 4 servings **SERVING SIZE:** 1 cup

Asparagus is a hardy vegetable, one of the first to pop out in the spring. When an asparagus sees the coast is clear of snow, he gets very excited and shoots straight through the ground. He is full of energy.

I wanted to reward this Tigger of the vegetable world for his enthusiasm, but not with anything heavy. Something bright and something green, so I chose Greek yogurt and parsley.

But bouncy asparagus, tangy yogurt, and naïve parsley could get into trouble—all that youthful energy without any experience or wisdom. So I finished this soup with toasted sliced almonds, the adult in the bowl.

1. Melt the butter in a large skillet over medium-low heat. Add the shallot and thyme and cook, stirring, until soft, about 4 minutes. Add the asparagus and cover with the chicken broth. Bring to a simmer and cook until bright green and tender, about 4 minutes for thin asparagus and 8 minutes for thick asparagus.

2. While the asparagus is cooking, place the almonds in a small skillet over medium heat. Cook, stirring gently, until the almonds are fragrant and lightly browned, about 3 minutes.

3. Add the torn bread and parsley to the asparagus mixture and submerge the bread. Put the asparagus mixture in a blender. Before you puree, be sure to remove the clear plastic disk in the center of the lid and cover with a kitchen towel. (If you leave the lid on, the pressure from the blender will build and pop the sealed top.) Blend the soup until pureed. Add the yogurt and blend to incorporate. Serve the soup warm, garnished with the toasted almonds.

NUTRITION INFORMATION
(PER SERVING):
CALORIES 158, CARBS 14G, FIBER 3G, PROTEIN 12G, TOTAL FAT 7G, SATURATED FAT 3G

- 1 tablespoon unsalted butter
- 1 large shallot, peeled and chopped
- ¾ teaspoon fresh thyme leaves, or ¼ teaspoon dried thyme
- 1 pound asparagus, trimmed and cut into 1½-inch lengths
- 2½ cups lower-sodium chicken broth
- ¼ cup sliced almonds
- 1 slice whole wheat or white bread, torn with your hands
- ¼ cup fresh parsley leaves
- 1 cup 2% Greek yogurt

KITCHEN TIP § Trimming Asparagus To figure out where to trim asparagus, bend the stalks until they break. Use the tip end for this soup, and discard the woody root end.

SKINNY TIP § Panada So as spritely and enthusiastic as this soup is, unfortunately, asparagus and 2 percent yogurt offer very little in the thickening department.

To address this, you're making a panada. Sounds sexy and mysterious, right? "Panada" is just a fancy term for wet bread.

The bread binds the soup and makes it thicker, and for less than 20 calories per serving. As a result, this tangy green soup will put a bounce in your step, not weigh you down.

And if you decide to tell your friends that you used a panada and make it sound all mysterious and sexy . . . well, go right ahead. You're the chef!

soulful chicken soup

PREP TIME: 30 minutes   **TOTAL TIME:** 1½ hours   **MAKES** 12 servings   **SERVING SIZE:** 1½ cups

Everyone needs a good chicken soup recipe. It is a well-known fact that men like women who make chicken soup. Women love men who make chicken soup. Friends enjoy friends who make chicken soup. You will like yourself more if you can make a good chicken soup.

Whether or not you believe that chicken soup can cure a cold, it is good for your social life, and that's good for your soul.

If you've never made chicken soup before, this is a gratifying starter recipe. If you've made chicken soup before, but your friends and family keep asking, "Where's the chicken?" this recipe solves that problem. You'll be hard pressed to take a spoonful without chicken in it. And chicken soup with chicken in it is always a little bit better.

NUTRITION INFORMATION (PER SERVING):

CALORIES 155, CARBS 8G, FIBER 2G, PROTEIN 20G, TOTAL FAT 4G, SATURATED FAT 1G

- 1   4- to 4½-pound chicken
- 3   carrots, peeled and sliced (about 1½ cups)
- 3   parsnips, peeled and sliced (about 1½ cups)
- 3   celery stalks, sliced (about 1½ cups)
- 2   small red onions sliced
- 2   bay leaves
- 1   tablespoon kosher salt, plus more to taste
- 12   cups water
- 1   cup frozen peas

1. Place the chicken in a deep pot and add the carrots, parsnips, celery, onions, bay leaves, and 2 teaspoons of the salt. Cover with the water. Bring to a simmer, skim as needed, and let the soup simmer gently until the chicken is cooked, about 45 minutes.

2. Remove the pot from the heat, remove the chicken from the pot, and set it aside in a bowl until it is cool enough to touch, 15 to 20 minutes. Remove the skin from the chicken and discard the skin. Remove the meat from the chicken and discard the bones. Shred the chicken meat using your fingers or two forks.

3. Skim the broth to remove any fat. Remove the bay leaves. Return the chicken meat to the pot with remaining teaspoon of salt. Return the pot to medium heat and bring to a simmer to heat the chicken through. Add the peas, and when they turn bright green, after about 2 minutes, remove the soup from the heat. Taste for salt and season as needed; serve warm.

SKINNY TIP § Skim the Fat but Leave the Gelatin Behind The best way to skim the fat from this soup is to refrigerate the soup overnight. The fat will solidify on top of the soup and will be very easy to remove. Also, is your refrigerated chicken soup thick, like the texture of soft jelly? If so, well done! That happens when the natural gelatin leaves the bones as they cook. That's the good stuff, the healing stuff.

KITCHEN TIP § More Chicken Flavor This is a starter chicken soup. Believe it or not, making a chicken soup in under 3 hours is hard to do. As a result, the broth has a mild flavor; most of the chicken flavor in this soup comes from the chicken itself. For a more intense broth, you have a few choices: You can add more chicken bones to the pot, or you can simmer the bones longer.

To add more bones, ask your butcher if he has any chicken back or neck bones lying around. Chop them into 3- or 4-inch pieces, and add with the chicken in step 1. Alternatively, you can remove all the vegetables when you remove the chicken, chop the chicken carcass (bones, minus the meat) into big pieces, and return them to the pot with the broth. Simmer the soup for an additional 2 to 3 hours; you'll get tremendous flavor from those bones.

Last thought, and let's keep this between you and me because some chefs would give me 30 lashes for even saying this: You could also toss in a bouillon cube or two to fortify the stock. They won't teach you that in culinary school, but it's done in kitchens around the world.

"Men like women who make chicken soup. Women love men who make chicken soup. Friends enjoy friends who make chicken soup. You will like yourself more if you can make a good chicken soup."

new england clam chowder

PREP TIME: 20 minutes **TOTAL TIME:** 30 minutes **MAKES** 5 servings **SERVING SIZE:** 1 cup

A few years ago, I had one of those autumn days when I hopped into my old convertible with a friend and drove north to see the leaves putting on their show. One turn, another turn, and there it was: a sign for a chowder festival in Ipswich, Massachusetts.

My car practically drove itself there. When I arrived, I found two dozen vendors offering their "chowdahs." I paid my entry fee and was handed a card to vote for my favorite. Now I had a responsibility. I couldn't just try a few chowders; I had to try *all the chowders*.

My most surprising finding? Some chowders are actually too creamy. On the one hand, chowders are supposed to be this rich-and-creamy, warm-you-on-the-dock experience. But sometimes all that cream just gets between you and the rest of the ingredients. I left the festival with a new goal: to make a chowder that was creamy but not so creamy that it covered up the other good chowder stuff.

By pureeing 2 cups of the potato, which is naturally starchy, I got that thick, rich texture without any cream. And without the cream heft, it was easier to taste the chewy clams and crispy bacon. Plus, by finishing the recipe with fresh herbs, this chowder is refreshing and will leave you eager for the next spoonful.

NUTRITION INFORMATION (PER SERVING):

CALORIES 212, CARBS 27G, FIBER 2G, PROTEIN 13G, TOTAL FAT 5G, SATURATED FAT 2G

- 2 strips bacon, cut into ¼-inch-thick pieces
- 1 medium onion, chopped
- 3 celery stalks, chopped
- 1 bay leaf
- ½ teaspoon fresh thyme, or ¼ teaspoon dried thyme
- ½ cup white wine or beer
- 2 russet potatoes, peeled and cut into ⅓-inch cubes
- 2 cups skim milk
- 2 6½-ounce cans chopped clams, with juice
- ¼ cup chopped fresh parsley
- 2 teaspoons chopped fresh tarragon (optional)
- 1 teaspoon kosher salt
  Freshly ground black pepper

1. Add the bacon to a large pot and turn the heat to medium. When the bacon is soft-crisp, after 3 or 4 minutes, remove the bacon and transfer to a paper towel-lined plate. Add the onion, celery, bay leaf, and thyme to the same pot; cover and sweat the vegetables, stirring occasionally, until the liquid is softened, about 4 minutes. Remove the lid, add the wine or beer, and cook until reduced by half, about 2 minutes.

2. Add potatoes to the pan along with the milk and clam juice from the cans. Bring to a simmer, reduce the heat if necessary, and simmer until the potato has softened, about 10 minutes.

3. Remove 2 cups of mostly solids from the pot and puree in a food processor or blender. You will need a little liquid to get the solids to catch. Return the puree to the pot, add the clams, and return to a simmer. Stir in the parsley, tarragon, salt, and black pepper to taste. Serve garnished with the reserved bacon.

KITCHEN TIP § The Best Clam Juice Many chowder recipes call for bottles of clam juice. Mine did, too, until I tasted the liquid that comes with canned clams. Seems sorta gross, right? It was a total "kissing the frog" moment, but it had to be done. I took a spoon to that cloudy liquid, closed my eyes, and gave it a try. *That stuff is liquid gold.*

Never discard that liquid. Use it in Bloody Marys, chowders, and linguine with clam sauce. It's delicious, and so flavorful that you can omit the bottle of clam juice. (Oh, and yes, I tried the jarred liquid clam juice, too; it tasted like water after experiencing that elixir that comes free in the can.)

KITCHEN TIP § Tarragon? Tarragon is a licorice-flavored herb that works really well with shellfish, but if you can't find it, skip it. Don't schlep from store to store looking for it—just make the soup. And if you've got a little licorice-flavored booze in the liquor cabinet like sambuca, Pernod, or ouzo, add a splash instead.

"I found two dozen vendors offering their 'chowdahs' . . . . Now I had a responsibility. I couldn't just try a few chowders; I had to try *all the chowders.*"

classic french onion soup

PREP TIME: 35 minutes **TOTAL TIME:** 1½ hours **MAKES** 6 servings **SERVING SIZE:** 2 cups

Almost anything worth doing is worth doing slowly. Speed, and less of it, is the key to good French onion soup. You cook the onions slow and low, so the flavor in the soup comes from properly caramelized onions, not a big ol' stick of butter. When the onions are ready, they'll be deep brown, and you'll have browned bits all over the bottom and sides of your pot.

French onion soup recipes traditionally call for homemade veal stock, and if you have access to some, by all means use it. I have yet to find a comparable beef broth on the market, so I use chicken stock, and beef up *(ahem)* the flavor of this soup with a cup of red wine.

NUTRITION INFORMATION
(PER SERVING):
CALORIES 351, CARBS 34G, FIBER 4G, PROTEIN 19G, TOTAL FAT 13G, SATURATED FAT 8G

2 tablespoons unsalted butter
3 pounds red onions, sliced ¼ inch thick (about 12 cups)
2 teaspoons kosher salt
1 6-inch baguette, cut into ⅓-inch slices (18 slices of bread)
1 cup dry red wine
7 cups lower-sodium chicken broth
1 teaspoon fresh thyme, or ¼ teaspoon dried thyme
2 bay leaves
   Freshly ground black pepper
6 ounces Gruyère cheese, shredded (about 1½ cups)

1. Preheat the oven to 375°F.

2. Melt the butter in a large pot over medium heat. Add the onions and 1 teaspoon of the salt, and stir to coat the onions with butter. Cook, stirring regularly, until the onions and the pan are brown, 35 to 45 minutes.

3. While the onions are cooking, arrange the baguette slices in single layer on a baking sheet and bake in the preheated oven until they are dry, crisp, and golden at the edges, about 10 minutes. Set aside.

4. After the onions have browned, add the red wine to the onion mixture and scrape the bottom of the pot with a wooden spoon to loosen any browned bits. Add the broth, thyme, and bay leaves and bring the liquid to a simmer. Reduce the heat if necessary and simmer for 10 minutes. Add the remaining teaspoon of salt and season to taste with black pepper.

5. Place the oven rack 6 inches from the broiler element and turn the broiler on. Set six individual broiler-safe crocks on the baking sheet. When the soup is done, divide the soup among the crocks (discard the bay leaves). Top each bowl with 3 toasted baguette slices (do not overlap) and top with Gruyère. Broil until the cheese is melted and bubbly around edges, 3 to 5 minutes. Serve immediately.

 KITCHEN TIP § No Cryin' in My Kitchen! Go grab an onion and put it in your hand. See the frizzy, hairy bits on the bottom, maybe with some dirt in them? That's the root end. This is where the tears come from. If you keep this intact, you won't cry.
Really.
Cut that onion in half (right now), straight through the root end. I realize that I told you to keep the root intact, but to safely cut onions you always need a flat side to cut on. So that's right, cut through the onion, skin and all. Now you have two halves, with the root end intact. Well done.
Peel one of the onion halves. Now, put the flat side on the cutting board, hold the root end to steady the onion, and begin slicing. No tears right? When you're almost down to the root end, like 1 inch left, toss the root end away. Your fingers are more valuable than this little nub.
The kitchen is a happy place; save your tears for real-life drama.

moroccan saffron chickpea soup

PREP TIME: 25 minutes **TOTAL TIME:** 55 minutes **MAKES** 12 servings **SERVING SIZE:** 1 cup

During the month of Ramadan, many Moroccans fast from sunrise to sundown, and this soup, traditionally called *harira*, is what is used to break the fast in the evening. It's soothing, hearty, and filling after a long day of fasting. With spices like cinnamon, ginger, and saffron, plus lemon and fresh herbs like parsley and cilantro, of course it's delicious. The soup will thicken as it sits, so feel free to add more liquid, or enjoy it as a flavorful side. It's terrific with grilled chicken or lamb.

1. Heat the oil in a large pot over medium heat. Add the onion and 1 teaspoon of the salt, and cook, stirring occasionally, until soft and golden, 6 to 8 minutes.

2. Add the saffron, cinnamon, ginger, and turmeric (if desired) to the pot; stir to combine and cook until fragrant, about 30 seconds.

3. Add the tomatoes, beans, lentils, and 1 teaspoon salt to the pot. Cover with the chicken broth and water, bring the mixture a boil, reduce the heat to a simmer, and

cook until the lentils have softened, about 30 minutes. Remove the pot from the heat.

4. While the soup is simmering, whisk together the eggs and lemon juice in a bowl. When the soup comes off the heat, stir this mixture into the soup. The soup will become lighter in color, and you may see strands of egg in the soup. Stir in the parsley, cilantro, and remaining teaspoon of salt. Serve warm.

NUTRITION INFORMATION
(PER SERVING):

CALORIES 237, CARBS 37G, FIBER 12G, PROTEIN 14G, TOTAL FAT 4G, SATURATED FAT 1G

- 2 tablespoons olive oil
- 1 large onion, sliced
- 1 tablespoon kosher salt
  Very large pinch of saffron
- 1 teaspoon ground cinnamon
- 1 teaspoon ground ginger
- 1 teaspoon turmeric (optional)
- 1 28-ounce can whole peeled tomatoes, crushed with your hands
- 2 15½-ounce cans garbanzo beans, rinsed and drained
- 1½ cups lentils
- 4 cups lower-sodium chicken broth
- 4 cups water
- 2 large eggs, lightly beaten
  Juice of 1 lemon
- ½ cup chopped fresh parsley
- ⅓ cup chopped fresh cilantro

KITCHEN TIP § Not Wild About the Price of Saffron? Saffron has a flavor like its color: bright, orange yellow, sunny, and bold. Not ditzy, flaky beach bum sunny, but deep, soulful Spain or Morocco sunny. Saffron is the stigma of a crocus flower, and the world's most expensive spice. But let's put expensive in perspective: one big pinch is enough for 12 cups of soup. Considering that each filament

has to be harvested from a crocus, how much would you pay for 15 crocuses? Twenty-five cents a flower? If that sounds right to you, saffron is a steal, one of those skinny kitchen ingredients where a little goes a long, memorable way.

KITCHEN TIP § Egg Liason
We add eggs, beaten with lemon juice, at the end of this recipe to thicken the soup, so

there's no need for cream. The eggs thicken the soup while the lemon juice brightens the flavor. You can actually see the soup turn a different color as you whisk in the eggs; it's exciting. By removing the soup from the heat first, you let the eggs thicken the soup, not scramble in it. For more on eggs and heat, see the tip with Pasta Carbonara, page 122.

new year's classic chili

PREP TIME: 10 minutes **TOTAL TIME:** 55 minutes **MAKES** 10 servings **SERVING SIZE:** 1½ cups chili without garnishes

A recipe with 13 ingredients can be intimidating, so let's break it down. Only two ingredients are fresh (the beef and the jalapeño), and you might already have ground beef in your freezer. The other 11 ingredients are pantry staples. Oregano, cumin, kidney beans, vegetable oil, salt —I'm willing to bet you've got half of those ingredients in your house already.

This is one of those highly sought-after, one-pot pantry dishes, the kind you can make a big pot of on a Sunday, freeze, and eat all winter long. My mom makes a pot of this very chili every New Year's Day. My sister-in-law makes it for the Super Bowl. Find your reason and have it whenever you like.

Garnish with the lower-calorie options I list below, and serve over You Can Make White Rice (page 169) for a total of 429 calories.

1. In a large pot, heat the oil over medium-high heat. Add the ground beef and cook, stirring occasionally, until browned, about 8 minutes. Season with 3 tablespoons of the chili powder, 2 teaspoons of the salt, the dried onions, the garlic powder, 1 teaspoon of the oregano, and 1 teaspoon of the cumin, stirring to combine.
2. Add the diced tomatoes, kidney beans, refried beans, jalapeño, and bay leaf. Stir to combine and cook until the sauce has thickened, 30 to 45 minutes.
3. Before serving, season with remaining tablespoon chili powder, teaspoon salt, teaspoon oregano, and teaspoon cumin. Remove and discard jalapeño and bay leaf. Serve warm, garnished as desired.

NUTRITION INFORMATION (PER SERVING):

CALORIES 325, CARBS 32G, FIBER 8G, PROTEIN 25G, TOTAL FAT 10G, SATURATED FAT 3G

- 1 tablespoon vegetable oil
- 2 pounds 90% lean ground beef
- 4 tablespoons chili powder
- 3 teaspoons kosher salt
- 1 tablespoon dried minced onion
- 1 teaspoon garlic powder
- 2 teaspoons dried oregano
- 2 teaspoons ground cumin
- 2 28-ounce cans diced tomatoes
- 2 15-ounce cans kidney beans, rinsed and drained
- 1 15-ounce can refried beans
- 1 jalapeño, stem removed, halved lengthwise, with seeds
- 1 bay leaf
  Finely chopped red onion, sliced scallions, cilantro, sliced pickled jalapeño, squeeze of fresh lime juice, for garnish

 SKINNY TIP § Refried Beans Are Naturally Low in Fat My mom buys a lot of low-fat products. I've even seen fat-free cream in her fridge, which frightens me since cream *is* fat. What can possibly be in that stuff? The low-fat label reassures her, which is fine, but when I sense she's being misled and buying products unnecessarily, I get frustrated. *Nobody messes with my momma.*

Low-fat refried beans are one of those low-fat products I find in her cabinet. If you have a can of refried beans in your cabinet, go get it. Look at that nutritional information label. My can, which does not have a "low-fat" label, has ½ gram of fat per serving. I bet yours has the same amount. Though my mother has been buying reduced-fat *refried* beans for years, calorically there's no reason to. I suppose the word "refried" makes people nervous. Don't be nervous; be smart. Canned refried beans are a naturally low-fat product; eat and enjoy.

 KITCHEN TIP § Slow-Cook It This recipe works well in the slow cooker. After you brown the beef, put it (and everything else in steps 1 and 2) in the slow cooker. Let it cook on high for 5 hours, or on low for 6 to 8 hours. When you're ready to serve, finish with the spices and salt in step 3.

pork chile verde

PREP TIME: 40 minutes **TOTAL TIME:** 1 hour 40 minutes **MAKES** 8 servings **SERVING SIZE:** 1¼ cups stew with 2 tortillas

You've heard of "knife and fork" soups? This is a "tortilla and spoon" stew. Hold a spoon in one hand and a piece of a warm, charred tortilla big enough to grab chunks of pork in the other. Pick up the tender pork chunks with your tortilla, spoon the sauce on top, and pop them into your mouth. When a piece of tortilla gets too small to be useful, toss it into the soup, let it get soaked with the sauce, and pick it up with a spoon.

This dish is really two meals in one: Pork Tacos with Tomatillo Salsa, and Tomatillo Tortilla Soup. Miss Manners, forgive me; this two-handed stew is bliss.

1. Heat the oil in a large pot over medium-high heat. Season the pork with salt, add to the pot, and cook in batches until brown, about 3 minutes per side. Be sure not to crowd the pan, and repeat until all the pork is cooked. Set the pork aside on a plate.

2. Add the onion, garlic, and chiles to the pot and reduce the heat to medium. Cook, stirring up any browned bits from the bottom of the pan, until the onion has softened, about 6 minutes.

3. Return the pork to the pot and add the broth and tomatillos. Bring the stew to a simmer. Cook, stirring occasionally, until the tomatillos have fallen apart and you can cut the pork with the side of a wooden spoon, about 1 hour.

4. While pork is simmering, cut two of the tortillas into ½-inch pieces and add to the stew. Just before serving, heat the remaining tortillas according to package directions, or see the charring tip on page 36.

5. Remove the stew from the heat and stir in the cilantro. Taste and adjust for seasoning. Serve with the warm tortillas.

NUTRITION INFORMATION
(PER SERVING):
CALORIES 453, CARBS 34G, FIBER 7G, PROTEIN 43G, TOTAL FAT 16G, SATURATED FAT 4G

- 2 tablespoons vegetable oil
- 3 pounds pork stew meat, trimmed of fat and cut into 1½-inch chunks
- 2 teaspoons kosher salt, plus more to taste
- 1 large onion, sliced
- 4 garlic cloves, coarsely chopped
- 4 large poblano chiles, cut into 1-inch pieces, with seeds
- 4 cups lower-sodium chicken broth
- 1½ pounds tomatillos, husked, rinsed, and cut into quarters
- 18 6-inch corn tortillas
- ½ cup coarsely chopped fresh cilantro

KITCHEN TIP § How Spicy Is This? Even though they're supposed to be on the mild side of the spicy continuum, poblanos are still spicy. *And you're using a lot of them.* Wear plastic gloves when handling the chiles, as even a little heat will stay on your hands and can be felt later, especially when you're taking out your contact lenses. Eeek!

If you don't want the heat, remove the seeds and veins from the peppers. When you add the peppers to the pot, and for the first 10 minutes or so of cooking, you're gonna feel the heat. The heat will mellow as the stew cooks, so for those of you who like it make-me-sweat spicy, keep the hot pepper sauce nearby.

SKINNY TIP § Tomatillos and Salsa Verde Tomatillos are unique looking, like small green tomatoes wrapped in a papery husk. They are the key ingredient in salsa verde.

If you can't find tomatillos, buy a few jars of salsa verde, brown the pork, pour the salsa over and let the pork simmer for an hour. Salsa is a good skinny ingredient; it's naturally low in calories.

chicken and andouille gumbo

PREP TIME: 30 minutes **TOTAL TIME:** 1 hour **MAKES** 10 servings **SERVING SIZE:** 1 cup

This is my favorite soup in the book. But it requires one component that can scare some home cooks: roux.

Let's break down the big bad roux. It's just two ingredients: flour and fat. Cook the flour in the fat until it becomes a paste, which gives it the ability to thicken liquid. There are light rouxs and dark rouxs, depending on how long you cook them. The darker the roux, the less it will thicken liquid. Gumbos require the darkest roux.

And what a dark roux lacks in thickening power it more than makes up for in flavor. It will put you right there on Bourbon Street, standing in front of a voodoo shop wondering if you should step in and let someone tell you your future.

I see your future now and it has a dark chocolate-colored roux in it, some sausage, chicken, and *flavor*. If you make this soup, people will look at you differently. Like you know something they don't. Which you will. You'll know how to make a roux.

Serve over You Can Make White Rice (page 169) and the total calorie count is just over 400 calories. This recipe was adapted from one taught to me by Corbin Evans, a talented New Orleans chef.

NUTRITION INFORMATION
(PER SERVING):

CALORIES 276, CARBS 18G, FIBER 2G, PROTEIN 12G, TOTAL FAT 17G, SATURATED FAT 3G

- 4 bone-in skinless chicken thighs (about 1 pound)
- ¼ cup Cajun seasoning
- ½ cup vegetable oil
- ¾ cup all-purpose flour
- 1 medium onion, cut into ¾-inch cubes
- 1 green bell pepper, seeded and cut into ¾-inch cubes
- 2 celery stalks, sliced
- ½ teaspoon kosher salt, plus more to taste
- 6 cups lower-sodium chicken broth
- 4 ounces andouille sausage, sliced
- 1 cup seeded and coarsely chopped tomatoes, canned or fresh
- 3 tablespoons minced garlic
- 3 bay leaves
- ¼ cup fresh parsley, coarsely chopped
- 3 scallions, thinly sliced, whites and greens divided
- 1 tablespoon Worcestershire sauce
  Hot sauce to taste

1. Preheat the oven to 400°F. Rub the chicken with the Cajun seasoning and place on a foil-lined baking sheet. Bake until cooked through, about 25 minutes.

2. Heat the oil in a large, wide pot over medium heat and whisk in the flour. Using a flat-bottomed wooden spoon, stir the roux until it turns milk chocolate brown (this should take about 12 minutes). Add the onion and continue to cook, stirring, until the roux is dark chocolate brown and the onion has softened, about 10 minutes.

3. Add the pepper, celery, and salt and cook, stirring, until softened, about 5 more minutes. Whisk the broth into the roux slowly, over the course of 3 to 5 minutes, so the broth can thicken as it heats with the roux. Add the sausage, tomato, garlic, bay leaves, and chicken; bring the broth to a simmer and cook for 20 minutes, stirring occasionally.

4. Remove the bay leaves and chicken from the pot and separate the chicken from the bones. Discard the bones, shred the meat, and return the meat to the pot. Add the parsley, scallion whites, and Worcestershire sauce and stir to incorporate. Taste and season with salt and hot sauce as needed. Serve hot, garnished with scallion greens.

KITCHEN TIP § Why You Makin' Me Fuss with Hot Thighs? You know I like a minimum of fuss in the kitchen. Fewer pots, fewer ingredients, less fuss. So if I'm making you fuss with hot thighs, there's a reason for it. Those thigh bones have good flavor. By simmering the chicken on the bone in the sauce, you're getting more flavor than you would if you took the chicken off the bone first. Also, though the recipe says 20 minutes of simmer time, you can let this soup simmer for 10 minutes, or even an hour. The longer the better. The flavor will deepen, and yes, like many soups and stews, this one is better the second day. I know it seems boneheaded, and in a way it is. There's flavor in them there bones.

 SKINNY TIP § Do You Andouille? Andouille is a smoky, spicy pork sausage that is found in Cajun dishes like gumbo and jambalaya. If they don't stock it in the sausage section of your grocery store, order it online: D'Artagnan makes a terrific version that can be found at www.dartagnan.com.

If you're impatient like me and can't wait for delivery, substitute kielbasa for andouille and be sure to add a few shakes of hot sauce to the soup pot. Calorically, be sure to reach for lower-calorie turkey kielbasa. Andouille has a low 120 calories per 2-ounce serving, so be sure your sausage is in that range. Slice that sausage thin so that you get a good number of slices in every serving. You'll be surprised how far 4 ounces of sausage can go, both in flavor and in quantity.

KITCHEN TIP § Canned Tomatoes If you have access to flavorful tomatoes in season, use them. But nine times out of ten, they're not. So grab that can of whole peeled tomatoes, discard the seeds, and chop the flesh. They're in season year-round.

"It will put you right there on Bourbon Street, standing in front of a voodoo shop wondering if you should step in and let some-one tell you your future."

something to munch:

snacks & dips

my college roommate,

Rachelle, is an amazing doctor. Happy in her work, devoted, and caring. But like so many of us, she puts herself last when it comes to taking care of her own needs.

At night, she comes home ravenous. So, while her most excellent husband is preparing their meal (good guy!), she eats the caloric equivalent of dinner *before* dinner. That's right, 500 calories of cheese and crackers plus a glass of wine before she even sits down. Are you nodding? Have you been there?

Not long ago, Rachelle asked me for my weight loss advice, and I gave her this prescription: *Eat more.*

Begin by adding 200 calories midafternoon, and if you feel it's needed, another 200 to 250 midmorning as well. *Take two snacks and that pre-dinner despiration will be a thing of the past.*

I know whereof I prescribe. When I worked as a cookbook editor and had three squares a day (plus 11 a.m. and 3 p.m. coffees), I gained weight. I ate big meals, fell into food comas, and was ravenous for the next feeding.

Get me off *that* roller coaster!

Prior to that, I worked in a test kitchen. I cooked and ate all day long; it was part of the job. *But I weighed less!* When it came time for dinner I had a smaller meal—what Europeans refer to as "supper"— mostly because I just wasn't hungry.

When I grazed all day long, forget the blood sugar crashes and coffee resuscitations: I ate little bits of everything and was rewarded for my efforts with good, even energy and a figure I liked. In fact, now that I think about it, all the women who worked in the test kitchen looked good. Healthy, curvy good.

And yes, I realize that not everyone can stand around cooking all day, but my point is this: If we want to look and feel our best, we've got to snack. In this chapter, I've got plenty of snacks and retro finger food that you can take to the office or enjoy at home. There's Buffalo Dip (page 97) and Parmesan Twists (page 101) for couch-potato football Sundays and Shrimp and Mango Summer Rolls (page 106) that look and taste like upscale restaurant food. Go retro with Stuffed Mushrooms (page 103) and Deviled Eggs (page 102), or try a Mediterranean mezze platter with Lemony Hummus with Parsley (page 108), Smoky Babaghanouj (page 111), and Romesco Spread (page 110).

Bring these snacks to work, and instead of the 3:30 yawn, you'll be chirping like a mynah bird. Your colleagues will wonder where you got the energy. And the new outfit. *And wait, there's something else that's different. Did you . . . lose . . . weight?*

Eat more and you'll be thinner. Counterintuitive yet true.

chicken satay with spicy peanut sauce

PREP TIME: 35 minutes TOTAL TIME: 50 minutes MAKES 8 servings SERVING SIZE: 3 skewers with 1 tablespoon dipping sauce

Chicken skewers with dipping sauce are irresistible. Who doesn't love tapping into their inner caveman and eating meat from a stick? Tame those Neanderthals with posh presentation: Lay the skewers on a platter with the dipping sauce in a small bowl.

   If you've got a peanut situation, try another sauce like the honey-mustard on page 52 in place of the peanut sauce.

1. For the chicken: Cut the chicken into ¼-inch strips across the grain. Lay the strips on a cutting board and gently flatten by pounding with your fist; they will be a variety of shapes and sizes. If some slices are very long (more than three bites), you may need to cut them in two. Place the chicken in a bowl with the oil and soy sauce and turn the chicken in the sauce to coat. Let the chicken marinate at room temperature for at least 20 minutes, or refrigerate overnight.

2. For the peanut sauce: Combine the peanut butter, soy sauce, lime juice, honey, scallions, garlic powder, and red pepper flakes in a bowl and whisk together.

3. Preheat a flat griddle over medium heat. Remove chicken from marinade, pat dry, and thread onto skewers; discard the marinade. Place the chicken on the hot griddle so that the skewers are positioned away from the direct heat and cook the chicken until golden brown, 2 to 3 minutes per side. Serve the skewers with peanut sauce for dipping.

NUTRITION INFORMATION (PER SERVING):

CALORIES 126, CARBS 4G, FIBER 0G, PROTEIN 12, TOTAL FAT 7G, SATURATED FAT 1G

FOR CHICKEN:

12 ounces boneless, skinless chicken breast (about 1 large)
2 tablespoons vegetable oil
2 tablespoons lower-sodium soy sauce

FOR PEANUT SAUCE:

3 tablespoons creamy peanut butter
2 tablespoons lower-sodium soy sauce
2 tablespoons fresh lime juice
1 tablespoon honey
1 tablespoon chopped scallion greens
⅛ teaspoon garlic powder
⅛ teaspoon red pepper flakes

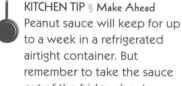

KITCHEN TIP § Make Ahead
Peanut sauce will keep for up to a week in a refrigerated airtight container. But remember to take the sauce out of the fridge about 30 minutes before serving to let it come to room temperature—you know how stubborn peanut butter can be.

KITCHEN TIP § Fire Up That Grill
If you want to grill the chicken, soak the skewers in water for 20 minutes before threading the chicken onto them. This will help prevent the skewers from charring when cooking over an open flame.

SKINNY TIP § Why Am I Pounding This Chicken? When you flatten the chicken with your fist, you make the pieces look bigger. Think about it; you're turning one big breast into 24 skewers, an appetizer that feeds eight. As a meal, you could probably eat that breast in one sitting, but would you ever sit and eat 24 skewers? Seems like a whole lotta food when it's reconfigured that way, doesn't it?

crab ravigote crostini

PREP TIME: 35 minutes   TOTAL TIME: 35 minutes   MAKES 16 servings   SERVING SIZE: 4 filled crostini

Ravigote is a perky little sauce whose name comes from the French word for "reinvigorate." Ravigote has a good amount of fresh herbs, onions, and vinegar and is served warm or cold, with fish or meat.

The nudge-and-wink legend of this sauce is that it's the one pro cooks turn to when the fish is getting a little past its prime and they need to resuscitate it, *Weekend At Bernie's*–style.

On the one hand, eeeew. But on the other, if the sauce is that magical, I want at it (but with fresh crabmeat, thank you very much). For those who love crab dip, this is a reinvigorating alternative. This recipe feeds a crowd; feel free to halve it or save some for lunch (see tip).

1. Preheat the oven to 375°F. Using a serrated knife, cut the baguette into sixty-four ⅓-inch slices and discard the ends. Transfer the bread slices to a baking sheet (you may need to do this in batches) and cook until crisp, about 8 to 10 minutes. Set aside until ready to use.

2. Meanwhile, place the mayonnaise, vinegar, chopped egg, shallot, capers, mustard, parsley, chives, and tarragon in a bowl and stir to combine. Gently fold in the cleaned crabmeat and season with salt as needed. Serve 1 tablespoon ravigote on top of each slice of toasted baguette.

NUTRITION INFORMATION
(PER SERVING):

CALORIES 148, CARBS 11G, FIBER 1G, PROTEIN 10G, TOTAL FAT 7G, SATURATED FAT 1G

1   24-inch baguette
½   cup mayonnaise
⅓   cup white vinegar
2   hard-boiled eggs, peeled and chopped (see Deviled Eggs, page 102)
1   small shallot or onion, finely minced
1   tablespoon capers, rinsed, drained, and chopped
1   tablespoon Dijon mustard
1   tablespoon finely chopped fresh parsley
1   tablespoon minced fresh chives
1   tablespoon chopped fresh tarragon
1   pound lump crab meat, picked over for shells
    Kosher salt

 KITCHEN TIP § Less-Expensive Lump? Sign Me Up! For the last year or so, I've been noticing 1-pound cans of jumbo lump pasteurized crabmeat in the refrigerator section of my seafood department for about $10 a can. That's much better than what I pay at the fishmonger for fresh-picked crab meat, which runs closer to $40 for a tub of the same size. Turns out the canned stuff is good, and I can find plenty of ways to spend that extra $30. If they don't carry pasteurized canned crab in the seafood section of your grocery store, ask your store manager if he or she might consider stocking it.

 SKINNY TIP § This Reminds Me of Tuna Salad, But Better Me, too! If you like, try Crab Ravigote as a meal. You'll save 40 calories per portion if you forgo the crostini: ¼ cup is only 103 calories per serving. Enjoy a cup of Crab Ravigote for lunch over greens and it's only 412 calories.

buffalo dip

PREP TIME: 10 minutes TOTAL TIME: 10 minutes MAKES 8 servings SERVING SIZE: 1 cup celery sticks with 2 tablespoons dip

Buffalo wings are a guilty pleasure and boy are they filled with calories. The calories aren't coming from the meat (or the bones). In fact, there's not much to a wing but some really high-calorie skin and sauce.

But I'm not eating wings for the meat or the skin, I'm eating them for the *crunch* and that sauce. So here's an alternative that has both. It's crunchy, saucy, and—with just three ingredients—a whole lot less fuss than making wings from scratch.

1. Combine the goat cheese and hot sauce in a bowl and whisk to combine. Serve with celery sticks.

NUTRITION INFORMATION
(PER SERVING):

CALORIES 50, CARBS 3G, FIBER 1G, PROTEIN 3G, TOTAL FAT 3G, SATURATED FAT 2G

1 4-ounce package fresh goat cheese, at room temperature
½ cup Frank's Red Hot Sauce
1 bunch celery, trimmed and cut into 4-inch pieces

 SKINNY TIP § How About Cream Cheese? Use it! If you use ½ cup cream cheese in place of the goat cheese, it will add 12 calories per serving. Whipped cream cheese is a lower-calorie option, since whipped cream cheese is really just regular cream cheese plus air. You can use ½ cup whipped cream cheese in place of the goat cheese and you'll save yourself 5 calories per serving.

 SKINNY TIP § Frank's Hot Sauce Frank's Red Hot is the original Buffalo hot sauce. You can use other hot sauces, you can make your own, but if you want authentic Buffalo wing flavor, it's got to be Frank's. Just open the bottle and combine with softened goat or cream cheese. Skinny Buffalo Bills fans, this one's for you!

"If you don't don't. enjoy

MAKING IT AND IT DOESN'T TASTE TERRIFIC, THEN WHO CARES IF IT'S LOWER IN CALORIES?"

parmesan twists

PREP TIME: 20 minutes   TOTAL TIME: 30 minutes   MAKES 12 servings   SERVING SIZE: 2 straws

I don't know which I like more about these Parmesan Twists: the way they look or the way they taste. If you put them out for a party, put them in a tall vase so they can splay out like a bunch of branches, or lay them on a tray. They're visually compelling, light, crisp, tasty, and have I mentioned how easy they are to make? Four ingredients and only 20 minutes of prep. Have at it!

1. Preheat the oven to 400°F. Cover two baking sheets with parchment paper and set aside.

2. On a lightly floured surface, unfold the puff pastry. Flour the side facing you and use a rolling pin to roll it to a 12-inch square. Brush the puff with egg mixture (you'll probably use less than half of what you've got, but that's fine).

3. Sprinkle the cheese and paprika evenly over the puff. Press the toppings gently but firmly into the puff to help them adhere.

4. Slice the puff into twenty-four ½-inch strips. Divide the strips between the prepared baking sheets, seasoned side up. Twist the strips twice, clockwise at the top and counterclockwise at the bottom, so that you've got one long spiral. Put the baking sheets in the oven and cook until the twists have puffed and are golden brown, about 18 minutes. Let cool and serve.

NUTRITION INFORMATION
(PER SERVING):

CALORIES 97, CARBS 7G, FIBER 0G, PROTEIN 3G, TOTAL FAT 6G, SATURATED FAT 3G

Small scattering of flour
1 8½-ounce sheet puff pastry, defrosted
1 large egg yolk, beaten with 1 tablespoon water
⅓ cup grated Parmesan cheese
1 teaspoon paprika

 SKINNY TIP § Can You Make a Low-Calorie Croissant? No, You Can't Well, you can, but it won't taste like a croissant. And puff pastry is basically one big sheet of croissant dough—lots of butter nestled between layers and layers of flaky pastry. So why is this insanely high-calorie ingredient in a skinny cookbook? Because it's good. And inexpensive. And easy to use. And my top priority is that terrific food comes out of your kitchen.

Check out the calorie count: 97 for two 12-inch cheese sticks. Because you're having a small portion, it's not bad at all. Oh, I know, you're going to be in the kitchen nibbling on all the broken pieces and cursing my name. Please don't! Because even if you have two portions, you're still under 200 calories. You could eat those calories without even thinking about it (or enjoying them) by drinking a soda. At least with this, you'll enjoy what you're eating and take time doing so. This naughty little treat will give you real pleasure. Enjoy it.

 KITCHEN TIP § Put That Knife Down Use a pizza wheel to cut strips of puff pastry. It makes a straight line without pulling at the puff.

deviled eggs

PREP TIME: 30 minutes TOTAL TIME: 1 hour 30 minutes MAKES 4 servings SERVING SIZE: 3 eggs

The devilishness in these eggs comes from their heat, which is typically from a spoonful of Dijon mustard. If this recipe were a hand of poker, you'd "see" that Dijon and raise it one pickled jalapeño (you know, those spicy pickled peppers that come on top of nachos). Pickled jalapeños are one of my favorite condiments because the flavor-to-calorie ratio is high. Twenty slices of pickled jalapeño are a measly 5 calories. Eat'em and weep.

1. Place the eggs in a small pot of cold water, covering by at least 1 inch. Bring to a simmer, cover, remove from the heat, and keep the eggs submerged until cooked through, 15 minutes. When done, place the eggs in a bowl of ice water until cool, about 10 minutes. Peel.

2. Halve the eggs lengthwise and remove the yolks. For a clean slice, wipe your knife with a damp towel between each cut.

Place the egg yolks in a bowl and the egg whites on a serving plate.

3. Mash the yolks with a fork. Add the mayonnaise, mustard, and lemon juice and mix well. Season to taste with salt and pepper.

4. Use a spoon to divide the filling among the egg halves. Top with pickled jalapeño and garnish with chives or a dusting of paprika.

NUTRITION INFORMATION
(PER SERVING):

CALORIES 135, CARBS 3G, FIBER 0G, PROTEIN 10G, TOTAL FAT 9G, SATURATED FAT 2G

6 large eggs
¼ cup light mayonnaise
1 tablespoon Dijon mustard
1 teaspoon fresh lemon juice
   Kosher salt and coarsely ground black pepper
12 slices pickled jalapeño, finely chopped
   Chopped fresh chives or paprika, for garnish

KITCHEN TIP § **Old Eggs Are Good Eggs** How do you tell the difference between an old egg and a young one? Put both in a bowl of water. Old eggs float, young eggs sink. As eggs age, they lose liquid through their shell. This forms an air bubble inside the shell that keeps them afloat.

A student of mine once told me that her mom used to have her to throw out the old eggs because they were, well . . . old. Where's the love? Old eggs are useful; they whip up into fluffier meringues (see Pavlova with Berries, page 252), and they are exactly what you want when cooking hard-boiled eggs, since that air

pocket makes them easier to peel. Peeling a fresh egg is like peeling yourself out of skintight jeans after dinner. *Avoid that.*

KITCHEN TIP § **The Trick to Peeling Eggs?** Here's the simplest way to peel hard-boiled eggs: Give them a light tap on the counter and roll them gently with the palm of your hand against the hard surface. Rolling will fracture the shell into what seems like a million little pieces. And yet, the pieces stay on the egg. That's because there's a thin membrane between the egg and the shell. That membrane is your friend; use it to remove those little bits of shell in one clean

pulling motion. You'll have fewer "egg white malfunctions" and more pristine egg white halves.

SKINNY TIP § **Light Mayo? But Didn't You Say...** Unlike the Caesar dressing (page 56), where full-fat mayo is the only option, for this recipe none of my tasters could detect a difference between low-fat and regular mayo (the spiciness of the filling takes over). So save those 36 calories per serving. If you choose to use full-fat mayo, the total per-serving calorie count is 148.

stuffed mushrooms

PREP TIME: 15 minutes **TOTAL TIME:** 40 minutes **MAKES** 4 servings **SERVING SIZE:** 3 mushrooms

Mushrooms are super-low in calories. So, when we stuff them, it's like being a kid in a calorie shop: We get to play.

To start this recipe, we need some fat to cook the garlic and shallots. Let's see: We've got butter, olive oil, vegetable oil, and . . . bacon.

Smoky bacon fat is a terrific complement to pecans and mushrooms. Plus, bacon gives us a bonus. In addition to the rendered fat we use for cooking, we get crispy bacon bits as texture in our caps.

Bacon can be a sensible choice for skinny eating. I know it's hard to think about eating bacon as a skinny thing, but if you're going to eat it (and I know you are), do it in a way that extends the flavor without guilt. Think about it: one piece of bacon for 12 mushrooms? It's nothing! So drink your water, exercise, and eat your bacon.

1. Preheat the oven to 375°F. Clean the mushrooms with a damp paper towel, remove the stems, and set aside. Place the caps top side down on a foil-lined baking sheet, and mince the stems.

2. Cook the bacon in a medium skillet over medium heat until it has rendered its fat and is beginning to crisp, about 3 minutes. Add the pecans, shallot, garlic, and salt. Cook until the shallot has softened, about 3 minutes more. Add the vinegar and use a wooden spoon to scrape up any browned bits from the bottom of the pan.

3. Spoon the stuffing into the caps and bake for 20 to 25 minutes. Garnish with chives and serve.

NUTRITION INFORMATION
(PER SERVING):

CALORIES 107, CARBS 6G, FIBER 1G, PROTEIN 4G, TOTAL FAT 8G, SATU-RATED FAT 2G

- 12 large white or cremini mushrooms (2 to 2½ inches in diameter)
- 1 strip bacon, chopped
- ¼ cup chopped pecans
- 1 large shallot, minced
- 1 garlic clove, minced
- ¼ teaspoon kosher salt
- 2 teaspoons cider vinegar
- 2 teaspoons chopped fresh chives

 KITCHEN TIP § Fresh 'Shrooms
When you choose mushrooms, pick ones with caps that are tightly closed over the gills, as those are the freshest. Since fresher mushrooms have more moisture, the cooking time will be closer to 25 minutes.

 KITCHEN TIP § In-cremin-ating
Cremini mushrooms look like white button mushrooms, but are darker. Their flavor is intense, almost as if that white button mushroom just had a big cup of coffee. And did you know that portobello mushrooms are actually just overgrown creminis? In fact, sometimes creminis are labeled "baby bellas." So if you like that rich, deep, I'm-in-a-forest portobello flavor, pick creminis.

shrimp and mango summer rolls

PREP TIME: 30 minutes **TOTAL TIME:** 45 minutes **MAKES** 4 servings **SERVING SIZE:** 2 rolls with 1 tablespoon Nuoc Chom

When this roll comes together, it's almost like a stained glass window. You can see the shrimp, mango, and herbs through the thin rice paper wrapper. If you like design, cake decorating, or accessorizing, this recipe is for you.

If you're not so much about presentation, you can still have fun. Just see the *Can't Wrap Your Head Around It?* tip below.

For extra flavor, serve this with the Spicy Peanut Sauce on page 94 (and you want to, you really, really want to!); it's an extra 47 calories per tablespoon. The Nuoc Chom is 11 calories.

NUTRITION INFORMATION
(PER SERVING):

CALORIES 97, CARBS 19G, FIBER 2G, PROTEIN 5G, TOTAL FAT 0G, SATURATED FAT 0G

- 12 large shrimp, cooked and halved lengthwise
- 1 small ripe mango, cut into long, thin matchsticks
- ⅔ cup fresh bean sprouts
- ½ cup fresh mint leaves
- ½ cup sliced fresh basil leaves
- ½ cup fresh cilantro leaves
- 4 large leaves Boston or red leaf lettuce, sliced in half
- 8 spring roll wrappers, plus a few as they're fragile (see tip below)
- ½ cup Nuoc Chom (recipe follows)

1. The easiest way to make summer rolls is with assembly-line precision, so let's set it up. Prepare the shrimp, mango, bean sprouts, mint, basil, cilantro, and lettuce leaves and organize the ingredients in individual bowls or piles on a larger platter or cutting board. Place a skillet of warm water on the counter, and be sure the skillet is wide enough so that each wrapper can lay flat. Lay a dry kitchen towel on the counter near the skillet; this is where you will make the roll. Prepare a platter with a slightly damp kitchen towel so that you can cover the completed rolls and prevent them from drying out.

2. Lay a wrapper in the warm water and remove when it feels like wet plastic wrap, 10 to 20 seconds depending on the heat of the water (you want it as hot as you can comfortably touch it, the hotter the better). Place the flexible wrapper on the dry towel and place 1 piece of lettuce in the bottom third of the wrapper. Top with 3 slices of shrimp and some mango, sprouts, and herbs. Roll up, tucking the sides in, burrito-style. Place on the platter and cover with the slightly damp towel. Repeat with the remaining wrappers.

3. Serve the rolls whole or slice on the bias. Serve with Nuoc Chom for dipping, if desired.

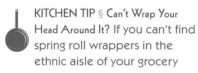 **SKINNY TIP** § Double Vision We slice the shrimp in half so that you end up with what looks like more shrimp per serving. Since you can see the shrimp through the wrapper, we want to emphasize that bounty.

 KITCHEN TIP § Can't Wrap Your Head Around It? If you can't find spring roll wrappers in the ethnic aisle of your grocery store, and you don't have an Asian market nearby, you can order them online from a number of sites, including Amazon.com.

If you can't be bothered with the wrappers or don't feel like assembling, divide the fillings among small Bibb lettuce leaves. Your rolls will be lovely, easier to prepare, and just as dippable.

KITCHEN TIP § Spring Roll Wrappers Are Fragile Wet, malleable spring roll wrappers are very fragile. You may tear a few when you work with them, but don't fret; everybody does. That's why they come so many to a package. Toss the wrecked wrapper to the side, pull out a new sheet, and try again.

nuoc chom

This classic Vietnamese dipping sauce is tangy, salty, spicy, and pungent. If you use fish sauce, it will be clear, and if you use anchovy paste it will be a bit cloudy. Since fish sauce is made from anchovies, the flavor is the same. Either way you go, Nuoc Chom is a tangy complement to Shrimp and Mango Summer Rolls.

1. Combine the vinegar, fish sauce, sugar, lime juice, garlic, and red pepper flakes in a small bowl and stir until the sugar dissolves.

NUTRITION INFORMATION
(PER SERVING):

CALORIES 11, CARBS 2G, FIBER 0G, PROTEIN 0G, TOTAL FAT 0G, SATURATED FAT 0G

¼ cup rice vinegar
¼ cup Vietnamese or Thai fish sauce, or 1 teaspoon anchovy paste mixed with ¼ cup water
2 tablespoons sugar
2 tablespoons fresh lime juice
1 garlic clove, peeled and smashed
¼ teaspoon red pepper flakes

 KITCHEN TIP § Is the Garlic Supposed to Be Like That? Yes. I just want you to get a bit of garlic flavor, so I made it easy. That smashed piece of garlic will leach its flavor into the sauce. Or, put all the ingredients in the food processor and let'er rip. That way you'll have lots of little pieces of garlic throughout the sauce.

endive leaves with smoked salmon, horseradish cream, and dill

PREP TIME: 15 minutes TOTAL TIME: 15 minutes MAKES 8 servings SERVING SIZE: 3 filled endive leaves

This is a perfect starter for a baby shower or brunch. It's elegant finger food without the fuss. For presentation alone, it's a winner.

And flavor-wise, sour cream and horseradish deliver the perfect counterpoints to rich smoked salmon, all cradled in a refreshing endive leaf. This one's feminine without being fragile; my kinda gal.

1. Combine the sour cream, mayonnaise, and horseradish in a small bowl and stir.

2. Separate the leaves from the endive. Lay a slice of salmon in the belly of each leaf and spoon ½ teaspoon of the sour cream mixture on top. Lay a small piece of dill on top of the sour cream mixture and arrange the filled leaves decoratively on a platter.

NUTRITION INFORMATION
(PER SERVING):

CALORIES 60, CARBS 5G, FIBER 4G, PROTEIN 4G, TOTAL FAT 3G, SATURATED FAT 1G

- 3 tablespoons sour cream
- 1 tablespoon mayonnaise
- 1 teaspoon prepared horseradish, drained
- 2 medium Belgian endive (enough for 24 leaves)
- ¼ pound sliced smoked salmon, cut into pieces (see ttip below)
  Dill leaves, to garnish

 KITCHEN TIP § "I Fought the Bulb, and . . . " When you wrestle with endive, endive wins, so don't try to tear the leaves from the head. Instead, trim the root end with a knife so the endive leaves fall away from the center and keep a clean edge. Use larger leaves for this presentation.

 KITCHEN TIP § Smoked Salmon Smoked salmon comes in 4-ounce (aka ¼-pound) packages, which are perfect for this recipe. My package contains 4 long pieces, which also makes the math easy: I divide each piece of salmon into 6 pieces so that I have enough to fill the leaves. If you buy smoked salmon in bulk (bless your heart and your palate), the smoked salmon portion is bigger than you might think, about 1½ inches by 2 inches.

 KITCHEN TIP § Don't Doubt Dill Dill looks delicate, but don't doubt its potency: Those fronds are flavorful. To garnish, choose the feathery fronds, and snip them from the firmer branches with scissors instead of a knife.

lemony hummus with parsley

PREP TIME: 15 minutes TOTAL TIME: 15 minutes MAKES 14 servings SERVING SIZE: 2 tablespoons

Why homemade hummus? You can buy it almost anywhere—even in the food section of some gas station convenience stores—and you know the brand you like. Why take the time or make the effort?

Well, if you were here I'd give you a spoonful and you'd see. But you're not, so here's my case: 1. Freshly squeezed lemon juice versus something the label refers to as "citric acid"; 2. I can buy a tub of hummus for $2.50. I can make three times that amount for that same $2.50; 3. Close your eyes and picture lemons growing on a tree. Now imagine yourself picking parsley from a garden. Now, imagine preservatives like potassium sorbate and sodium benzoate. Which do you want to eat?

Listen, I'm not a cook-aholic, and I certainly enjoy grocery store conveniences. I just want you to have options for making food that's even better. You're busy; if you want to take store-bought hummus to work, you've got my blessing. You snack, I'm happy.

Try the hummus with carrots, celery, cauliflower, and broccoli florets for dipping.

1. Combine the garbanzo beans, lemon zest and juice, tahini, garlic, and salt in a food processor; pulse until you have a thick paste. If you have puree on the bottom and whole beans on the top, use a flexible spatula to scrape those beans into the bowl and pulse again. With the processor running, add the olive oil and water and puree until smooth. Add the parsley leaves and pulse 2 or 3 times to incorporate.

NUTRITION INFORMATION (PER SERVING):

CALORIES 77, CARBS 8G, FIBER 2G, PROTEIN 2G, TOTAL FAT 5G, SATURATED FAT 1G

- 1 15½-ounce can garbanzo beans (chickpeas), drained and rinsed
  Zest and juice of 1 lemon (about 2 tablespoons)
- 2 teaspoons tahini (sesame seed paste)
- 1 small garlic clove
- ¼ teaspoon kosher salt
- ¼ cup extra-virgin olive oil
- ¼ cup water
- 1 cup coarsely chopped parsley leaves

KITCHEN TIP § D.I.Y. Tahini
Tahini is a common Middle Eastern ingredient that's less common in the U.S. If you can't find it in the supermarket, try a health food market. If you strike out in both places but have access to sesame seeds (look in the spice aisle or the ethnic food aisle, especially near the Japanese foods), you can make tahini yourself. Toast 1 cup sesame seeds in the oven at 375°F until fragrant and light golden, 10 to 15 minutes. Add to a food processor and grind. Cover with ¼ cup vegetable oil and grind until the mixture is a smooth paste. Tahini is a key ingredient in this hummus and in Smoky Babaghanouj (page 111).

 KITCHEN TIP § Parsley Bleeds
When you add the parsley, pulse it just a few times to incorporate. If you pulse more than that, it will start to bleed and your hummus will go green. Alternatively, take the pre-parsley hummus out of the food processor, finely chop the parsley, and stir it in.

KITCHEN TIP § Hummus from Scratch: You've Been Warned If you want to take this recipe to another level, use the rehydration process in the recipe for Black Beans from Scratch (page 175) and rehydrate a bag of dried garbanzos. Use 1¾ cups rehydrated garbanzos in place of the canned. Garbanzos take a bit longer to cook than black beans, so figure an extra 30 minutes of simmer time. A word of caution: Once you try homemade hummus, there's no going back.

 SKINNY TIP § Red Pepper Hummus?
Sure you can! Just use ¾ cup roasted red peppers, rinsed, drained, and chopped, in place of the parsley. Your hummus will be red and very smooth, since the red peppers add a lot of moisture to the mix. Or, in addition to the lemon and parsley, add chopped sun-dried tomatoes to this recipe. They are just 5 calories per tomato, and you know how flavorful they are.

"I'll take healthy and happy over scrawny and cranky any day."

romesco spread

PREP TIME: 15 minutes TOTAL TIME: 15 minutes MAKES 10 servings SERVING SIZE: 2 tablespoons

When I made this recipe, I gave it the ultimate test: I shared it with a friend from Spain. *Salsa romesco*, as it's called over there, is a Catalan specialty. As soon as she saw that bright red color, she said, "Ahhhhhhh, *R-r-r-r-r-r-r-omesco!*" and rolled her tongue in a way I could never hope to. She told me that in Spain she likes to grill long onions (like our scallions) till they are sweet and chewy, dip them in Romesco, tilt her head back sword-swallower style, and eat them bite by bite. Romesco also makes a terrific accompaniment to grilled fish.

As a snack, spread Romesco on crostini (see Gazpacho tip on page 66 for recipe). The flavor is intense and vivid, rich with roasted peppers and toasted almonds. When it comes together, the individual elements are hard to place, a *what-is-that?* kind of delicious.

1. Tear the bread into pieces with your hands and add it, the toasted almonds, and garlic to the food processor. Pulse until almonds are finely ground, about 20 seconds. Add the roasted peppers, vinegar, salt, and red pepper flakes to the food processor and puree to make a paste. While the food processor is running, add the oil and water.

NUTRITION INFORMATION
(PER SERVING):

CALORIES 59, CARBS 3G, FIBER 1G, PROTEIN 1G, TOTAL FAT 5G, SATURATED FAT 1G

- 1 slice sandwich bread (white or whole wheat), crusts and all
- ½ cup sliced almonds, toasted (see tip below)
- 1 small garlic clove, peeled
- ½ cup jarred roasted red peppers, rinsed, drained, patted dry, and coarsely chopped
- 2 tablespoons red wine vinegar
- ½ teaspoon salt
- ¼ teaspoon red pepper flakes (or more to taste)
- 2 tablespoons extra-virgin olive oil
- ¼ cup water

 SKINNY TIP § A Little Goes a Long Way Romesco is an ideal skinny dip. Even though it has calorie-dense almonds, bread, and olive oil, those ingredients have healthy fats and vitamins your body needs. Plus, the roasted red peppers add bulk and flavor with very few additional calories—an ideal skinny ingredient.

Romesco tastes so rich, a little goes a long way. You couldn't sit down and eat a tub of Romesco the way you could, say, a pint of mint chocolate chip. You'll be content after a few bites.

 KITCHEN TIP § Toasting Almonds: Take Two In the Asparagus Soup recipe (page 76), I described one method for toasting almonds. It's a method I like to use when I'm toasting a small amount of nuts, seeds, or spices, like pine nuts or sesame or cumin seeds. For this Romesco, we need to toast ½ cup sliced almonds. With bigger nuts, or bigger amounts of nuts, it's easier to get even toasting in an oven or toaster oven. Set yours to 350°F, place the nuts in one even layer on a skillet or baking sheet, and cook until golden brown and fragrant, 12 to 15 minutes.

smoky babaghanouj

PREP TIME: 25 minutes TOTAL TIME: 1 hour 10 minutes MAKES 20 servings SERVING SIZE: 2 tablespoons

This eggplant dip is a sister to hummus and incorporates many of the same ingredients, like garlic, lemon juice, olive oil, and tahini. But instead of chick-peas, this dip uses an even lower-calorie leading lady: eggplant.

By broiling the eggplant, we give it an intense, smoky flavor, and when we puree it in the food processor, it becomes so creamy it's almost fluffy. If you like hummus, you'll love smoky baba.

1. Turn the broiler on. Put the eggplants on a foil-lined sheet pan and place under the broiler. Let the eggplants blacken on all sides, turning periodically with tongs, 30 to 40 minutes. Let the eggplants cool in a large bowl until you can handle them, about 10 minutes.

2. Peel the skin from the eggplants. Discard the skin and reserve the flesh. There will be a lot of smoky liquid settling in the bottom of your bowl; be sure to keep it. Use a spoon to scoop out the larger seed pods, but don't let those little seeds make you crazy; you don't need to remove them all.

3. Transfer the eggplant and liquid to a food processor fitted with a metal blade and puree. Add the olive oil, lemon juice, tahini, garlic, and salt. Process until smooth. Spoon the baba into a serving dish and garnish with parsley.

NUTRITION INFORMATION
(PER SERVING):
CALORIES 48, CARBS 4G, FIBER 2G, PROTEIN 1G, TOTAL FAT 4G, SATURATED FAT 0G

- 3 small, heavy eggplants (about 3 pounds)
- ¼ cup extra-virgin olive oil
- 6 tablespoons fresh lemon juice, or more to taste
- 2 tablespoons tahini (sesame seed paste)
- 1 small garlic clove, peeled
- 1 teaspoon salt
- ¼ cup finely chopped fresh parsley, for garnish

 KITCHEN TIP § Choosing Eggplant
When you choose eggplant, pick the small, heavy ones, as they tend to have more flesh and fewer seeds.

 KITCHEN TIP § Make-Ahead Baba
If you plan to serve this baba at a dinner party, make it ahead (I always try to leave as little to do as possible on the day of a party). It's best slightly warm or at room temperature, so be sure to leave it out for at least an hour before serving. If it's coming from the fridge, add salt, lemon juice, or both to perk up the flavors. Flavors get inhibited when cold and need a little coaxing to come out (don't we all?).

 SKINNY TIP § Baba and Bread
This is a soft, velvety spread. Pick a dipping partner like warm pita or something firm and crisp, like bagel chips or flatbread. Since baba has fewer calories than Romesco Spread (page 110) or Lemony Hummus with Parsley (page 108), you can afford to go with a higher-calorie partner.

twirl your fork:
pasta & noodles

"Good. Fast. Cheap. Pick two."

This manufacturing philosophy can also be used to describe healthy home cooking. If it's fast and good, it's rarely cheap. Good and cheap takes time. Cheap and fast doesn't usually taste good.

The exception to that rule is pasta. We all know it's fast and cheap. But it's also one of those rare things that can be fast, cheap, *and* good when done right.

Look, there's no way around it: Pasta is a caloric ingredient. In fact, a 2-ounce portion of pasta, $\frac{1}{8}$ of a 1-pound box, is 200 calories. *Before you add sauce.* If we're going to grant those calories permission to enter our bodies, we need to be sure they're delicious. If they're not delicious, why waste all those calories on flour and water? I'd rather eat two 100-Calorie Cookies (page 259). Wouldn't you?

Making a good bowl of pasta is about technique. It requires no additional calories or Italian ancestry. You just have to follow My Four Commandments of Pasta:

1. Use a lot of water. *More than you think.* When pasta packages ask for 6 quarts of water, they mean it. Fill that pasta pot and bring it to an aggressive boil so the pasta can move like John Travolta on the dance floor in *Saturday Night Fever*. You gotta let your pasta shake its noodle.

2. Use a lot of salt. *Way, way more than you think.* When you salt the pasta water, you want it to be salty like the sea. Ever get a mouthful of ocean? Blech. That stuff is salty. But that's what you want.

Not a pinch, not a tablespoon. At least 3 tablespoons of salt. Yes, I'm serious. Remember, salty water doesn't lead to salty pasta—it leads to flavorful pasta. The pasta takes what it needs and nothing more.

3. Sauce the pasta in the pan. *Like they do it in Italy.* When you cook pasta, cook it al dente, which is Italian for "to the tooth." Keep it chewy, with some personality.

In these recipes, you make the pasta sauce while you boil the pasta. When the pasta is done, take it straight from the pot and drop it into the sauce (you'll need big pans). Then, with a wooden spoon or plastic-coated tongs, turn the pasta in the sauce to coat it well. Cook the pasta and sauce together over very low heat for just a minute or two and the sauce will cling to the pasta.

We do not serve a bowl of naked pasta with sauce on top. I don't care if this is how your husband likes it or how his mom did it. Get a new husband. *You think I'm kidding?* I don't kid about pasta.

4. Save the pasta cooking water. *It's the secret ingredient.* To help the sauce adhere to the pasta, add a little of the pasta cooking water when you mix the pasta and the sauce. The water has starch in it, which helps sauces cling to the noodles. This magic water is the esprit de pasta—the secret ingredient you can't buy, *you have to make.*

If you follow these four rules, you will make good pasta. Which is key, because if you have a dull bowl of pasta, you'll actually end up eating more of it, passively, hoping that at some point flavor will come. Or you'll put it down and rifle through the fridge or the pantry until you find something that tastes better, like crackers, chips, or ice cream. That's not a skinny way to eat.

If you're going to eat pasta, it's your obligation to cook it well. *Capeesh?*

rigatoni with sausage and broccoli rabe

PREP TIME: 30 minutes TOTAL TIME: 30 minutes MAKES 6 servings SERVING SIZE: 2⅓ cups

In the time it takes you to boil a pound of rigatoni, you can make a homemade pasta sauce. I am always surprised by how expensive jarred pasta sauces are, especially when you can buy a 28-ounce can of crushed or whole peeled tomatoes for just over a dollar. It takes relatively little effort to add garlic and a couple of pantry pinches to the sauce, which—in addition to being cheaper—gives you that whole "I made it myself" swagger. What's better than that?

1. Bring a large pot of salted water to a boil. Cook the pasta according to the package directions until al dente. During the last 3 minutes that the pasta is cooking, add the broccoli rabe to the pot with the pasta.

2. While the pasta is cooking, heat the oil over medium heat in a pot large enough to hold the cooked pasta. Add the garlic and cook, stirring, until it begins to soften, about 1 minute. Add the oregano and red pepper flakes, and cook until fragrant, about 30 seconds. Add the crushed tomatoes, sausage, and salt, and stir to combine. Bring to a simmer and cook, stirring occasionally, for 10 to 12 minutes.

3. Drain the pasta and rabe and add to the sauce. Gently turn the pasta and rabe in the sauce to coat. Serve warm, topped with the Parmesan cheese.

NUTRITION INFORMATION
(PER SERVING):
CALORIES 453, CARBS 65G, FIBER 6G, PROTEIN 26G, TOTAL FAT 10G, SATURATED FAT 2G

1   pound dried rigatoni
1   large bunch broccoli rabe, trimmed and cut into 2-inch lengths
1   tablespoon olive oil
2   large garlic cloves, sliced
½   teaspoon dried oregano
    Large pinch of red pepper flakes
1   28-ounce can crushed tomatoes
12 ounces chicken sausage, sliced into ¼-inch rounds (see tip, page 31)
½   teaspoon kosher salt
2   tablespoons grated Parmesan cheese

SKINNY TIP § You Want More Vegetables? Since rigatoni is big, bulky, and full of air, these portions look huge. This little trick of the eye makes this dish naturally less caloric, as air is calorie-free. If you like, bulk out this pasta even more with extra rabe or with vegetables like roasted red peppers, grilled zucchini, or sautéed mushrooms. If you want a rainbow in your bowl, add some of those delicious Beet Greens with Pine Nuts (page 149). Heated up the second day, this is even better.

linguine vongole (clam sauce)

PREP TIME: 15 minutes TOTAL TIME: 20 minutes MAKES 8 servings SERVING SIZE: 1 cup

Though *vongole* sounds exotic, this dish is simple and takes just 20 minutes to make. The star ingredient, chopped clams, is inexpensive and easy to find; it's next to the canned tuna in most grocery stores. Don't overthink the vongole: It's a straightforward pasta.

1. Cook the pasta in a large pot of salted water according to the package directions until al dente. Reserve 1 cup pasta cooking liquid before you drain the pasta.

2. Heat the oil in a large skillet over medium heat. Add the garlic and red pepper flakes and cook, stirring, until fragrant, 30 seconds to a minute. Add the parsley and stir until wilted, about 30 seconds. Stir in the clams along with their juice and white wine, and bring to a simmer. Cook until the liquid is reduced by half, about 2 minutes.

3. Add the pasta to the skillet with the clam sauce, reduce the heat to low, and turn the pasta in the sauce. Add the cheese and salt. Add the pasta cooking liquid ¼ cup at a time, as needed, to help the sauce adhere. Serve warm.

NUTRITION INFORMATION
(PER SERVING):

CALORIES 347, CARBS 47G, FIBER 2G, PROTEIN 14G, TOTAL FAT 10G, SATURATED FAT 2G

1 pound dried linguine or fettuccine
⅓ cup extra-virgin olive oil
6 garlic cloves, minced
Large pinch of red pepper flakes
2 cups fresh parsley leaves, chopped
3 6½-ounce cans chopped clams
½ cup dry white wine
¼ cup grated Parmesan cheese
2 teaspoons kosher salt, plus more for water

 SKINNY TIP § How Low Can You Go? This recipe is very low in calories. It makes a delicious, satisfying bowl of pasta, meant to be enjoyed as part of a meal. If you just can't get enough, have a bigger portion. If you divide this pasta among six instead of eight, each portion is 1⅓ cups and 463 calories. You'll still have room for a glass of white wine.

KITCHEN TIP § Oh, Happy Day, I Have Fresh Clams! Then let's put them to use! Figure about ½ to ¾ pound of clams per person, as clams are pretty much all shell anyway. You'll need to use a bigger skillet, or even a pot, to make room for all those shells, plus extra room so the clams can open. Add the clams to the sauce as above, cover, and cook over medium-high heat until the shells open, 5 to 6 minutes, depending on the number of clams. I like to use tiny cockles for this recipe, as they're sweet and plump, and they contribute a delicious juice to the sauce.

 KITCHEN TIP § Garlic, Gently At first, you might think vongole is just about the clams. That makes sense, as it is a clam sauce. But in reality, vongole is also about the garlic, gently cooked in a good amount of olive oil. Chop the garlic very finely (a mini chop works well for this), and be sure to submerge the garlic in oil when you cook it, as that will keep it from browning.

cavatappi with basil pesto, tomatoes, and green beans

PREP TIME: 20 minutes **TOTAL TIME:** 35 minutes **MAKES** 8 servings **SERVING SIZE:** 1¾ cups

This is a bouncy, happy pasta dish. Start by making a fresh pesto, which takes 5 minutes. Don't get nervous, trust me: It'll be the best pesto you've ever had and you'll be surprised at how easy it is. Next, cook the pasta and green beans together in one pot, with the green beans coming straight from the freezer. Totally fuss-free. Finally, toss everything together with grape tomatoes, which will cook just a bit from the heat of the pasta.

As those tomatoes cook, they wilt, as if to say, "*Oy, you don't know the day I've had!*" and contribute their sweet just-warm tomato flavor to the dish. Grape tomatoes always make me smile; they look like little clown's noses. When you eat this pasta, you'll smile, too.

1. Bring a large pot of salted water to a boil. Add the pasta and cook according to the package directions until al dente. Add the frozen green beans during the last 3 minutes of cooking. Reserve 1 cup pasta cooking water, drain the pasta and beans, and place in a large, wide bowl.

2. While the pasta is cooking, combine the walnuts, pine nuts, garlic, and salt in the bowl of a food processor and blend to a paste. Add the basil and oil and process until smooth. Add the cheese and blend once more.

3. Toss the hot pasta and beans with the pesto and tomatoes; add reserved cooking water as needed. Serve warm or at room temperature.

NUTRITION INFORMATION (PER SERVING):

CALORIES 434, CARBS 49G, FIBER 5G, PROTEIN 13G, TOTAL FAT 21G, SATURATED FAT 4G

- 1 pound dried cavatappi pasta (see tip below)
- 1 9-ounce box frozen green beans
- ¼ cup walnuts
- ¼ cup pine nuts
- 1 garlic clove, peeled and smashed
- 1 teaspoon kosher salt, plus more for pasta water
- 2 cups fresh basil leaves
- ⅓ cup extra-virgin olive oil
- ½ cup grated Parmesan cheese
- 1 pint grape tomatoes, halved

 SKINNY TIP § Pesto Possibilities
It's pretty easy to make homemade pesto, isn't it?

If you want to use this pesto for other dishes, this recipe makes 1 cup pesto, 78 calories per tablespoon. *Eeek! That's a whole lotta calories.* But a little goes a long way with pesto. It's concentrated, so be sure to dilute the pesto with pasta cooking water or hot tap water when you use it and spread the love around. It makes a terrific dressing for roasted vegetables.

To store, put pesto in a resealable container and place plastic wrap directly on the surface of the pesto to keep it from discoloring. Seal the container and refrigerate the pesto for up to 1 week.

 SKINNY TIP § All Twisted Up?
Having a hard time finding cavatappi? Don't sweat it. I just want you to use a twisty pasta, whether it's cavatappi, gemelli, fusilli, or rotini. Those swirly pastas give the pesto lots of curves to cling to, and they are a terrific visual contrast to the straight green beans and round tomatoes. Plus, cavatappi is bulky; all that bulk is big in the bowl, which gives great visual appeal and helps you enjoy your pasta s-l-o-w-l-y.

gemelli with asparagus, prosciutto, and goat cheese

PREP TIME: 15 minutes TOTAL TIME: 25 minutes MAKES 8 servings SERVING SIZE: 1¼ cups

This is a pasta dish for the spring: bright green asparagus and tender pink prosciutto blanketed by a creamy goat cheese sauce. Try this with your favorite springy coiled pasta, like fusilli or rotini, and add a cup or two of frozen peas for even more bounce.

A gentle warning: Asparagus is an aphrodisiac, and prosciutto isn't far behind. Birds do it, bees do it. You wanna blame the pasta for your . . . *ahem* . . . desire to burn calories? Go right ahead.

1. . Cook the pasta in salted water according to the package directions until al dente. Toward the end of the cooking, add the asparagus to the pot to cook with pasta, just 2 minutes for skinny asparagus and up to 4 minutes for thicker asparagus. Drain the pasta and asparagus.

2. In a large skillet, melt the butter over medium heat. Add the shallot and thyme, and cook until the shallot has softened, 2 to 3 minutes. Add the prosciutto and stir to coat with butter. Add the goat cheese and milk to the skillet, stir to make a smooth sauce, and reduce the heat to low.

3. Add the drained pasta and asparagus to the skillet with the goat cheese sauce. Turn the pasta to coat with the sauce and season with salt and plenty of black pepper.

NUTRITION INFORMATION
(PER SERVING):
CALORIES 316, CARBS 46G, FIBER 3G, PROTEIN 15G, TOTAL FAT 8G, SATURATED FAT 4G

1 pound dried gemelli pasta
1 pound fresh asparagus, trimmed and cut into 3-inch lengths
1 tablespoon unsalted butter
1 shallot, sliced
1 teaspoon fresh thyme leaves
4 ounces thinly sliced prosciutto
4 ounces soft goat cheese
½ cup whole milk
½ teaspoon kosher salt
   Coarsely ground black pepper

SKINNY TIP § Prosciutto
Prosciutto is a super-skinny ingredient. It tastes best when it's thinly sliced, and of course when it is, ¼ pound of it seems like it could last forever.

SKINNY TIP § If You Like These Flavors . . . Prosciutto-wrapped asparagus is a classic appetizer. If you like the flavors in this pasta, steam or blanch some asparagus (as above), and wrap it in prosciutto. Take it one step further by using a goat cheese dipping sauce, with equal parts goat cheese and milk. Add a little lemon zest and coarsely ground black pepper to that creamy goat cheese dip, for no extra (caloric) charge. And yes, it's best to eat this aphrodisiac with your hands. *The rest is up to you.*

pasta carbonara

PREP TIME: 25 minutes **TOTAL TIME:** 30 minutes **MAKES** 8 servings **SERVING SIZE:** 1 cup

Carbonara has all the ingredients we love but tend to deny ourselves, like bacon, whole eggs, cheese, and of course pasta. Life's too short for all that deprivation. Somebody's going to eat good pasta—it might as well be you.

1. Bring a large pot of salted water to a boil and cook the spaghetti according to the package directions until al dente. Add the frozen peas to pot during the last 3 minutes of cooking. Reserve 1 cup of the pasta cooking water before draining the pasta and peas.

2. In a wide skillet large enough to fit the cooked pasta, cook the bacon over medium heat until slightly crispy, 3 to 4 minutes. Remove the bacon from the pan with a slotted spoon and drain on paper towels. Remove excess bacon fat from the skillet; leave just enough to coat the bottom of the pan.

3. Remove the skillet from the hot burner and let the pan cool for about 2 minutes (see tip). Add the eggs and cheese to the skillet and whisk together, scraping up the browned bits from the bottom of the pan. Add the drained pasta and peas to the egg mixture and coat the pasta with the sauce; use tongs to turn the pasta in the sauce. Add the pasta cooking water, $\frac{1}{4}$ cup at a time, to thin the sauce and help it coat the pasta more evenly.

4. Toss the reserved bacon with the pasta. Season the pasta with salt and black pepper as needed.

NUTRITION INFORMATION
(PER SERVING):

CALORIES 399, CARBS 45G, FIBER 2G, PROTEIN 21G, TOTAL FAT 14G, SATURATED FAT 6G

1   pound dried spaghetti or linguine
½   cup frozen baby peas
8   ounces bacon, cut into ¼-inch pieces (about 8 strips)
4   large eggs, lightly beaten
1½ cups grated Parmesan or Pecorino Romano cheese (about 6 ounces)
    Kosher salt and coarsely ground black pepper

"Somebody's going to eat good pasta—it might as well be you."

SKINNY TIP § Delicious Illusion or Delusion? Though this sauce feels intensely creamy, it has no cream; all that indulgence comes from thickened—but not scrambled—eggs.

Here's how it's done: Since raw eggs thicken at 160°F and turn into scrambled eggs at 180°F, the game is to keep the egg temperature between 160° and 180°F, using the heat of the pan and the just-cooked spaghetti to warm the eggs. (Remember, boiling water is 212°F, so you want the pan and pasta hot, but not crazy hot.)

Don't break out your thermometers; it's easy to get the feel of this. You know the difference between a raw egg and a thicker one, and you certainly know what a scrambled egg looks like. Give it a shot, and err on the side of caution; you can always turn up the heat, but you can't take it away.

SKINNY TIP § How Caloric Is Bacon? Old-fashioned pork bacon has lost a whole lot of fans to turkey bacon. Now I love turkey, but I can't help but wonder why we are always so anxious about our pork bacon. I did a little grocery-store research to get to the bottom of this, and was quite surprised about what I learned. It turns out that a 1-ounce slice of cooked pork bacon has about 40 calories. Since bacon surrenders its fat during cooking, many of bacon's calories are left in the pan. (Ah, if only I could to jump into a skillet and surrender my fat as easily.) *Only 40 calories?* You can burn off those calories taking your dog for a walk.

Oh, and that turkey bacon? Also 40 calories per slice. Of course, with turkey bacon, you'll end up with a bigger slice, since it's less fatty and therefore less fat is left in the sauté pan. In the end it's a question of quantity: big piece of turkey bacon or smaller piece of pork bacon; slice per slice, they are caloric equals. Either way, bacon is not something to forgo for the sake of extra calories. No, you don't want to make yourself a bacon sandwich with blue cheese sauce; but in small amounts, go for it. Yes, Virginia, you can have that bacon!

SKINNY TIP § One Cuppa Pasta? Fuggheddaboutit! Listen up folks, you're eating pasta carbonara. The recipe doesn't call for whole wheat pasta, egg substitutes, or fat-free condensed milk to faux-thicken the thing—you're having the real deal.

Now I love this dish, but personally I can't eat more than a cup of the stuff because it's *that* filling. I can have Linguine Vongole (page 118) on a weekly basis, but Carbonara is an indulgence.

That said, if you plonk these noodles into a bowl straight out of the measuring cup, you're going to get sad faces. So serve it restaurant-style: Use your tongs to grab the noodles and pull them high into the air. Let the noodles hang over the plate and turn them as you put them on the plate so you get squiggles and height. Repeat until you've got a tall mound; this tight cupful of noodles will stand proud.

And if you serve it family-style, be sure to serve this in a wide bowl or platter. It'll make it look like you've got enough to feed an army, which in fact you do.

"YOU DON'T GO TO VEGAS &
SIT IN THE HOTEL ROOM, & YOU
DON'T HAVE LOW-CALORIE MAC
& CHEESE. YOU SHOULDN'T FAKE
ANY OF

life's
greatest
PLEASURES."

three-cheese mac and cheese

PREP TIME: 20 minutes TOTAL TIME: 30 minutes MAKES 8 servings SERVING SIZE: 1 cup

Mac and cheese is two things: It's macaroni. It's cheese. Neither of these is low in calories. You don't go to Vegas and sit in the hotel room, and you don't have low-calorie mac and cheese. You shouldn't fake *any* of life's great pleasures.

When I was thinking about how to make a lower-calorie mac and cheese, I could have added steamed cauliflower or butternut squash, or used nonfat cream or evaporated milk. Hey, I could draw you a picture of mac and cheese and you could chew on that, but that's no way to live.

So let's not mess too much with mac and cheese. Get the best, most flavorful cheese you can find. Or just grab those little nubs of cheese in your fridge; they're just sitting in there waiting to make you happy. Want an assertive blue cheese instead of the cheddar? Pepper Jack instead of the Gruyère? Go for it. This recipe is a framework; make it your own. The more flavorful the cheeses, the better the dish.

And no, this mac and cheese is not what you "should" have if you think you "should" be denying yourself. So have a small portion. You'll be satisfied, 'cause it's that good.

NUTRITION INFORMATION
(PER SERVING):

CALORIES 474, CARBS 49G, FIBER 2G, PROTEIN 25G, TOTAL FAT 19G, SATURATED FAT 11G

1 pound dried elbow macaroni
2 tablespoons unsalted butter
2 tablespoons all-purpose flour
1½ teaspoons dry mustard
1 teaspoon fresh thyme leaves
¼ teaspoon freshly ground nutmeg (optional)
3 cups skim milk
2 cups grated cheddar cheese (about 8 ounces)
1 cup grated Gruyère cheese (about 4 ounces)
½ cup grated Parmesan cheese (about 2 ounces)
2 teaspoons kosher salt, plus more as needed
  Coarsely ground black pepper
  Hot sauce, for serving

1. Bring a large pot of salted water to a boil and cook the pasta according to the package directions until al dente.

2. Meanwhile, in a saucepan large enough to fit the pasta, melt the butter over medium heat. Stir in the flour, mustard, thyme, and nutmeg. Cook until mixture is bubbly, about 2 minutes. Slowly whisk in the milk and cook until the mixture thickens. Reduce the heat to low, whisk in the cheeses, and salt.

3. Add the pasta to the sauce and stir to coat until sauce is clinging to pasta, about 3 minutes. Season with black pepper and serve with hot sauce to taste.

 SKINNY TIP § Want a Bigger Portion? **If you did want to bulk out this recipe with a little vegetable love, here are my two recommendations: try broccoli or tomato. Broccoli and cheddar go together like, well, broccoli and cheddar. Ever had that combo as soup?** *Oooh. Mmmm. Yes.* **Feel free to add some frozen or fresh florets to the pasta toward the end of the cooking time, and give yourself a much bigger serving size.**

The same goes for grape tomatoes; just toss a pint (or two) of halved tomatoes into the mix when you're saucing the pasta. I've always loved a nice slice of ripe tomato in my grilled cheese sandwich; this is the same sort of yum.

pasta bolognese

PREP TIME: 25 minutes TOTAL TIME: 1 hour 15 minutes MAKES 8 servings SERVING SIZE: 1½ cups

Ground beef is a beautiful thing. You can use it to make Fuss-Free Meatballs (page 225), Classic Chili (page 85), Sloppy Joes (page 222), or this Bolognese sauce—four very different, crowd-pleasing dishes. It's gratifying to cook these favorites because you know that your meal won't just get eaten, it'll get slurped down with vigor. Your people will be happy. There may be calls for an encore. (Not to worry; desserts start on page 234.)

When you choose ground beef, select 90 percent lean, which has the same calorie count as ground turkey. Or choose a fattier cut and drain the fat to keep the calories the same. Or go with ground turkey. As you like!

1. Add the bacon to a large, heavy skillet and cook over medium heat until the fat has rendered and the bacon is beginning to crisp, about 3 minutes. Add the carrot, onion, garlic, and rosemary and cook, stirring, until the vegetables are translucent and soft but not browned, about 5 minutes.

2. Add the beef and 1 teaspoon salt to the vegetables. Increase the heat to high and use a wooden spoon to break up the meat, cooking until the meat is no longer pink, 3 to 5 minutes. Add the milk, reduce the heat to medium-high, and cook until the milk has almost simmered away, about 10 minutes. Add the wine and cook until it has almost simmered away, another 10 minutes.

3. While liquids are cooking, squish the whole tomatoes with your hands to break them up, or pulse several times in a food processor. Add tomatoes to the almost-dry meat mixture, bring to a gentle simmer, and cook until flavorful, 30 to 45 minutes. Season with the remaining teaspoon salt and pepper to taste.

4. Cook the pasta in salted water according to the package directions until al dente. When cooked, reserve 1 cup of the pasta cooking liquid, drain, add the pasta to the Bolognese, and stir until the pasta is evenly coated with the sauce. Add the pasta cooking liquid, as needed, to help distribute the sauce. Serve warm.

NUTRITION INFORMATION
(PER SERVING):

CALORIES 414, CARBS 53G, FIBER 3G, PROTEIN 23G, TOTAL FAT 9G, SATURATED FAT 3G

2 strips bacon, chopped
1 carrot, grated
1 small onion, grated
1 garlic clove, sliced
1 tablespoon chopped fresh rosemary
1 pound 90% lean ground beef
2 teaspoons kosher salt
1 cup whole milk
1 cup white wine
1 28-ounce can whole peeled tomatoes, drained
  Freshly ground black pepper
1 pound dried penne or ziti

KITCHEN TIP § Smooth as Milk
In this recipe, I ask you to boil away liquids twice. Seems sort of fussy considering how relaxed these recipes usually are. Here's why: Milk curdles in the presence of heat and acid, whether that acid is wine or tomato juice. By cooking the milk first, you can add the other ingredients, building layers of flavor.

So why are you cooking down the wine? Wine gives terrific *background* flavor. In the foreground, the alcohol becomes too dominant, so you simmer it away before you add another liquid.

SKINNY TIP § Get Saucy
This sauce is intense because we cook away so much of the liquid that it's tight and clings to the pasta. If you like your sauce saucier, add more pasta cooking liquid and let the Bolognese love flow.

soba noodles with shiitakes and bok choy in a spicy coconut broth

PREP TIME: 15 minutes TOTAL TIME: 25 minutes MAKES 6 servings SERVING SIZE: 1½ cups

Sometimes people save certain ingredients for eating out because they're not sure how to prepare them at home. Soba noodles and coconut milk are two of those ingredients. If you can boil pasta, you can cook soba; they're a noodle, too. Lite coconut milk can be found in the Asian section of the grocery store, and it has 60 percent less fat than the regular kind; I don't know how they remove all those calories and still keep it so flavorful, but they do. In this recipe we use it to make a slightly spicy broth for the noodles.

1. . Heat the oil in a medium, wide saucepan over medium heat. Add the shallot and lemongrass and cook, stirring, until the shallots are translucent, about 3 minutes. Add the sliced shiitakes and cook, stirring, until they begin to release their liquid, about 6 minutes. Add the bok choy and chile, and cook, stirring, until the greens begin to wilt, about 1 minute. Add the coconut milk, mirin, soy sauce, and lime zest to the saucepan and bring to a simmer. Cook until the sauce thickens, 3 to 5 minutes.

2. Meanwhile, prepare the soba noodles according to the package directions. Divide the noodles among bowls. Remove the sauce from the heat and stir in the cilantro and basil. Serve the vegetables and coconut broth over the noodles with a lime wedge.

NUTRITION INFORMATION (PER SERVING):
CALORIES 378, CARBS 68G, FIBER 2G, PROTEIN 12G, TOTAL FAT 7G, SATURATED FAT 4G

1 tablespoon vegetable oil
1 shallot, sliced
1 plump stalk lemongrass, trimmed and smashed
10 ounces shiitake mushrooms, trimmed and sliced
1 large head bok choy, cut crosswise into ½-inch ribbons
1 serrano chile, sliced
1 13.6-ounce can lite coconut milk
¼ cup mirin (see below)
2 tablespoons lower-sodium soy sauce
   Grated zest of 1 lime, plus a second lime cut into wedges
8 ounces dried soba noodles
1 cup fresh cilantro leaves, chopped
1 cup fresh basil leaves, chopped

SKINNY TIP § Bet on Brassicas
Bok choy is in the cabbage family, just like broccoli, cauliflower, and Brussels sprouts. The brassicas, as the cabbage family is called, are reputed to have terrific cancer-fighting properties. I like bok choy because it has a crisp, refreshing flavor; the stems are sweet while the greens have a slightly bitter flavor. If you can't find bok choy, try escarole or spinach in this dish.

SKINNY TIP § Got Mirin?
Mirin is a sweet Japanese rice wine used for cooking. It has 25 calories per tablespoon and is sometimes used in place of sugar or honey in recipes.

spicy peanut noodles with shrimp

PREP TIME: 25 minutes **TOTAL TIME:** 40 minutes **MAKES** 10 servings **SERVING SIZE:** 2 cups with shrimp

I was recently asked to bring a noodle dish that would feed a crowd with a variety of eating needs. One guest didn't do cheese, another was a fish-eating vegetarian (pescatarian), another was allergic to shellfish, while the rest were total carnivores.

Oy vey. Feeding Jack and Mrs. Sprat would have been simpler. But in the end, this was the dish to take. Noodle dishes without cheese can be hard to find, unless you go with Asian flavors, like this recipe. The fish-eating vegetarian was happy, and to be sure that our guest with the shellfish allergy stayed safe, I cooked the shrimp in the pasta water after the pasta was out. That way, I could serve the shrimp on the side for those who wanted it. No extra work, no extra time.

Even the carnivores enjoyed this dish and said it was filling and satisfying. As for me, I was just grateful that no one had a peanut allergy.

1. Bring a large pot of salted water to a boil and cook the pasta according to the package directions until al dente. To cook the shrimp, add it during the last 3 minutes while the pasta is cooking, or cook it separately, after you've removed the pasta.

2. In a large bowl, whisk together the peanut butter, soy sauce, rice vinegar, sesame oil, honey, ginger, garlic powder, and red pepper flakes. Add the pasta and turn to coat in the sauce. Add the cabbage, bell peppers, apple, cilantro, and scallion greens and toss to combine. You may need to add the vegetables in batches, or use two bowls—you're making 20 cups of noodles! Serve the noodles garnished with the shrimp and chopped peanuts. Serve with lime wedges.

NUTRITION INFORMATION
(PER SERVING):

CALORIES 454, CARBS 50G, FIBER 6G, PROTEIN 30G, TOTAL FAT 15G, SATURATED FAT 3G

- 1 pound dried linguine
- 2 pounds frozen shrimp, defrosted
- ½ cup creamy peanut butter
- ⅓ cup lower-sodium soy sauce
- ¼ cup rice vinegar
- 2 tablespoons toasted sesame oil
- 1 tablespoon honey
- 1 tablespoon grated fresh ginger
- ¼ teaspoon garlic powder
- ¼ to ½ teaspoon red pepper flakes, depending on your preferred spiciness
- 1 small napa cabbage, thinly sliced crosswise (8 cups)
- 2 red bell peppers, seeded and thinly sliced
- 1 Granny Smith apple, cut into matchsticks, or 1 cup mung beans
- ½ cup chopped fresh cilantro
- Greens of 4 scallions, chopped
- ½ cup chopped roasted peanuts
- 1 lime, cut into 8 wedges

KITCHEN TIP § Shrimp Size
If you're buying frozen shrimp, don't just look to the size (large, extra-large, jumbo), look to the count. All frozen shrimp will have a number on the bag, like 16–20 or 21–26, which indicates the number of shrimp you can expect to get per pound. In this recipe, if you were to use a pound of 16–20 shrimp, you'll have really big shrimp, but just about 3 per portion. If you want more shrimp per serving, go for a smaller shrimp with a bigger count.

KITCHEN TIP § Napa Cabbage
Napa cabbage is a fragile cabbage and wilts easily, which makes it perfect for this dish. When you look for it in the grocery story, select a long cabbage with crinkly leaves, as opposed to green cabbage that is round with smooth leaves.

tuna noodle summer salad

PREP TIME: 30 minutes **TOTAL TIME:** 30 minutes, plus 4 hours to chill **MAKES** 10 servings **SERVING SIZE:** 2 cups

This pasta salad says summer to me. It's what I crave when I come off the beach and need something filling but don't want something that will make me feel heavy. I was never one of those girls who could sit in a teeny bikini on the beach, inhale a burger and fries, then bound down to the water without a jiggle. *Who are those girls, anyway?*

My mom has made this pasta salad every summer since I can remember. Though I love it for the flavor, I think she likes it for the convenience: It makes 5 quarts of food. Momma's no fool; she wanted to be out of the kitchen and on the beach with the rest of us.

1. 1. Cook the pasta in salted water according to the package directions until al dente. Drain and rinse with cold water.

2. In a large bowl, combine the mayonnaise, dressing, and mustard. Mix well. Add the tuna, cucumber, tomatoes, bell peppers, scallions, salt, pepper, and cooked pasta shells and toss to coat the salad with dressing.

3. Put in an airtight container and refrigerate until chilled; overnight is best. But if hungry people are standing between you and the fridge, don't stand on ceremony; let them eat.

NUTRITION INFORMATION (PER SERVING):

CALORIES 462, CARBS 41G, FIBER 3G, PROTEIN 23G, TOTAL FAT 23G, SATURATED FAT 3G

- 1 pound dried medium pasta shells
- ¾ cup mayonnaise
- ½ cup Italian vinaigrette-style dressing
- 1 tablespoon Dijon mustard
- 4 5-ounce cans solid tuna packed in oil, drained
- 1 English cucumber, sliced into half-moons
- 2 pints grape tomatoes, sliced
- 3 bell peppers (green, red, and yellow), seeded and diced
  Greens of 4 scallions, chopped
- 1½ teaspoons kosher salt
- ½ teaspoon coarsely ground black pepper

SKINNY TIP § Why Oily Tuna? As I was preparing this recipe, I was listening to an interview on the radio with celebrity chef Mario Batali. The host was asking him about oil-packed vs. water-packed tuna, and mentioned that when Julia Child was on the show, she said that she used only oil-packed tuna because she thought the water took the flavor out. Batali agreed. He added that water-packed tuna can't be found outside the United States; most countries only use oil-packed.

I agree with these experts; oil-packed is the way to go. For this recipe, simply drain the oil, and use the full-flavored tuna. Since you're draining, the remaining oil is minimal, but the flavor difference is not.

SKINNY TIP § My Momma Said . . . *Store-Bought* Salad Dressing? Yep, that's what she said. I'm typically a homemade kinda gal, but I'm not messing with Momma on this one. For this recipe, pick your favorite brand of Italian dressing; maybe it's already in the fridge. And instead of chopping garlic and herbs to make your dressing from scratch, put that energy into the mountains of vegetables on your counter: You've got tomatoes, peppers, cucumbers, and scallions to chop. Come on, hop to it. And remember: you won't have to cook for days.

lemon-herb orzo with feta

PREP TIME: 25 minutes **TOTAL TIME:** 35 minutes **MAKES** 8 servings **SERVING SIZE:** 1¼ cups

This Greek-inspired cold pasta salad is one of my favorites. A flavorful vegetarian main, it makes a terrific dinner partnered with a simple salad on a hot summer night. Or try it as a side dish with a skewer of grilled shrimp or Seared Chicken with Lemon and Rosemary (page 188). It's tangy and lemony, with assertive feta, kalamata olives, and handful after handful of fresh herbs. This salad commands attention in a most refreshing way.

1. Cook the orzo in salted water according to the package directions until al dente. Drain and rinse with cold water until the orzo is firm.

2. In a large bowl, whisk together the olive oil, lemon juice, and zest. Add the crumbled feta and whisk to combine. Add the cooked orzo and toss to coat with the sauce.

3. Add the olives, parsley, basil, mint, dill, and scallions to pasta. Season with salt and black pepper; toss to combine.

NUTRITION INFORMATION
(PER SERVING):
CALORIES 325, CARBS 45G, FIBER 3G, PROTEIN 10G, TOTAL FAT 12G, SATURATED FAT 3G

- 1 pound dried orzo
- ¼ cup extra-virgin olive oil
  Juice and grated zest of 2 lemons (about ⅓ cup juice)
- 1 cup crumbled feta (about 4 ounces)
- ½ cup kalamata olives, pitted and chopped
- 1 cup chopped fresh parsley
- ⅓ cup chopped fresh basil
- ¼ cup chopped fresh mint
- ¼ cup chopped fresh dill
  Greens of 4 scallions, thinly sliced
- 1 teaspoon kosher salt
- ½ teaspoon coarsely ground black pepper

SKINNY TIP § Orzo Orzo comes in a tiny box. I'm always surprised by how much it grows when I cook it. So let's think about that for a second. Dried orzo: teeny tiny. Cooked orzo: big and plump. What happens?

We know what happens; the pasta rehydrates. But I never realized just how much. When I took the orzo out of the pasta pot with a strainer, a third of my water was gone. *The orzo had absorbed almost 2 quarts of water.*

That's some bloated pasta. But puffy pasta has a perk: When we eat those noodles, that means we're "drinking" a whole lot of water, too. Pasta puffs so we stay skinny.

veg out:
veggie sides

"do your homework!"

"Make your bed!"

"Eat your vegetables!"

Three commands I heard a lot as a kid, each backed up with the rationale of parents everywhere, "Because I said so!" *Ugh.*

And yet, when I want to lose weight, I follow this one command: fill half the plate with vegetables. *At every meal.* When I do that, I fill up on fiber and water, and just don't have the room for the more caloric stuff.

Since I'm not into trickery and deception, I don't "sneak" vegetables into food. Instead, we're going to make vegetables taste so good you won't *have* to eat them, you'll *want* to eat them. You'll *ache* for Satisfying Slaw (page 155) to enjoy with your Baby Back Ribs (page 217). You'll want to devour the Braised Cabbage with Apples, Caraway, and Mustard (page 145) snuggled next to your sausages. Roast Rack of Lamb (page 215) just won't be the same without Moroccan Carrots (page 140). Plus, these vegetable dishes don't just taste good—they *look* good. They're the prettiest bowls at the table and will be missed if they aren't there.

To get the best flavor from your vegetables, we're going to sauté or roast them. *No steaming, folks. That's not the way to make vegetables taste scrumptious.* Each vegetable serving is about 100 calories—the same as a tablespoon of butter. And believe me, we pack a lot into those 100 calories.

As a bonus for eating your veggies, here's more good news: Most recipes in this chapter require no more than 15 minutes of prep. Plus, some have more than 200 percent of your daily requirement for vitamins in a single serving (Garlicky Sautéed Spinach, page 139). I'm not a nutritionist, but that sounds like a win to me. When you eat your vegetables, you're doing your body good, and not just for skinny purposes.

So leave your bed unmade. Forget the homework. But *eat your vegetables!* And not because anybody said so, but because they are easy to make, they fill you up, and they taste so good.

crispy roast broccoli

PREP TIME: 10 minutes **TOTAL TIME:** 30 minutes **MAKES** 4 servings **SERVING SIZE:** 1 cup

This is a magical recipe. The ingredients are simple and familiar: broccoli, olive oil, and salt. So what makes this broccoli recipe different from all other broccoli recipes? Strong, dry heat.

When you roast broccoli in a screaming hot oven, you'll end up with crispy edges on the florets that crunch in an irresistible way. This natural crispness does not require deep-frying or caloric bready coatings. It is heat driven, so you can enjoy the crispy texture without any additional calories.

1. Preheat the oven to 450°F. Use a knife to separate the florets from the broccoli stems and cut the florets into bite-size pieces (keep in mind that they will shrink as they cook). Use a vegetable peeler to peel the dry exterior from the broccoli stems, and slice the stems into ⅛-inch pieces.

2. Place the broccoli in a large roasting pan, drizzle with the oil, and sprinkle with the salt. Use your hands to toss the broccoli in the oil; be sure it is coated evenly.

3. Put the broccoli in the oven and cook until crispy brown, about 20 minutes total, stirring the broccoli after 12 minutes (you should already start to see the crisp edges). Serve warm or at room temperature.

NUTRITION INFORMATION
(PER SERVING):

CALORIES 82, CARBS 10G, FIBER 4G, PROTEIN 4G, TOTAL FAT 4G, SATURATED FAT 1G

1 head broccoli
1 tablespoon olive oil
¾ teaspoon kosher salt

KITCHEN TIP § Frozen Florets
Lots of busy parents like to keep frozen broccoli around because the "little trees" are the only vegetables their kids will eat. If you want to use frozen instead of fresh, use 6 cups of defrosted florets.

KITCHEN TIP § One Less Pan to Clean Some people avoid roasting because that roasting pan can be a bear to clean. Solution: Cover the pan with aluminum foil. You'll still get those crispy edges, and you can toss the foil for minimal cleanup. You wouldn't be the first person to put that used-but-clean roasting pan back in the cabinet.

garlicky sautéed spinach

PREP TIME: 10 minutes TOTAL TIME: 10 minutes MAKES 4 servings SERVING SIZE: ⅔ cup

Spinach is the incredible shrinking vegetable. A big bunch of the stuff will shrink down to an amount so small you'll find yourself wondering who ate it while you looked away.

But that now-you-see-it, now-you-don't quality has an upside: A single serving of this recipe supplies you with 210 percent of your vitamin A requirements and 54 percent of your vitamin C.

Spinach wilts so you stay perky.

1. Heat the oil in a large skillet over medium heat. Add the garlic and tilt the pan to submerge the garlic in the oil. Cook until garlic is softened but not browned, about 1½ minutes.

2. Add the spinach in batches and use tongs to turn the spinach and coat with the oil. Cover the pan and let the spinach cook until it wilts, about 2 minutes.

3. Remove the lid and cook the spinach, turning with tongs, until the water has evaporated and the spinach has completely wilted, about 1 minute longer. Season to taste with salt and red pepper flakes, and serve warm.

NUTRITION INFORMATION
(PER SERVING):

CALORIES 90, CARBS 5G, FIBER 3G, PROTEIN 3G, TOTAL FAT 7G, SATURATED FAT 1G

- 2 tablespoons extra-virgin olive oil
- 4 garlic cloves, sliced
- 2 large bunches spinach, trimmed (about 1 pound)
  Kosher salt and red pepper flakes

SKINNY TIP § Texture Trivia
Too much of the same texture can be monotonous, which is why people put raisins in rice pudding and chips in ice cream. For this dish, sprinkle pine nuts or sunflower seeds over the top for a refreshing, crisp contrast to the soft texture.

SKINNY TIP § Which Spinach Is Best? My choice for this recipe is fresh spinach because it has the most intense flavor. If you'd prefer to use frozen, use 3 cups of defrosted spinach. Avoid baby spinach for this recipe because it's fragile and best enjoyed raw in a salad. Use the grown-up spinach, as it can handle the heat.

KITCHEN TIP § Spinach Prep
When my friend Aaron tasted this recipe, he said, "It's good, but it's not a real recipe, because there's no trick to it." Ironically, Aaron learned to make cocktail sauce the day before (equal parts ketchup and prepared horseradish) and thought it was a revelation.

The true technique of sautéed spinach isn't in the cooking, it's in the prep. Here are two spinach secrets.
1. Spinach grows in the ground and can be full of sand and soil. If you rinse it in a colander under running water the sand and dirt will cling to the leaves. Instead, place the spinach in a big bowl and fill it with water. Swish the spinach around and the dirt will fall to the bottom of the bowl. Lift the leaves from the water, leaving the dirt behind. Let water cling to the leaves; it helps them steam.
2. Sometimes when I eat raw spinach, I get a weird squeaky sensation on my teeth. To avoid it, dunk the spinach in boiling water until it wilts, about 30 seconds, and proceed. You'll be squeaky-free.

moroccan carrots

PREP TIME: 20 minutes   **TOTAL TIME:** 30 minutes   **MAKES** 4 servings   **SERVING SIZE:** Generous ½ cup

Serve this side when you're feeding friends who like flavor. These carrots bring their own point of view to the table, popping with the intense flavors of scallions, cumin, cinnamon, and mint. They're a terrific accompaniment to roast meats; plus, they're pretty, especially on a family-style platter with Crispy Roast Broccoli (page 138) or Roasted Cauliflower Steaks (page 142).

1. Bring a pot of salted water to a boil. Add the carrots, return to a boil, and cook until the rawness is gone and the carrots are still firm, 2 to 3 minutes. Drain the carrots.

2. Meanwhile, in a bowl, combine the parsley, scallion, mint (if desired), lemon juice, olive oil, honey, salt, cinnamon, cumin, and red pepper flakes. Pour the marinade over the cooked carrots and stir to coat. The carrots will soak up the liquid as they sit. Serve at room temperature or chilled.

NUTRITION INFORMATION (PER SERVING):
CALORIES 84, CARBS 13G, FIBER 3G, PROTEIN 1G, TOTAL FAT 4G, SATURATED FAT 1G

1 pound carrots, peeled and cut into ¼-inch-thick slices on the bias (about 2½ cups)
½ cup fresh parsley leaves, roughly chopped
1 scallion, green and white parts thinly sliced
1 tablespoon thinly sliced mint leaves (optional)
Juice of 1 lemon
1 tablespoon olive oil
1 teaspoon honey
½ teaspoon kosher salt
Big pinch of ground cinnamon
Big pinch of ground cumin
Pinch of red pepper flakes

KITCHEN TIP § **Easy Peeling**
To peel carrots efficiently, lay each carrot on a cutting board, start at the center, and peel to the end, turning the carrot until you've peeled one half. Then flip the carrot and peel the other side. Believe it or not, this twice-peel method is more efficient, as your hands can move faster when working on a smaller area.

SKINNY TIP § **Moroccan Smarts**
In Morocco, there's typically a platter of small vegetable dishes served before the meal, including grilled eggplant, marinated tomatoes (not too different from the ones on page 43), pickles, olives, and carrots like these. Yes, they're tasty, but it's also a smart way to fill up on flavorful low-calorie dishes before hitting the main meal.

roasted cauliflower steaks

PREP TIME: 5 minutes **TOTAL TIME:** 35 minutes **MAKES** 4 servings **SERVING SIZE:** 1½ cups

Slicing cauliflower into steaks is fun. Plus, it should take no more than 2 minutes, which is much less time-consuming than dealing with individual florets.

When you paint the cauliflower steaks with olive oil and place them in a hot oven, you'll be rewarded with beautiful golden steaks that are naturally sweet. Try this recipe once, and it will become one of your most requested.

1. Preheat the oven to 425°F.

2. On a cutting board, stand the cauliflower on its stem end, and cut lengthwise into ½-inch-thick slices. The slices should hold together relatively well, like little cross-sections of a tree.

3. Place the slices on a large sheet pan, brush with olive oil, and season with salt on both sides. Cook for 20 minutes, until the underside is golden brown. Remove from the oven, turn the cauliflower over, and continue cooking until the second side is golden, about 10 minutes more. Enjoy warm or at room temperature.

NUTRITION INFORMATION (PER SERVING):

CALORIES 82, CARBS 8G, FIBER 4G, PROTEIN 3G, TOTAL FAT 5G, SATURATED FAT 1G

1   head cauliflower, core trimmed and outer leaves removed
1½ tablespoons olive oil
    Kosher salt

 SKINNY TIP § Roasting with Oil
When you roast, you're cooking with dry heat at a high temperature. And what do you do when you visit a dry place? You moisturize. Same goes for vegetables: You've gotta give those girls something to keep them supple, and that's oil. To get the most coverage with the least calories, spritz the vegetables with oil before roasting, or do my favorite: Drizzle the oil on top of the cauliflower, and brush to coat. Your roasted vegetables stay moist, and you use as much oil (calorically speaking) as you need to. Your food will taste—and look—delicious.

buttery green beans with shallots and sliced almonds

PREP TIME: 20 minutes **TOTAL TIME:** 35 minutes **MAKES** 4 servings **SERVING SIZE:** Generous 1 cup

Green beans were meant for butter; together, they are an intoxicating combination. If you see long, skinny green beans in the grocery store, grab them. They are *haricots verts*, or French green beans (the French have always had a thing for thinness). Haricots will cook after a few minutes in a sauté pan; they don't need to be pre-softened by blanching (boiling), so you can skip step 1.

NUTRITION INFORMATION
(PER SERVING):
CALORIES 120, CARBS 11G, FIBER 4G, PROTEIN 4G, TOTAL FAT 8G, SATURATED FAT 3G

1. . Bring a large pot of salted water to a boil and add the green beans. Cook until bright green yet still crisp, 1 to 2 minutes. Remove the beans from the water and set to the side while you cook the almonds.
2. Add the butter to a large skillet over medium heat and cook until the butter foams, about 1 minute. Add the almonds and shallot and cook, stirring, until the shallots are softened, about 3 minutes.
3. Add the beans to the almonds, season with the salt, toss, and cover. Cook until the beans are warmed through, 2 to 3 minutes. Add the lemon juice (a squeeze at a time), taste, adjust the seasonings as needed, and serve warm.

1 pound green beans or haricots verts, stem ends trimmed
1½ tablespoons unsalted butter
⅓ cup sliced almonds
1 shallot, thinly sliced
½ teaspoon kosher salt, plus more as needed
Juice of ½ lemon

KITCHEN TIP § Do I Have to Boil the Beans? Good question. And trust me, I've tried to figure out a way around this. Green beans are pretty dense, so if you just sauté them in the butter, they'll look mottled, partially uncooked and partially cooked. If you dunk them in water, there's no place to hide, so they cook evenly. If you don't want to blanch them in boiling water, steam them in a covered microwave-safe bowl with ¼ cup of water at the bottom for 2 to 3 minutes.

This is a good dish to make when you've already got a pot of boiling water going (say, for pasta). You can blanch these beans, take them out of the water, and use the water for the pasta. Blanched green beans (like most vegetables) will keep in the refrigerator for 3 to 5 days; just be sure to shock (cool) them in a large bath of icy cold water as soon as they're out of the boil to stop the cooking process.

Don't have the right tool to fish out the green beans? Ask your local kitchen or restaurant supplier if they have "spiders." These are wide, flat implements, somewhere between a spoon and a spatula, with a bamboo handle and woven metal bowl. They are terrific for pulling items out of a deep fryer or boiling water. Or, you can place the beans in a big strainer or colander, then dunk them into the boiling water. After the beans have cooked out their rawness, simply pull out the strainer and add the beans to the buttery almonds and shallots.

roasted delicata

PREP TIME: 15 minutes **TOTAL TIME:** 40 minutes **MAKES** 6 servings **SERVING SIZE:** 1½ cups squash wedges

Poor, poor delicata. She's the vegetable equivalent of the really cute woman no man ever approaches. You've seen delicatas before, next to the other, more popular squashes like butternut and acorn. She's small and yellow with green stripes, like a stout mini football. You may have even picked her up and thought *Hmmm, what can I do with this?*

Don't hate her because she's beautiful! The overlooked delicata is easy to manage (you won't have to wrestle with her on the cutting board like butternut) and that pretty skin is edible, so you won't have to remove it.

Take the pretty vegetable home. She tastes even better than she looks.

1. Preheat the oven to 425°F.

2. Cut the squash in half lengthwise and remove the seeds with a wooden spoon. Put the squash on a cutting board flat side down, and cut into 1-inch-wide slices.

3. Put the squash on a sheet tray or roasting pan and brush with oil. Season with salt and pepper and lay the thyme sprigs on top. Place in the oven.

4. Roast the squash until you can easily insert the tip of a paring knife into the squash, about 25 minutes. Let the squash cool for a minute so that it releases from the pan easily (don't force it), and remove with a spatula; serve warm.

NUTRITION INFORMATION
(PER SERVING):

CALORIES 89, CARBS 15G, FIBER 2G, PROTEIN 1G, TOTAL FAT 4G, SATURATED FAT 1G

2 delicata squash
1½ tablespoons olive oil
5 sprigs fresh thyme
1 teaspoon kosher salt
¼ teaspoon freshly ground black pepper

KITCHEN TIP § An Even Tan
If you want your squash to get golden brown on both sides, flip after the first 15 minutes in the oven.

KITCHEN TIP § Soft like a Wooden Spoon Wooden spoons are the tool to use when you want to scrape seeds from an uncooked squash. They have soft edges so they don't scrape the uncooked flesh as metal does. Remember this tip when it's time to make your Halloween jack-o-lantern.

braised cabbage with apples, caraway, and mustard

PREP TIME: 15 minutes TOTAL TIME: 35 minutes MAKES 8 servings SERVING SIZE: 1 cup

This recipe is like dating three people at the same time and not needing to choose. Cabbage has three perfect partners: apples, mustard, and caraway seeds. This recipe allows her to flirt with all three at the same time, and somehow everyone wins.

Serve warm with your favorite grilled sausages.

1. Melt the butter in a large pot over medium heat. Add the onion and caraway seeds, and cook, stirring, until the onion has begun to soften, about 3 minutes. Add the cabbage and 2 teaspoons of the salt, and stir to coat the cabbage with butter.

2. Add the wine and partially cover; cook until the cabbage has softened a bit, about 15 minutes. Add the apples, cider vinegar, mustards, and remaining teaspoon salt and stir to incorporate. Cook until the apples are warmed through yet firm and the cabbage is tender, 5 to 10 minutes.

NUTRITION INFORMATION
(PER SERVING):
CALORIES 91, CARBS 13G, FIBER 4G, PROTEIN 2G, TOTAL FAT 3G, SATURATED FAT 2G

- 2 tablespoons unsalted butter
- 1 sweet onion, like Vidalia or Walla Walla, sliced
- ½ teaspoon caraway seeds
- 1 2- to 2½-pound green cabbage, trimmed and shredded
- 1 tablespoon kosher salt
- ½ cup white wine
- 1 Granny Smith apple, peeled and chopped
- 2 tablespoons cider vinegar
- 2 teaspoons grainy mustard
- 2 teaspoons Dijon mustard

 SKINNY TIP § Generous Cabbage There's a reason I included three different cabbage recipes in this chapter: Cabbage recipes are tasty, filling, inexpensive, and versatile. From the Sweet and Sour Red Cabbage (page 147) to Satisfying Slaw (page 155) to this recipe, you'll have your hands full.

And when I say hands full, I mean it: One 2½-pound cabbage yields bowls full of shredded vegetable. Shredding a cabbage is like seeing that teeny car with all the clowns piling out. You know what's coming but still . . . it's hard to believe how much a single cabbage yields.

 KITCHEN TIP § How Do You Shred Cabbage? I like to shred cabbage by hand. First, remove any wilty outer leaves and trim the stalk end. Then slice the cabbage in half, cutting through the core. With the cabbage on the board flat side down, start with the part furthest from the core and slice, almost shaving the cabbage into ¼-inch-thick lengths. You can also shred the cabbage in the food processor, but this hand method is so easy you can do it in the time it takes to get the processor out of the cupboard.

sweet and sour red cabbage

PREP TIME: 15 minutes **TOTAL TIME:** 45 minutes **MAKES** 8 servings **SERVING SIZE:** ¾ cup

The Italians call this sweet and sour sauce *agrodolce,* literally the combination of agro (sour) and dolce (sweet).

This sauce reminds me of a complex person, someone who can be both spicy and sweet at the same time. And is exactly why I've partnered the *agrodolce* with a *red head* (bah-dum-cha!).

1. Heat the oil in a large saucepan over medium heat and add the onion. Cook, stirring, until softened, about 3 minutes. Add the cabbage, sugar, water, 2 teaspoons of the salt, and the thyme. Bring to a simmer, reduce the heat to medium-low, and cook, partially covered, until softened, about 30 minutes.

2. Check the cabbage periodically to be sure there is enough water. Remove the pot from the heat, and add the vinegar, red pepper flakes, and remaining teaspoon of salt.

NUTRITION INFORMATION
(PER SERVING):

CALORIES 99, CARBS 20G, FIBER 3G, PROTEIN 2G, TOTAL FAT 2G, SATURATED FAT 0G

- 1 tablespoon vegetable oil
- 1 red onion, sliced
- 1 2½- to 3-pound red cabbage, shredded (see tip, page 145)
- ¼ cup sugar
- ½ cup water
- 1 tablespoon kosher salt
- 1 teaspoon fresh thyme leaves
- ½ cup red wine vinegar
- Big pinch of red pepper flakes

 SKINNY TIP § Do-Si-Do Your Partner In this recipe, we're using red wine vinegar to provide the sour part of the sweet and sour. Vinegar has only 2 calories per tablespoon, so feel free to experiment. If you use white vinegar, go easy, as it's tangier than the others. The opposite goes for rice wine vinegar, which is milder. Be sure to add the vinegar once the pot has been removed from the heat, so the color stays vivid.

As for sweetness, we're using sugar and sautéed red onion. Sweet onions have only 100 calories per onion, while sugar has 50 calories per tablespoon. That makes sautéed onions a terrific skinny ingredient: more sweetness for fewer calories. Adjust the sweet and sour balance until it works for you.

roasted brussels sprouts with crispy purple onion

PREP TIME: 15 minutes **TOTAL TIME:** 45 minutes **MAKES** 4 servings **SERVING SIZE:** ¾ cup

This delicious side dish is visual therapy for the cook. After you place the ingredients on the baking sheet, take a moment to look at them. The deep and light green of the sprouts contrasts with the purple onions, plus you have all those curves to look at, from the tight round Brussels to the open arcs of the onions. This kitchen moment makes cooking as rewarding as eating.

1. Preheat the oven to 425°F.

2. Place the Brussels sprouts, onion, and thyme on a large rimmed baking sheet, drizzle with the oil, and season with the salt. Turn the sprouts so that they are cut side down.

3. Cook until the sprouts are golden brown and soft, 25 to 30 minutes. If the sprouts brown before they soften, cover with aluminum foil and continue cooking. Remove and discard the thyme and serve.

NUTRITION INFORMATION (PER SERVING):

CALORIES 114, CARBS 15G, FIBER 5G, PROTEIN 4G, TOTAL FAT 5G, SATURATED FAT 1G

- 1 pound Brussels sprouts, trimmed and halved
- 1 large red onion, cut into ¾-inch wedges
- 8 sprigs fresh thyme
- 1½ tablespoons olive oil
- 1 teaspoon kosher salt

 SKINNY TIP § Loveable Brussels Brussels sprouts are so cute! They're tiny cabbages, and the food lovers I know love them passionately, whether partnered with chorizo, shredded in a raw salad, or sautéed with maple syrup and mustard seeds.

But others I know hate them with an equal passion.

Why? Because they've had overcooked sprouts, which can turn a person off for life. Brussels sprouts, like any cabbage, get sulfurous and funky if you cook them too long.

Because Brussels are dense, many recipes ask you to boil them before you roast or sauté them. Unfortunately, they

can go army green and icky if they cook too long. In this recipe, halve the sprouts, then roast at a high temperature to get them tender inside and golden brown on the cut side. Prepared this way, your Brussels will be bright green and delicious.

beet greens with pine nuts

PREP TIME: 15 minutes **TOTAL TIME:** 15 minutes **MAKES** 4 servings **SERVING SIZE:** 1 cup

I like getting something for nothing. At my farmers', market, they sell a lot of root vegetables with their tops on, like carrots, parsnips, and beets. The jury is still out on carrot greens, but beet greens make a spectacular side dish. The stems are a bit thicker than the leaves, so you'll want to cook them first, then add the leaves and let them wilt a bit, like spinach. Beet green stems have a sweet flavor with a refreshing crunchy texture, almost like bok choy.

And what makes them even sweeter is that they're free. It's like turning wrapping paper into a whole new present.

NUTRITION INFORMATION
(PER SERVING):
CALORIES 63, CARBS 5G, FIBER 4G, PROTEIN 3G, TOTAL FAT 4G, SATURATED FAT 1G

1 pound beet greens
1 tablespoon olive oil
  Kosher salt
1 teaspoon chopped garlic
1 tablespoon pine nuts, toasted

1. Prepare the beet greens by separating the greens from the stems. Chop the stems into 2- to 3-inch lengths and roughly chop the greens.

2. Heat the oil in a large skillet over medium-high heat. Add the beet stems and season with salt. Cook, stirring, until they begin to soften, about 5 minutes. Add the garlic and cook until fragrant, about 30 seconds. Add the beet greens, season with salt, and cook, stirring, until wilted, about 2 minutes more; if your pan is dry, a splash or two of water will help the beet greens wilt.

3. Meanwhile, add the pine nuts to a small skillet and toast over medium heat until lightly browned and fragrant, 2 to 3 minutes. Serve the beet greens topped with the toasted pine nuts.

KITCHEN TIP § How to Toast Pine Nuts Put the pine nuts in a small, dry skillet and place over medium heat. Cook, shaking the pan every 30 seconds or so, until lightly browned and fragrant, 2 to 3 minutes. Be sure to remove the pine nuts from the skillet after cooking or they will continue to cook in the hot skillet. Keep toasted pine nuts in the freezer until you are ready to use them.

SKINNY TIP § Fiber Is Your Friend Beet greens are all fiber, which means exactly what you think it means. I know, it's not polite cookbook chatter, so I'll leave it at that, but I wanted you to know so you're not alarmed. *Moving on.*

If you like doing yummy things with unexpected foods, beet greens are for you. If you like pretty food, this recipe is a gem, and tastewise, though it looks like a big mound of greens, it has the mild, sweet flavor of beets. Plus there's that (ahem) health benefit. Enjoy.

SKINNY TIP § Swiss Chard Simpatico If you like this cooking method, try it with Swiss chard. It comes in several colors: red, white, and psychedelic rainbow. This cooking method lets you enjoy the crisp stems with the wilted greens.

fennel gratin

PREP TIME: 15 minutes **TOTAL TIME:** 30 minutes **MAKES** 4 servings **SERVING SIZE:** 1 cup

Fennel is unique looking, like a pregnant bunch of celery. It has an anise flavor that can be bracing when raw but becomes mild, sweet, and nutty when cooked.

When you cut the fennel bulb, halve it lengthwise and place it flat side down, then cut it into wedges. By incorporating the core into your slices, you'll keep the pieces together. Fennel has a lovely shape; show it off.

1. Preheat the oven to 425°F.

2. Place the fennel in a 9x13-inch baking dish and toss with the olive oil, thyme, salt, and pepper. Cover with aluminum foil and cook until the fennel has softened, 15 to 20 minutes. Remove the foil, return to the oven, and cook until the edges are golden brown and crisp, another 15 minutes.

3. Remove the baking dish from the oven and preheat the broiler. Sprinkle fennel with the cheeses and cook until cheese has melted and is bubbling, 3 to 5 minutes. Serve warm.

NUTRITION INFORMATION
(PER SERVING):

CALORIES 110, CARBS 9G, FIBER 4G, PROTEIN 5G, TOTAL FAT 7G, SATURATED FAT 2G

- 2 medium bulbs fennel, cut into ⅓-inch wedges (5½ cups)
- 1 tablespoon olive oil
- ½ teaspoon fresh thyme leaves
- ½ teaspoon kosher salt
  Pinch of freshly ground black pepper
- ⅓ cup shredded Gruyère cheese (about 1½ ounces)
- 2 tablespoons grated Parmesan cheese

KITCHEN TIP § No Gratin Dish? No Fennel? No Problem If you don't have a gratin dish, use a 9-inch pie plate or 8-inch square baking dish. And if you don't have fennel, try this dish with endive. Instead of roasting it, slice it in half and gently braise it in a little chicken stock for 5 to 10 minutes. Endive won't get golden brown like fennel, but it will offer a bittersweet counterpoint to gooey melted cheese.

crispy kale chips

PREP TIME: 15 minutes   TOTAL TIME: 45 minutes   MAKES 8 servings   SERVING SIZE: 2 cups

At a party, a mound of **Crispy Kale Chips** quickly becomes a conversation piece, as guests wonder what it is and how you did it.

Kale chips are the crispiest chips I've ever had. Bright green and translucent, they crinkle in the mouth like cellophane. They are a terrific accompaniment to a sandwich (or better yet, piled *inside* a sandwich). You won't be able to keep your hands off them, and at 88 calories for a 2-cup serving, you won't have to.

1. Preheat the oven to 325°F.

2. Use a knife to remove the stems from the kale leaves and tear the leaves into big pieces, 3 to 4 inches wide. Discard stems, or reserve for another use (see tip below).

3. Drizzle the kale leaves with the olive oil and season with the salt and pepper. Toss the leaves with your hands to coat with oil. Divide the leaves between two baking sheets so that they are in one layer. Bake until crispy, 18 to 20 minutes.

NUTRITION INFORMATION (PER SERVING):

CALORIES 88, CARBS 6G, FIBER 1G, PROTEIN 2G, TOTAL FAT 7G, SATURATED FAT 1G

- 1 pound kale
- ¼ cup olive oil
- 1 teaspoon kosher salt
- ½ teaspoon freshly ground black pepper

KITCHEN TIP § Stem Stamina
Al Di La is a well-loved Italian restaurant in my neighborhood, and one of their most popular dishes is ricotta gnocchi with Swiss chard (for more on Al Di La, see tip, page 231). For that dish, they use the chard leaves, but what to do with the mountains of stems? Compost seems a little heartless, so instead they apply some restaurant ingenuity. They toss the stems with olive oil, salt, and pepper, grill them, then serve them as a side dish. As with the beet greens (page 149), Al Di La makes a whole new dish from an ingredient that others might discard. Try the same approach with your kale stems.

spaghetti squash with brown butter sauce

PREP TIME: 15 minutes **TOTAL TIME:** 1 hour 20 minutes **MAKES** 8 servings **SERVING SIZE:** ¾ cup

Before I wrote this book, I had never tried spaghetti squash. It always sounded like diet food to me, and ingredients that scream "diet" make me want to run in the opposite direction. I like my food to be what it is.

Oh, spaghetti squash, forgive my impertinence! You are most decidedly squash, not a faux bowl of pasta. And you are one groovy squash, a natural curiosity like the sea horse, the hummingbird, the platypus. Your long strands are a gift of nature that I waited too long to admire. You fill me, visually and actually.

Spaghetti squash is just waiting for a little honest love at a grocery store near you. Cook one, open it up, and take a peek. You won't believe it until you see it yourself.

NUTRITION INFORMATION (PER SERVING):
CALORIES 91, CARBS 10G, FIBER 2G, PROTEIN 1G, TOTAL FAT 6G, SATURATED FAT 4G

- 1 2½- to 3-pound spaghetti squash
- 4 tablespoons (½ stick) unsalted butter
- 10 fresh sage leaves, sliced
- ¼ cup fresh lemon juice (1 to 2 lemons)
- 1 teaspoon kosher salt

1. Preheat the oven to 400°F.

2. Poke holes all over the spaghetti squash using the tines of a fork (trust me, you don't want that bad boy to burst). Place the squash on a baking sheet and cook until it's soft, about 1 hour. Remove from the oven.

3. While the squash is cooking, melt the butter in a medium skillet over medium heat. The butter will foam and the milk solids will fall to the bottom of a pan (best to avoid black pans for this, as you'll want to see the solids brown). The milk solids will turn a deep brown in 1 to 2 minutes after you've seen them fall. Add the sage leaves and allow them to cook until fragrant, about 10 seconds. Add the lemon juice all at once and carefully, as the butter will enthusiastically greet the lemon juice, and stir to combine. Remove the sauce from the heat and set it aside.

4. When the squash is cool enough to touch, slice lengthwise, scoop out the seeds and discard, and use a spoon to remove the squash strands. Neat-o! Place the strands in a bowl and toss with the brown butter sauce and the salt until the strands are coated. Serve warm or at room temperature.

KITCHEN TIP § Cooking Spaghetti Squash I cook spaghetti squash whole for one reason: it's a pain in the neck to cut, like maneuvering a heavy, dense rugby ball on your cutting board. No, thank you. Sure it'll cook faster, but nah, not worth it.

As an alternative to roasting, you can boil the squash for half an hour or microwave it for 10 to 12 minutes. But roasting is the best way to intensify the natural flavors. Cooks, start your ovens!

shiitakes and snow peas with ginger

PREP TIME: 10 minutes **TOTAL TIME:** 20 minutes **MAKES** 4 servings **SERVING SIZE:** ½ cup

Mushrooms are a challenging skinny-cooking ingredient. Raw, they're fine, but when cooked, they absorb a surprising amount of fat and become caloric (and yummy). Plus, they shrink to one-quarter of their raw volume when cooked. *If only we could suck in all that fat and still lose 75 percent of our volume!* 'Shrooms are an alternate reality.

In this dish I'm using less oil than usual, so they dry-roast in the skillet. I'm balancing shiitakes with crisp, crunchy snow peas, which lose no volume when cooked. Those two combine with a ka-POW of fresh ginger, and we're riding the tasty train to a lower-calorie mushroom side dish.

1. Heat the oil in a medium skillet over medium-high heat. Add the garlic and ginger and cook, stirring, until fragrant, about 1 minute. Add the shiitakes and season with ½ teaspoon of the salt. Cook, stirring, until the shiitakes release liquid, about 5 minutes.

2. Add the snowpeas, water, and remaining ½ teaspoon salt. Cook until the snowpeas turn bright green and the water is almost completely evaporated, about 2 minutes. Serve warm.

NUTRITION INFORMATION (PER SERVING):

CALORIES 76, CARBS 10G, FIBER 2G, PROTEIN 2G, TOTAL FAT 4G, SATURATED FAT 0G

- 1 tablespoon vegetable oil
- 2 garlic cloves, sliced
- 1½ inch cube fresh ginger, cut into matchsticks
- 5 ounces shiitake mushrooms, sliced
- 1 teaspoon kosher salt
- 2 cups fresh snow peas or sugar snap peas, gently packed
- ¼ cup water

KITCHEN TIP § For Matchsticks, It's Best to Be Square When preparing fresh ginger, snap off a knob, bring it to your nose, and inhale deep. *Aaaaahhhh.*

After you've had your moment, put the ginger on the cutting board. Begin by "squaring off" the piece, using your knife to trim that round tube into a square (this also removes the papery outer skin). Once you have your 1-inch cube, slice it into thin planks, divide them into two piles, and cut the planks into thin matchsticks. The ginger makes this dish sing.

SKINNY TIP § No Snow? Snow peas and sugar snap peas are terrific skinny ingredients, weighing in at 41 calories per packed cup. They arrive in my grocery store in the spring and stay for most of the summer. If you don't have them (or can't wait), try using canned water chestnuts. They're crisp, sweet, and about 70 calories per cup. They can be found in the Asian section of the grocery store.

satisfying slaw

PREP TIME: 15 minutes TOTAL TIME: 15 minutes MAKES 8 servings SERVING SIZE: ½ cup

For a slaw to be satisfying, it has to do two things. First, it has to look inviting, colorful, and vibrant. Second, it's gotta be tangy. I need a little attitude to balance that mayo; I need perk.

After all, coleslaw is meant to be refreshing. I serve it with baby back ribs (page 217) and pulled pork (page 218) so that it can cut through the richness of the meat. Slaw to ribs is like ginger to sushi.

This slaw earns its name; it's all that and a bag of cabbage.

1. In a large bowl, whisk together the mayonnaise, vinegar, mustard, sugar, and celery seeds. Add the coleslaw mix, red onion, and jalapeño to the bowl and toss to coat with the dressing. Season with salt and pepper. Chill until ready to serve. Slaw can be kept covered in the refrigerator for up to 5 days.

NUTRITION INFORMATION
(PER SERVING):

CALORIES 81, CARBS 4G, FIBER 1G, PROTEIN 1G, TOTAL FAT 7G, SATURATED FAT 1G

⅓ cup mayonnaise
¼ cup cider vinegar
2 tablespoons Dijon mustard
1 teaspoon sugar
½ teaspoon celery seeds
1 14-ounce package coleslaw mix
½ small red onion, thinly sliced on a mandoline (see tip, page 55)
1 jalapeño, chopped, with seeds
½ teaspoon kosher salt
¼ teaspoon freshly ground black pepper

 KITCHEN TIP § What Does Coleslaw Have in Common with a Bloody Mary? I'll give you a guess: It's one of those "why do I have this?" items in your pantry. Celery seeds are often listed in both Bloody Mary and coleslaw recipes. The seeds have a brassy, green flavor, like concentrated celery. And the texture is fun, too; they pop

in your mouth like tiny poppy seeds. It gives your slaw an edge.

 SKINNY TIP § Substitution, Ref! Bagged cabbage is easy to use. It has two ingredients: cabbage and carrots. It's easy, and is part of why this slaw takes 15 minutes to make. If your grocery store doesn't

carry it, simply shred a head of green cabbage and grate a carrot. You'll want 7 cups of homemade coleslaw mix for this recipe. And if your cabbage makes more than 7 cups of shredded leaves (highly likely), just double the sauce recipe. Trust me, you'll find plenty of takers for this slaw.

can-do carbs:

starchy sides

when you think *carbs,*

what comes to mind—mashed potatoes? rice? French fries?

Those are some of the more popular carbs. And sadly, we've been having a love/hate battle with carbs for a few decades now. Carbs have found themselves in the unlucky position of obesity scapegoat. *Aw carbs, poor carbs.*

In some ways, carbs have taken an underserved bad rap, like blaming a hyper kid for his energy instead of letting him join a sports team and get his ya-ya's out.

It's not that carbs are bad, it's that we're focusing on their weaknesses instead of their strengths. For example, check this out:

  1 cup dried long-grain white rice: 699 calories
  1 cup dried couscous: 651 calories
  1 cup dried black beans: 662 calories
  1 cup dried quinoa: 626 calories
  1 cup dried bulgur wheat (for tabouli): 479 calories

Dried carbs are the second-most calorie-dense food category on the planet (fat is the first). And though carbs and protein are calorically equivalent, we rarely sit down to a bowl of shredded chicken with the enthusiasm with which we sit down to a bowl of rice, noodles, or mashed potatoes. Carb calories go down quick.

Plus, when you eat these carbs, you rarely eat them on their own; you usually combine them with butter or olive oil, maybe you'll top the black beans with a dollop of sour cream, or add nuts and dried fruit to the quinoa.

Now, remove your negative carb hat for a second and look at this from a different perspective. Here's a basic home economics and massive global geopolitical question: *How do I feed myself for the least amount of money?*

Rice, beans, and cornmeal are some of the least expensive calories in the grocery store. Plus, they taste good. Who doesn't love mashed potatoes, creamy polenta, or fried rice? Carbs are inexpensive, delicious, and if properly chosen, nutritious.

Which is why I could never ask you to go without carbs. Taking them away would be like *not* celebrating your birthday just because it falls near New Year's; it's just mean. Instead, I've reworked some of your favorite carb side dishes so that you can have a satisfying portion for under 150 calories.

That means you *can* have a serving of Fluffy Mashed Potatoes (page 160) or Fried Rice (page 174) for less than 130 calories per serving. In fact, go ahead and have a double portion of Fried Rice, add some shrimp, and call it dinner.

I have a foolproof Popovers recipe (page 172) that will show you how to make a puffy popover to go with your Sunday roast for under 100 calories. Or, enjoy two (or three) with jam or a little lemon curd (page 251) for breakfast.

You'll also find well-loved whole grain sides like Tabouli (page 163), as well as Quinoa with Orange, Ginger, Parsley, and Pine Nuts (page 178). By partnering calorie-dense bulgur and quinoa with fresh fruit and vegetables, you can have a larger portion without the caloric impact.

And after enjoying these dishes, you might just be inspired to do something physical. That's good, because carbs are your best friend when you need energy. Just be sure to say thank you to the quinoa that helped you run up that hill, the rice that helped you hit your foul shot, and the potato that had you surfing the waves all day. See what I mean? Life is better with carbs.

fluffy mashed potatoes

PREP TIME: 15 minutes TOTAL TIME: 40 minutes MAKES 8 servings SERVING SIZE: ½ cup plus 2 tablespoons

Though it's easy to make mashed potatoes taste good with a stick of butter and a cup of cream, it's also easy to make them taste good without those caloric crutches. Simply choose the right potato; a nice, sweet waxy potato like Yukon Gold or Red Bliss is the potato of choice for my mash, as they're sweet and have a thin skin that does not need to be removed before mashing if you like a "rustic" look.

Calorically, waxy potatoes are the same as starchy potatoes (Idaho, russet), so if you prefer the texture and flavor of russets, by all means use them. Some women like men with hairy chests and some don't; everyone's entitled to an opinion.

NUTRITION INFORMATION
(PER SERVING):
CALORIES 129, CARBS 22G, FIBER 2G, PROTEIN 3G, TOTAL FAT 4G, SATURATED FAT 2G

- 2 pounds Yukon Gold or other waxy potatoes, peeled and cut into ½-inch slices
- 1 tablespoon plus 1 teaspoon kosher salt
- 2 tablespoons unsalted butter
- ¾ cup whole milk
  Freshly ground black pepper, or 1 tablespoon prepared horseradish (optional)

1. Put the potatoes in a medium pot, cover with water, and add 1 tablespoon salt. Bring to a boil, reduce to a simmer, and simmer gently until potatoes are tender when pierced with the tip of a paring knife, 20 to 25 minutes.

2. Drain the potatoes and return to the pot (over low heat). Add the butter and mash the potatoes until crumbly. Slowly whisk in the milk and season with the remaining teaspoon salt. Season with black pepper or horseradish, as desired. Serve warm.

KITCHEN TIP § Fluffing Techniques
Don't have a potato masher? Neither do I. Here are some alternatives:
1. Use a slotted spoon. If you do this, be sure to use a really wide pot so that you have a good angle to smash those 'taters.
2. Get a really enthusiastic kid to do it for you. I've been known to put the potato pot on the ground and have an eight-year-old go at it with whatever blunt object I can find. It tires 'em out and makes 'em happy.
3. Do you have a ricer? If not, how about a colander? Pro chefs use a tool called a ricer to literally push the cooked potatoes through holes that

are similar in size to those of a colander. It purees and lightens the potato without adding extra fat. You can press the potato through a colander for the same effect, but your best bet is to . . .
4. *Whip it real good.* After you've got those potatoes crumbly, add a bit of milk and whip them with a whisk. Not too much milk—just enough to smooth the edges without weighing it down. And be sure to mash those potatoes to crumbly before adding any liquid.

SKINNY TIP § Pools of Butter
Though butter is always nice in a recipe, this mashed potato recipe is so creamy it can stand

on its own. But if you want to "show off" the indulgence, make a little indentation in the center of the warm mashed potatoes and put the butter right in it. The butter will melt into the potatoes, leaving a little pool of flavor. You can also use this presentation technique for individual servings.

SKINNY TIP § Mash with Cauliflower
Several low-carb diets cut the calories in mashed potatoes by introducing a new ingredient: cauliflower. It cuts the calories, and personally, I like the flavor a lot. If you like that approach, add cauliflower florets to the simmer pot along with the potatoes.

peas with shallots and bacon

PREP TIME: 10 minutes TOTAL TIME: 15 minutes MAKES 4 servings SERVING SIZE: ½ cup

Certain foods, like bacon, chocolate chip cookies, or just-made coffee, are as much about the aroma as they are about the eating. If someone says he or she isn't hungry for dinner, start cooking the bacon in step 1 and that person will come running.

1. Place the bacon in a medium skillet over medium heat. Cook the bacon until soft-crisp, about 2 minutes per side. Remove from the pan and drain on paper towels. Pour out some of the fat so that you've got 1 tablespoon of fat remaining in the pan. If you need more fat, add a little butter.
2. Put the shallots in the skillet, season with ½ teaspoon of the salt, and cook until they begin to soften, about 2 minutes. Add the frozen peas and water, and cover. Cook until the peas are warmed through, about 2 minutes. Remove the cover and remove from the heat.
3. Roughly chop the bacon and return it to the peas. Mix and season with the remaining ½ teaspoon salt and a few grinds of pepper. Serve warm.

NUTRITION INFORMATION
(PER SERVING):

CALORIES 108, CARBS 11G, FIBER 3G, PROTEIN 5G, TOTAL FAT 5G, SATURATED FAT 2G

2 strips bacon
1 tablespoon unsalted butter (if needed)
2 shallots, thinly sliced
1 teaspoon kosher salt
1 10-ounce package frozen peas (2 cups)
2 tablespoons water
   Coarsely ground black pepper

KITCHEN TIP § Baby Peas
When purchasing frozen peas, look for baby peas or petits pois. They are smaller than regular peas and tend to be sweeter and less starchy. Buy frozen peas instead of canned, as they have the best flavor, texture, and vibrant color.

SKINNY TIP § Big Bacon?
For calorie-counting purposes, I estimate that 1 slice of bacon is 1 ounce, as that's what 1 regular slice of bacon typically weighs. If you're seduced by thick-cut bacon (I know I am), use ⅔ of a slice.

tabouli (middle eastern bulgur wheat salad)

PREP TIME: 20 minutes TOTAL TIME: 25 minutes MAKES 6 servings SERVING SIZE: ⅔ cup

Tabouli is the first recipe I ever made on my own. We were having an international potluck at school, and this was my contribution. I probably chose to make tabouli because it came in a cool box with a seasoning packet. As a kid, I was always a sucker for a seasoning packet.

These days I get my kicks from fresh herbs, lemons, and tomatoes. The flavors in this version are just as good (dare I say better?) than the seasoning-mix version, and the dish has significantly less sodium.

1. Put the bulgur wheat in a large bowl. Pour the boiling water over the bulgur and cover with plastic wrap. Let it stand until the bulgur is tender and the water is absorbed, about 20 minutes.

2. Add the tomato, parsley, mint, scallion, olive oil, lemon zest, lemon juice, and salt; toss to combine. Serve immediately or refrigerate for up to 3 days. The flavor will improve as it sits, though the mint will discolor slightly, so add the mint just before serving.

NUTRITION INFORMATION
(PER SERVING):
CALORIES 133, CARBS 21G, FIBER 5G, PROTEIN 4G, TOTAL FAT 5G, SATURATED FAT 1G

1 cup dried bulgur wheat
1 cup boiling water
1 cup chopped tomato
1 cup roughly chopped fresh parsley
¼ cup chopped fresh mint
1 scallion, green and white parts thinly sliced
2 tablespoons olive oil
   Grated zest and juice of 1 lemon
1 teaspoon kosher salt

 SKINNY TIP § More Tabouli; Fewer Calories If you want a bigger portion, add cucumber to the tabouli. If you add 1 medium cucumber, peeled, seeded, and chopped, you can have a 1 cup serving for 135 calories. Amazing, right? A cucumber adds another 2 cups of volume to the dish and only 2 calories per serving. Kinda blows my mind.

 SKINNY TIP § Atlantic Avenue Tabouli I live in Brooklyn. On Atlantic Avenue, not far from my apartment, there is a collection of outstanding Middle Eastern bakeries, butchers, grocery stores, and restaurants. When developing this recipe, I visited these shops (twist my arm) to investigate how they make tabouli. Though we use the same ingredients, we use them in very different amounts. Their version is predominantly chopped tomatoes and parsley. Make it as you like—starchy or veggie side.

northern polenta/southern cheese grits

PREP TIME: 5 minutes TOTAL TIME: 15 minutes MAKES 5 servings SERVING SIZE: ½ cup

My friend Gabe loves to cook. He's a single dad, so at dinnertime he cooks for two: himself and his 9-year-old son. Polenta is one of his specialties. This is his recipe:

"I get my son started with his homework. I bring some milk to a boil and I whisk in the cornmeal. I don't use instant—never use instant because as soon as I get the cornmeal in the pot, he needs some help with his homework. So for 20 minutes, I go back and forth—help him with his homework, stir the polenta. Homework, stir, homework, stir. That's how you make polenta. If it were instant, my son would never get his homework done."

1. Bring the milk and water to a simmer in a medium saucepan. Add the salt and slowly whisk in the cornmeal. Cook at a gentle simmer, whisking occasionally, until thickened, about 25 minutes.

2. Whisk in the cheeses and chives, and remove from the heat. Season with pepper to taste.

NUTRITION INFORMATION
(PER SERVING):

CALORIES 133, CARBS 15G, FIBER 1G, PROTEIN 8G, TOTAL FAT 5G, SATU-RATED FAT 3G

2 cups skim milk
1 cup water
2 teaspoons kosher salt
½ cup coarse-ground cornmeal
½ cup shredded cheddar cheese (about 2 ounces)
2 tablespoons freshly grated Parmesan cheese
1 tablespoon chopped fresh chives or scallion greens
   Freshly ground black pepper

KITCHEN TIP § Polenta, Grits, or What? And How About Instant? Polenta and grits are the same dish: cornmeal cooked in a liquid (milk, broth, water) until it becomes a thick and creamy porridge. Good corn is sweet, as we know from munching on a just-picked ear in the middle of summer. Polenta (or grits) can be a real treat as part of a meal, served the same way you'd serve mashed potatoes.

Polenta is an Italian term, while *grits* originates in the southern United States. Grits used to be made exclusively from hominy, but now any corn will do. The term refers to the gritty nature of coarse-ground hulled dried corn kernels.

Though you can make polenta with a cornmeal of the coarseness you desire, grits should be made using coarse cornmeal. And yes, you can use instant, which is typically parcooked (like instant rice) or just more finely ground (as with rolled oats, which also cook faster than coarse oats).

KITCHEN TIP § *Best Cornmeal* I like to buy local and have become friendly with Billy Robinson, the owner of a grist mill in Supply, North Carolina. When I visit my parents (who live nearby), I buy bags of Billy's grits and keep them in the freezer until I need them. In the grocery store, I like the sweet flavor of Goya coarse-ground cornmeal.

SKINNY TIP § *Can I Skip the Cheese?* Of course! Cornmeal is a skinny ingredient because when you cook it, ½ cup of meal grows to 2½ cups of delicious side dish. Polenta is a sweet, creamy side dish that compliments mains that bring their own flavorful sauces to the party, like Seared Chicken with Lemon and Rosemary (page 188) or Skirt Steak with Chimichurri Sauce (page 226). With entrées like these, you can omit the cheddar, which saves you 50 calories per serving.

KITCHEN TIP § *What's Better than Creamy Polenta? Grilled Polenta* Tasty on its own, this polenta becomes transcendental when grilled. Make the polenta without the water, so it's thicker, and when you're done with the simmering let it cool in an 8-inch pan or loaf pan coated with plastic wrap, or any size plastic container. It should take about an hour to cool and become firm.

Remove the cooled polenta from the container and cut it into ½-inch-thick pieces. Cook on a well-oiled grill until you can see the grill marks, 3 to 4 minutes per side. The outside will be crisp and the inside creamy. It's delicious on its own and exceptional with a little chimichurri dipping sauce (page 226).

If you don't have time for grilling, you can also sauté the firm polenta in a nonstick pan with a little olive oil.

KITCHEN TIP § *Breakfast, Too?* Gabe likes to serve leftover grilled polenta for breakfast. He pops the pieces in a toaster to warm them and serves them with soft-scrambled eggs.

"It's not that carbs are bad, its that we're focusing on their weaknesses instead of their strengths."

steakhouse sweet potato wedges

PREP TIME: 10 minutes TOTAL TIME: 35 minutes MAKES 6 servings SERVING SIZE: 4 or 5 wedges

Talk about finger food! These sweet potato wedges look incredible stacked high on a platter. They are soft and sweet, as much candy for the mouth as they are for the eyes. Chili powder makes this deliciously easy, but experiment with other seasonings like cumin and garlic powder, chopped fresh rosemary, or thyme. For dunking, ketchup always works (at 15 calories per tablespoon), or try a squeeze of fresh lime juice for a British chips-and-vinegar effect.

1. Preheat the oven to 425°F. Cut each sweet potato in half lengthwise, and place it flat side down on a cutting board. Cut the potato halves into 1-inch-wide wedges.

2. In a small bowl, combine the oil, chili powder, and 1 teaspoon of the salt. Place the potatoes on a roasting pan and brush with the oil mixture. Lay the potatoes flesh side down on the pan and put the pan in the oven.

3. Cook until potatoes, turning once, until soft, 20 to 25 minutes. Remove the pan from the oven and season with remaining ½ teaspoon salt. Let the wedges cool for a bit, and serve warm.

NUTRITION INFORMATION
(PER SERVING):

CALORIES 171, CARBS 30G, FIBER 5G, PROTEIN 2G, TOTAL FAT 5G, SATURATED FAT 1G

- 2 pounds sweet potatoes (about 4 small)
- 2 tablespoons olive oil
- 1½ teaspoons chili powder
- 1½ teaspoons kosher salt

KITCHEN TIP § Tan Taters
If you want your wedges to get some color, the potato flesh has to be in contact with the roasting pan. To get that flesh blistered and golden brown, cook your potatoes on one side without turning.

KITCHEN TIP § Sweet Potato Puree
If you like the flavor of sweet potatoes and want to try them mashed, try this recipe for sweet potato puree: Poke holes in the flesh of 2 pounds of sweet potatoes (any size) and roast in a 400°F oven for 30 to 45 minutes, until they are soft. Remove the sweet potatoes from the oven and

allow them to cool until you can handle them. Remove peel, transfer the naked sweet potatoes to a food processor, and add ¾ cup milk and 2 tablespoons of butter. Taste the sweet potato puree and season with salt as needed. Calorically, they're the same as Fluffy Mashed Potatoes (page 160).

red potato salad with herb vinaigrette

PREP TIME: 30 minutes TOTAL TIME: 45 minutes MAKES 9 servings SERVING SIZE: 1 cup

I grew up on deli potato salad, which is one part boiled potatoes and one part mayonnaise. Blech. I *hated* the stuff, and unfortunately I vetoed the entire potato salad category for most of my life.

And then I learned about German potato salad. In place of mayo, it calls for a vinaigrette made with herbs, vinegar, and mustard, a tangy contrast to starchy potatoes. It can be served warm or cold and always tastes better the second day.

See what happens when you swear off entire categories of food? I missed out.

1. Add the potatoes to a medium saucepan and cover with salted water by 1 inch. Bring to a boil and cook until you can easily pierce potatoes with the tip of a knife, 20 to 30 minutes.

2. Meanwhile, in a large bowl, make the dressing: Whisk together the cider vinegar and mustard; slowly add the oil. Stir in the parsley, onion, celery, pepperoncini, scallion greens, tarragon, capers, and caraway seeds. Season with the salt.

3. After you have cooked and drained the potatoes, as soon as humanly possible cut the potatoes into ⅓-inch slices. Fold the hot potatoes into the dressing as you go. Taste and adjust for seasonings. Note: If you plan to serve this cold, the recipe may need additional salt.

NUTRITION INFORMATION
(PER SERVING):

CALORIES 125, CARBS 18G, FIBER 3G, PROTEIN 3G, TOTAL FAT 5G, SATURATED FAT 1G

- 2 pounds baby red potatoes
- ½ cup cider vinegar
- 2 tablespoons mustard
- 3 tablespoons vegetable oil
- ⅔ cup roughly chopped fresh parsley
- 1 small red onion, very thinly sliced and soaked in ice water for 15 minutes and drained (about ½ cup; see tip, page 47)
- 6 celery stalks (inner stalks, if possible) with greens, sliced
- 4 pickled pepperoncini peppers, roughly chopped
- 2 scallion greens, sliced on the bias
- 1 tablespoon chopped fresh tarragon
- 2 teaspoons capers, rinsed and drained (optional)
- ¼ teaspoon caraway seeds
- 1 tablespoon kosher salt, plus more for water

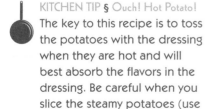

KITCHEN TIP § Ouch! Hot Potato! The key to this recipe is to toss the potatoes with the dressing when they are hot and will best absorb the flavors in the dressing. Be careful when you slice the steamy potatoes (use tongs to steady them) and you will be rewarded for the effort.

A moment of sanity: This reminds me of a friend who prepared herself for the pain of natural childbirth by holding her hands in ice water for up to 20 minutes at a time. I thought she was nuts. If you don't want to handle hot potatoes, don't. Do what works for you. That said, what doesn't kill you . . .

you can make white rice

PREP TIME: 15 minutes TOTAL TIME: 30 minutes MAKES 6 servings SERVING SIZE: ½ cup plus 2 tablespoons

Rice is the most popular starch in the world. People have been preparing rice since the beginning of human time (predating modern conveniences like rice cookers and stoves). Cave people did it. *You can do it, too.*

When you make rice, your goal is to ever-so-gently put moisture back into something that has been dehydrated. It's like when you put wilting tulips in water and they perk up. When you use heat, rehydrating rice becomes faster and more efficient (don't try that with the tulips), but you want to do it gently, or the rice will get frazzled.

If you're nervous about rice, give this recipe a try. After all, it's only rice. If it's not perfect, the worst thing that can happen is you toss it out and try again.

NUTRITION INFORMATION (PER SERVING):

CALORIES 129, CARBS 25G, FIBER 0G, PROTEIN 2G, TOTAL FAT 2G, SATURATED FAT 1G

1¾ cups water
1 tablespoon unsalted butter
1 teaspoon kosher salt
1 cup long-grain rice

1. In a small saucepan, bring the water, butter, and salt to a boil. Add the rice, return the water to a simmer, reduce the heat to low, cover, and cook until steam holes are evident, about 15 minutes. Remove the covered pan of rice from the heat and let the rice steam, covered, for another 5 minutes.

2. Using a fork, gently fluff the rice and serve. Rice will keep in an airtight container for 1 week; reheat as needed in a small amount of water.

KITCHEN TIP § Don't Peek! So if you aren't supposed to peek, how are you supposed to see those steam holes? Trust me. Or use one of those nifty see-through glass pot lids. If you keep your heat real low, the steam holes will appear at 15 minutes. So don't peek until the rice has cooked, covered, for 15 minutes, and *then* lift the lid. See? Told ya. Replace the cover, remove the rice from the heat, and let it steam for another 5 minutes. Look at you, cooking rice!

KITCHEN TIP § Cook It Like Pasta You can cook rice the same way you cook pasta. Add the rice to boiling, salted water and after 15 minutes, drain the rice in a strainer. That's it! Sure, you cooked it a little aggressively, so the rice might have blunt edges, but that's okay. Sometimes a loss of elegance is worth the efficiency; like when you're trying to feed a table full of kids.

"if you can't taste THE BUTTER WHY EAT ALL THOSE BUTTER CALORIES? IT'S LIKE PAYING FOR A MOVIE & WEARING A BLINDFOLD."

popovers

PREP TIME: 15 minutes   TOTAL TIME: 55 minutes   MAKES 12 servings   SERVING SIZE: 1 popover

Popovers are a blast to make. They look innocent enough when you put them into the oven, but then—KA-POW!—they more than double their size. The trick is that they're hollow inside, which lets us put this puffball on our plates for 84 calories. They are best straight out of the oven while they're still hot, so plan accordingly.

1. Preheat the oven to 425°F. Divide the butter among the empty muffin cups in a standard-size 12-cup muffin or popover tin and place the tin in the oven until the butter melts and the pan is hot, 2 to 3 minutes.

2. Combine the flour, chives, and salt in a medium bowl. In a separate bowl, whisk together the milk and eggs. Gradually whisk the milk mixture into the flour mixture.

3. Carefully remove the hot muffin tin from the oven. Fill each section with batter, working quickly. Bake until puffed and golden, 20 minutes. Reduce the heat to 350°F and continue to cook for another 20 minutes.

NUTRITION INFORMATION
(PER SERVING):
CALORIES 84, CARBS 11G, FIBER 0G, PROTEIN 4G, TOTAL FAT 2G, SATURATED FAT 1G

1	tablespoon unsalted butter
1¼	cups all-purpose flour
1	teaspoon dried chives
1	teaspoon kosher salt
1¼	cups skim milk
3	large eggs

KITCHEN TIP § Did Your Pops Flop? **Are you peeking at the popovers while they cook? Restrain yourself! Do not open the oven door while the pops are cooking. They will catch a chill and fall.** *They will know if you peek.*

In many popover recipes, you cook the popovers at a high heat, which really tempts fate. Sometimes the pops are raw on the inside which causes them to fall minutes after they're out of the oven.

In this recipe, we inflate the pops at high heat, then use a lower heat to stabilize. This way, your pops are a lot less likely to flop.

KITCHEN TIP §Tall Pops
Let your ingredients come to room temperature before cooking. The less cold they are, the higher they'll pop.

SKINNY TIP §Pop Swaps
I added dried chives for flavor and color. If you want something milder and just as colorful, go for dried parsley. If this dried herb thing is keeping you from making the Popovers, proceed without.

Popovers are a classic partner to Classic Roast Beef (page 223), and in place of the butter, you use pan juices from the roast to grease the pan. If you're making the roast beef, please use the juices that settle out as the roast cooks to make your Popovers.

Alternatively, for a breakfast pop, serve the popovers (minus the chives) with orange marmalade or strawberry jam. And try a little soft butter; you've got (caloric) space for it!

fried rice

PREP TIME: 10 minutes TOTAL TIME: 15 minutes MAKES 3 servings SERVING SIZE: ½ cup

Next time people tell you they don't do leftovers, feed them this. By using ginger, garlic, toasted sesame oil, and scallion, you can turn the leftover steamed rice into terrific fried rice. It's all in there, except the massive amounts of oil.

1. Heat the vegetable oil in a small nonstick skillet over medium-high heat. Add the garlic, ginger, and scallion whites and cook, stirring, until fragrant, about 1 minute. Add the rice and stir to combine. Let the rice reheat, without stirring, until hot and the grains on the bottom are beginning to brown, about 3 minutes (you may need to add a tablespoon or two of water if the rice is very dry).

2. Add the peas and stir to incorporate. Push the rice to the edges of the pan and add the egg in the center. Let the egg begin to cook and stir to incorporate. When the egg has cooked, the peas are bright green, and some of the rice is beginning to brown, after about 2 minutes, remove the skillet from the heat and stir in the scallion greens, sesame oil, and soy sauce. Serve warm.

NUTRITION INFORMATION
(PER SERVING):

CALORIES 129, CARBS 17G, FIBER 1G, PROTEIN 4G, TOTAL FAT 4G, SATURATED FAT 1G

1 teaspoon vegetable oil
1 teaspoon minced garlic
1 teaspoon minced fresh ginger
1 scallion, whites and greens thinly sliced
1 cup leftover white rice (see You Can Make White Rice, page 169)
¼ cup frozen baby peas
1 large egg
¼ teaspoon toasted sesame oil
1 teaspoon lower-sodium soy sauce

 SKINNY TIP § Skinny Fried Rice for Dinner? Why not! Make yourself a double (or triple) portion, and add shrimp or ham for a little extra flavor. *Mmmm.*

 SKINNY TIP § What Makes Fried Rice Taste Good? The key to that fried-rice flavor is a little toasted sesame oil, which is not a cooking oil but a flavoring oil, so add it *after* the rice has cooked. Toasted sesame oil, plus the fresh flavors of garlic, ginger, and scallion, delivers tasty fried rice.

Also, when you fry in a nonstick skillet, you can use less oil. In a regular skillet, you'll have to use a lot more oil to prevent the rice from sticking.

 KITCHEN TIP § Nonstick Care
When you're cooking with nonstick pans, be sure to reach for a soft tool for stirring, like a wooden spoon or a heatproof spatula, to avoid scratching the surface.

black beans from scratch

PREP TIME: 10 minutes TOTAL TIME: 1½ hours, plus an overnight soak MAKES 12 servings SERVING SIZE: ½ cup

It's gratifying and cost-effective to make beans from scratch. Feel free to swap in pinto, white, kidney—really, any bean you like. It takes some time, but it's not hands-on; the beans rehydrate when you're asleep and can be a back-burner item (literally) while you're doing other things.

1. Put the beans in a large bowl and cover with water by 2 inches. Let soak for 8 hours or overnight.

2. Drain and rinse the beans. Place the soaked beans in a large pot and cover with 4 quarts of water. Add the onion, garlic, thyme, bay leaves, 1 teaspoon salt, the oregano, and red pepper flakes. Bring

to a simmer and simmer gently until beans are soft, creamy, and firm without being mushy, about 1 hour 15 minutes. Season with the remaining 2 tablespoons salt and serve, or store, covered in their liquid, in a sealed container in the refrigerator for up to 2 weeks.

NUTRITION INFORMATION (PER SERVING):
CALORIES 90, CARBS 19G, FIBER 6G, PROTEIN 7G, TOTAL FAT 0G, SATURATED FAT 0G

- 1 16-ounce bag dried black beans
- 1 large onion, peeled and cut in half
- 4 garlic cloves, peeled and smashed
- 5 sprigs fresh thyme
- 2 bay leaves
- 1 teaspoon plus 2 tablespoons kosher salt
- 1 teaspoon dried oregano
   Generous pinch of red pepper flakes

 SKINNY TIP § Black Bean Meal As many vegetarians know, a bowl of beans and rice gives you all the amino acids you need, making it a complete protein. For a simple dinner, I love to make rice, then top it with homemade beans, salsa, cilantro, some pickled jalapeños, and a poached egg (page 34). Try it; it's soothing and simple and totally homemade—something you're unlikely to find in a restaurant.

 KITCHEN TIP § Quick-Soak Method If you don't want to let the beans soak overnight, try the quick-soak method. Put the beans in a pot and bring them to a boil. As soon as they come to a boil, drain them and proceed with step 2. You won't have to let the beans soak overnight, but you will have to bring them to a simmer twice.

 KITCHEN TIP § Slow Cooker Black Beans Want to make black beans in a slow cooker? Go for it. Put all the ingredients listed in this recipe in a slow cooker and cover the beans with 8 cups of water. Cook for 5 hours on high or 6 hours on low. If you're new to slow cooking, be warned: It's addictive.

sue's easy cheesy black beans

PREP TIME: 10 minutes   TOTAL TIME: 10 minutes   MAKES 4 servings   SERVING SIZE: ⅓ cup

Sue Park tested the recipes in this cookbook. On Mondays, she would come to the test kitchen with samples of her cooking from the weekend. As I would take a bite of her tiramisù, Parisian macaroons, or chocolate cupcakes, she'd smile and say, "You won't *believe* how much butter is in that!"

She was right; I was always shocked. And *if you can't taste the butter, why eat all those butter calories?* It's like paying for a movie and wearing a blindfold.

She thought that her signature black beans would be good for the book, so she made them for me. They were good, *real good*, but at over 200 calories for ⅓ cup serving, there was no way they would work. We refined the recipe and we were thrilled when tasters preferred the 133-calorie version.

1. Heat the black beans and salsa in a small saucepan over medium-low heat. When the mixture comes to a simmer and the beans are hot, after about 3 minutes, add the cheese. Stir the beans until the cheese has melted; about 1 minute. Serve warm.

NUTRITION INFORMATION
(PER SERVING):

CALORIES 133, CARBS 17G, FIBER 7G, PROTEIN 8G, TOTAL FAT 3G, SATURATED FAT 2G

1   15½-ounce can black beans, rinsed and drained, or 1¾ cups Black Beans from Scratch (page 175)
⅓   cup salsa verde (or your favorite salsa)
⅓   cup grated sharp cheddar cheese (about 1½ ounces)

SKINNY TIP § Poblano Rice
Sue serves her Cheesy Black Beans with poblano rice, which is easy to make if you've mastered You Can Make White Rice (page 169). Instead of cooking the rice in plain water, she makes poblano water. She sautés chopped poblano chile, garlic, and onion in a tablespoon of oil. When they're soft, she purees them in the blender with water or chicken stock. She uses this liquid *in place* of the water and butter when steaming the rice. By using this flavorful poblano broth instead of water, she makes a *how-did-you-do-that?* rice, adding negligible additional calories for the flavor.

SKINNY TIP § Huevos Rancheros
Sue loves these beans in the morning on a Mexican Breakfast Tortilla (page 36). By adding beans, you'll have a real stick-to-your-ribs breakfast, perfect if you're hitting the ski slopes or are on your feet cooking all day, like Sue.

But you're also halfway to one of my favorite brunches: *huevos rancheros*, a combination of eggs (however you like them), warm tortillas, cilantro, salsa, and beans. Sometimes restaurants add tasty calorie bombs, like sour cream, guacamole, or tons of cheese. If you have your cheese in your beans, as you do with your recipe, you'll get the flavor without tons of calories. Plus, this is an easy-to-assemble meal if you're short on time and want to serve an impressive brunch.

ten-minute couscous with almonds and parsley

PREP TIME: 10 minutes TOTAL TIME: 10 minutes MAKES 6 servings SERVING SIZE: ½ cup

Couscous is a tiny pasta. As such, it can be very caloric (651 calories for a cup of dried couscous). In this recipe, you rehydrate this pasta with water, and toss it with fresh herbs, currants, and sliced almonds. In so doing, you turn ¾ cup of dried couscous into 3 delicious cups of flavorful side dish.

1. Place the couscous and currants in a bowl and pour the boiling water over. Cover with plastic wrap and let sit for 5 minutes.

2. Remove the plastic wrap from the bowl and fluff the couscous using the tines of a fork. Add the parsley, almonds, lemon zest, juice, oil, and cinnamon and toss with the couscous. Season with salt to taste and serve warm, room temperature, or chilled.

NUTRITION INFORMATION
(PER SERVING):
CALORIES 126, CARBS 21G, FIBER 2G, PROTEIN 4G, TOTAL FAT 3G, SATURATED FAT 0G

¾ cup dried couscous
2 tablespoons dried currants
1 cup boiling water
1 cup roughly chopped fresh parsley (or other fresh herbs, like basil, mint, and scallion greens)
2 tablespoons sliced almonds, toasted (see tip, page 110)
   Grated zest and juice of 1 lemon
1 tablespoon olive oil
¼ teaspoon ground cinnamon
   Kosher salt

KITCHEN TIP § Fluff Your Food
Many couscous and rice recipes ask you to "fluff using the tines of a fork" after the starch has steamed. I know it seems precious, but fluffing has its purpose. Once rice (or pasta, in the case of couscous) is rehydrated, it's fragile. If you stir it with a spoon, it can get mashed. Use the gentle tines of a fork to lift and separate.

Maybe it is a little precious. But so are those pieces of couscous.

SKINNY TIP § Fruit Pops
If you don't have dried currants in your pantry, use dried apricots, raisins, cherries, or cranberries. Since dried fruits are expensive, calorically speaking (about 500 calories per cup), you

want to distribute them evenly throughout the dish. I use currants because I like their flavor and size. They're so tiny you'll end up with lots of little flavor bursts throughout the dish. If you opt for raisins or dried cherries, be sure to chop them before using.

quinoa with orange, ginger, parsley, and pine nuts

PREP TIME: 15 minutes **TOTAL TIME:** 35 minutes **MAKES** 6 servings **SERVING SIZE:** ⅔ cup

Quinoa is called a miracle grain because it has eight essential amino acids and is considered a complete protein. It's also way high in calories, weighing in at 180 calories per cooked ½ cup. Yowza!

How can we have our quinoa and a sexy body, too? Create a mini miracle of your own, and combine quinoa with fresh ingredients like oranges and parsley.

1. Add the quinoa to a medium pot and cover with the water. Bring to a simmer, cover, reduce the heat to medium-low, and simmer until you can see the opaque ring of the grain, 15 minutes. Let the quinoa steam in the covered pot, off the heat, until all the water is absorbed, 10 to 15 minutes.

2. Meanwhile, in a large bowl, combine the parsley, chopped orange, orange and lemon zests, lemon juice, pine nuts, scallion, ginger, olive oil, and salt. Toss to combine.

3. Add the cooked quinoa to the dressing and mix well. Serve chilled or at room temperature.

NUTRITION INFORMATION
(PER SERVING):

CALORIES 124, CARBS 19G, FIBER 3G, PROTEIN 4G, TOTAL FAT 4G, SATURATED FAT 1G

- ¾ cup dried quinoa
- 1½ cups water
- 1 cup roughly chopped fresh parsley
- Grated zest of 1 seedless orange, plus orange sections, roughly chopped
- Grated zest of 1 lemon, plus 1 tablespoon lemon juice
- 2 tablespoons pine nuts, toasted (see tip below)
- 1 scallion, green and white parts thinly sliced
- 1 teaspoon grated fresh ginger
- 1 tablespoon olive oil
- 1 teaspoon kosher salt

KITCHEN TIP § How to Toast Pine Nuts Put the pine nuts in a small, dry skillet and place over medium heat. Cook, shaking the pan every 30 seconds or so, until lightly browned and fragrant, 2 to 3 minutes. Be sure to remove the pine nuts from the skillet after cooking or they will continue to cook in the hot skillet. Keep toasted pine nuts in the freezer until you are ready to use them.

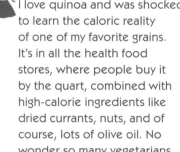

SKINNY TIP § Keen on Quinoa? I love quinoa and was shocked to learn the caloric reality of one of my favorite grains. It's in all the health food stores, where people buy it by the quart, combined with high-calorie ingredients like dried currants, nuts, and of course, lots of olive oil. No wonder so many vegetarians gain weight when they forgo meat and eat high-protein starches instead. Cup for cup, quinoa is way more caloric than chicken or fish.

If you like quinoa, try making it Greek-style, with the flavorings from the Lemon-Herb Orzo with Feta (page 133). Or, combine quinoa with chopped green, red, and yellow peppers, along with scallions, olive oil, and lemon juice. Both recipes add fresh vegetables and herbs to your quinoa, not dense calories.

roasted baby potatoes with caramelized garlic

PREP TIME: 10 minutes TOTAL TIME: 40 minutes MAKES 4 servings SERVING SIZE: 1 cup

Roasted baby potatoes are a popular restaurant side dish and simple to make at home. In this recipe, you can take it one step further by adding a head of roasted garlic. A single garlic clove has four calories, spreads *like buttah*, and gives intense flavor.

1. Preheat the oven to 425°F.

2. In a small bowl, combine the olive oil, rosemary, salt, and pepper.

3. Remove the top third of the garlic with your knife so that you can see the cloves. Discard the top and brush the exposed cloves with the rosemary oil (not too much; you want to save most of it for the potatoes). Place the garlic on the roasting pan, cut side down.

4. Put the potatoes on the roasting pan with the garlic and brush with the remaining rosemary oil. Place the potatoes cut side down in the pan and bake for 30 minutes. Use a paring knife to check if the potatoes are done; the tip of the knife should move in and out of the potato with ease: If they are still quite firm, return the pan to the oven for an additional 5 to 10 minutes.

5. Remove the pan from the oven and let the potatoes cool in the pan for 5 minutes (it takes a bit of time for the potatoes to relax and release from the pan; give them their time, as you don't want to leave that crispy edge on the pan). Remove the potatoes and garlic from the pan.

6. Remove the garlic cloves from the papery shell. You can use the tip of the paring knife or a grapefruit spoon to do this, and feel free to tear the papery skin. The cloves are soft, so try to keep them intact. Combine the roasted garlic cloves with the roasted potatoes in a bowl and serve warm.

NUTRITION INFORMATION
(PER SERVING):

CALORIES 157, CARBS 26G, FIBER 3G, PROTEIN 3G, TOTAL FAT 5G, SATURATED FAT 1G

- 2 tablespoons olive oil
- 1 tablespoon finely chopped fresh rosemary
- 1 teaspoon kosher salt
- ¼ teaspoon freshly ground black pepper
- 1 head garlic
- 2 pounds small red potatoes, cut in half

SKINNY TIP § Magical, Mystical Roasted Garlic Ah, roasting. The magic of this technique is evident with garlic, something you'd hesitate before eating raw but is hard to resist when roasted. If you've made it, you know how easy it is (and cheap—a head of garlic usually costs around 19 cents), so you might want use it in other ways. Spread it on bread or a cracker: It's like butter, but better. Try it as part of a pasta sauce, or better yet, use roasted garlic as part of your Lemony Hummus with Parsley (page 108) or Smoky Babaghanouj (page 111). If you're looking for a quick and easy appetizer, just put it out with crostini (page 96) and crudités, caramelized side up to show off the color. Try it in the Roasted Tomato Soup (page 74), or really anytime you want to amp up flavor.

 KITCHEN TIP § Garlic: Which End Is Up? If you sit the garlic head on your counter, it will balance best on its root end (the side with the hairy bits, just like an onion). That's the base. You want to keep that intact, and remove the top third from the other side.

KITCHEN TIP § How Big Is Small? Red-skinned baby potatoes are marketed under so many names, from baby potatoes to new potatoes to teeny-tiny potatoes. And small, compared to a big honkin' 1½-pound sweet potato, becomes a question of perspective, *as is so often the case* when it comes to size. I tested this recipe with two different kinds of "small" red potatoes, one that yielded 3 potatoes per pound and another that yielded 12.

Magically, the recipe worked just as well for both kinds of small. Both sizes were perfectly cooked through, though the smaller ones had a crispier edge (might want to keep those big potatoes going just a bit longer for optimal crispness).

"A single garlic clove has four calories, spreads *like buttah*, and gives intense flavor."

much depends on dinner:

meats & mains

In the summer, I like to

walk around the neighborhood and guess who is cooking steak, who is grilling a leg of lamb, and who is slow-cooking ribs over wood chips. In the winter, I can do the same thing walking up the stairs of my apartment building: *We've got sausage and peppers on the first floor, roast chicken on the second . . .*

Meat calls to me.

And here's a happy little secret about cooking meats or other proteins: *They're the easiest part of the meal to prepare.*

All you really need to do is get a high-quality piece of protein, season it properly, cook it respectfully, and get out of the way. Marinades and spice rubs evolved as part of our pre-refrigeration history, about as necessary today as the appendix. They covered up the flavors of inferior meat so that we could satisfy our protein needs while eating meat that may have been past its prime. We'd hide those off flavors, spoonful-of-sugar style.

But we're not living in medieval Europe. We have refrigeration. We have access to delicious organic meat, day-boat fish, frozen-at-their-peak shrimp, and fresh-from-the-farm chicken. We can go easy on the caloric coatings, marinades, and sauces and still enjoy delicious meat.

For the best-quality meat, go Prime. Choice is okay and typically what you can find at the grocery store. That's fine if you are going with something saucy, like Thai Beef (page 228), but less fine if you're enjoying meat on its own, as in Classic Roast Beef (page 223). Prime is the best-quality meat, the most marbled and delicious.

When I pick chicken, I opt for organic. Free range is less important to me. I've been to chicken farms and seen the birds on their "free range," but chickens are more the couch-potato type; they like to snuggle. It's as if these free-range chickens have an unused gym membership—theoretically active but practically inert.

I use chicken thighs when braising (Quick Chicken Mole, page 192) or stir-frying (Chicken Stir-Fry with Pineapples and Cashews, page 196), as they stay moist. No use for the skin in those situations, so toss it. Breast meat is delicious when roasted (Sage-Roasted Turkey with Apples and Onions, page 197); just be sure to keep that skin on so the breast meat stays moist (Seared Chicken with Lemon and Rosemary, page 188).

A meat thermometer is a critical tool when you want a perfectly Seared Duck Breast (page 198), moist Herb-Marinated Pork Tenderloin (page 214), or any other kind of roast. It's the definitive way to read your meat's mind.

If you're looking for main dishes with sauces and dips, try Crispy Fish Sticks with Tartar Sauce (page 210), Slow Cooker Pulled Pork (page 218), and Baby Back Ribs with 30-Minute Barbeque Sauce (page 217). These dishes have flavorful sauces that are worth the calories.

There are plenty of fish dishes, and I keep them simple. I have three salmon recipes, one sweet (Salmon with Teriyaki Glaze, page 206), one spicy (Simplest Salmon, page 205), and one with a creamy fresh herb sauce (Slow-Roasted Salmon with Lemon-Dill Sauce, page 207). The sauces have no more than four ingredients each and take about 5 minutes to prepare.

Here's another skinny secret: mains are not that caloric on their own. *It's the way we eat our mains* thats the problem. Historically, Americans have enjoyed "meat plus three," a big chunk of meat on one side of the plate, with three sides taking up the other side.

We're going to change that. For weight loss and maintenance, you want to fill half your plate with vegetables, while starchy carbs and proteins can divvy up the rest.

Think back to the size of the sections in a TV dinner: There was one big section for the protein and three little ones for the starch, veggies, and dessert. Flip it around. Use the big section for vegetables and one of the smaller sections for protein. With that one flip of the mental switch, you'll get closer to the portion size you want to have and the weight you want to be.

Really. Just shift the plate 180 degrees, and put your veggies where your meat is.

Some of these main dishes are very low in calories, like Shrimp Scampi (334 calories, page 201) or Sausage and Peppers (298 calories, page 212). Since they're not a complete meal on their own, you'll want to serve them over pasta or with a piece of bread. However, some *are* complete meals that are still low in calories, like Baked Chicken Murphy (294 calories, page 194). You can enjoy a larger portion or dessert.

Flip through the following pages: The recipes seem easy, don't they? They *are* easy. Making a main dish doesn't have to be hard. As a cook, you're the host of a party, helping your carefully selected guests (the ingredients) mingle and get to know one another. Make the introductions and let the guests do their thing while you relax and enjoy.

seared chicken with lemon and rosemary

PREP TIME: 15 minutes TOTAL TIME: 35 minutes MAKES 4 servings SERVING SIZE: 1 breast, 2 to 3 thighs, or a combo, with sauce

Boneless, skinless chicken breasts are tough love. They are popular because they're low in fat and look like they'd be easy to cook. No bones, no carcass, no problem. In fact, it's a challenge—even for pro chefs—to cook boneless, skinless breasts without adding lots of fat or drying them out. Unless you time it perfectly, they'll be undercooked or dry.

Who needs that stress? I like to coat skinless chicken breasts (see page 190 for a Chicken Milanese recipe) or keep their skins on while cooking to keep them from drying out. It's like a reverse raincoat: That jacket keeps the moisture inside. If you want to discard the skin after cooking, go for it—just be sure to keep that jacket on while you cook.

If you're prone to drying out boneless, skinless chicken breasts, don't fret. *It's not you, it's them.*

NUTRITION INFORMATION
(PER SERVING):

CALORIES 392, CARBS 3G, FIBER 0G, PROTEIN 31G, TOTAL FAT 28G, SATURATED FAT 8G

2½ pounds skin-on bone-in chicken (breasts and thighs)
1 teaspoon kosher salt
1 tablespoon olive oil
3 garlic cloves, minced
1 tablespoon chopped fresh rosemary
⅓ cup fresh lemon juice (from 2 big lemons)
¼ cup chopped fresh parsley

1. Preheat the oven to 375°F.
2. Season the chicken all over with salt. Heat the oil in a large ovenproof skillet over medium-high heat. Add the chicken pieces, skin side down, and cook until golden brown, about 8 minutes. Turn the chicken over and add the garlic and rosemary to the pan. Cook until fragrant, about 30 seconds. Add the lemon juice, stir to incorporate, and transfer the skillet to the oven.
3. Cook until the chicken is cooked through, about 20 minutes. Remove the pan from the oven and stir in the parsley. Serve the chicken with the sauce.

KITCHEN TIP § Juicier Lemons
Let your lemons come to room temperature before you squeeze them, and you will get a lot more juice. If you go through them pretty quickly, keep your citrus in a bowl on the counter. Pretty and useful.

To get the best yield, use a reamer or stick a fork inside the lemon half and wiggle the tines side to side to release the juice.

KITCHEN TIP § Golden Child
To get that golden, crispy restaurant-style chicken skin, there's one rule: Don't touch the chicken while it cooks. Just put it in the pan and let do its thing. Let it cook for 8 minutes before you flip it, and your patience will be rewarded.

SKINNY TIP § How Can Chicken Skin Be Skinny? Bone-in, skin-on chicken has optimal flavor and moisture. Before you worry yourself unnecessarily about the skin, just look at that

calorie count! A lot of chicken fat renders from the skin when you cook it and will appear in the pan when you do that initial cooking in step 2. We need about ¼ cup of the fat to make the sauce or it will be too tangy.

If you want less fat, remove some from the pan. One tablespoon of chicken fat is 115 calories and 13 grams of fat. Calculate accordingly. And when you put your abacus down, remember the real point of this dish: It tastes good.

chicken diablo (devil's chicken)

PREP TIME: 15 minutes TOTAL TIME: 50 minutes MAKES 4 servings SERVING SIZE: 2 thighs

Chicken Diablo is juicy, crisp oven-baked chicken with a hint of heat. The mustard mellows as it cooks, so you'll find yourself biting in, enjoying the flavor, then fanning yourself like Scarlett O'Hara, saying, "Oh my, is it hot in here or is it me?" It's not you. *Devil made you do it.*

I love this dish both straight out of the oven—juicy, crisp, and hot—and as a picnic food enjoyed at room temperature. Instead of making a decision, prep a double batch and have it both ways. *Fiddle-de-dee.*

1. Preheat the oven to 400°F. Cover a baking sheet with aluminum foil and spray with cooking spray.

2. Place the cornflakes in a plastic bag and crunch with your fingers until crumby; put the crumbs in a shallow bowl. In a small bowl, combine the mustard, parsley, thyme, and cayenne and mix well.

3. Remove the skin from the chicken.

Discard the skin and season the chicken with salt. Brush the mustard mixture onto the chicken, covering all sides. Dip the chicken in the cornflake crumbs and coat well. Place the coated chicken, flesh side up, on the prepared baking sheet. Bake until cooked through, about 30 minutes Serve warm.

NUTRITION INFORMATION
(PER SERVING):
CALORIES 307, CARBS 19G, FIBER 1G, PROTEIN 29G, TOTAL FAT 12G, SATURATED FAT 3G

3 cups cornflakes (or 1 cup cornflake crumbs)
⅓ cup Dijon mustard
¾ teaspoon dried parsley
¾ teaspoon dried thyme
½ teaspoon cayenne
3 pounds skin-on, bone-in chicken thighs (about 8 thighs)
1½ teaspoons kosher salt

KITCHEN TIP § Cornflake Crumbs
Cornflakes make a terrific alternative to bread crumbs when baking in the oven. They are crisp and golden, plus their natural sweetness is a perfect counterpoint to the spicy mustard sauce in this recipe. The cornflakes cool your mouth while keeping it stimulated with a sweet crunch.

SKINNY TIP § Faux Fried Chicken
If this seems like the cheater's way to make fried chicken, that's because it is. Instead of doing the whole flour, egg, bread-crumb thing (which is great, don't get me wrong; see Chicken Milanese, page 190), we're just slathering those chicken pieces with a flavored mustard and dunking them in breakfast cereal. We're cheating calories and unnecessary labor while delivering flavor and kitchen fun. Score one for the devil.

chicken milanese

PREP TIME: 20 minutes TOTAL TIME: 40 minutes MAKES 4 servings SERVING SIZE: 1 breaded cutlet

As a teenager, I became obsessed with chicken cutlets and had them for lunch on a roll with salt, pepper, mayo, lettuce, and tomato almost every day. Plus chips. Plus soda. Plus a big chocolate chip cookie. It's a wonder I fit through the door.

When I figured out how to make chicken cutlets at home that were better than the ones I was addicted to as a teenage girl, I was one happy woman. And if there's one truth to cutlets, it's this: When you pan-fry chicken cutlets, you can't cut corners. If you want to make them taste good, you've got to make them right.

Which is why this recipe uses more fat than any other in the book, and it's worth every drop. To successfully pan-fry the cutlets, you've got to cook them in a good amount of fat (put away those spritzers and misters). But here's the key: Don't just take your chicken breast out of the package, bread it, and fry it. You've got to pound those breasts first, which will help them cook evenly and give you a better coating-to-chicken ratio.

Plus, when you pound the chicken, it will seem like you have more chicken. You'll take longer to eat, and you will be satisfied with fewer calories in the end.

NUTRITION INFORMATION
(PER SERVING):

CALORIES 394, CARBS 11, FIBER 1G, PROTEIN 42G, TOTAL FAT 20G, SATURATED FAT 3G

- 1 cup all-purpose flour
- 2 large eggs
- 1½ cups panko bread crumbs (see tip right)
- 1 tablespoon dried parsley
- 1½ pounds boneless, skinless chicken breast halves (4 pieces)
- 1½ teaspoons kosher salt
- ⅓ cup olive oil
- 1 lemon, cut into wedges

1. In three separate shallow plates (pie plates are ideal), place the flour, lightly beaten eggs, and bread crumbs. Add the parsley to the bread crumbs and stir to combine.

2. Place the chicken breasts, one at a time, between two sheets of plastic wrap (or one big piece, folded over the chicken). Using a meat mallet or a small skillet, gently pound the breasts, starting with the thickest part, until they are ⅓ inch thick. Season both sides of each cutlet with salt.

3. One at a time, coat the chicken with flour, shaking off any excess, then coat with beaten eggs. Finally, coat the chicken with the bread crumbs.

4. Heat half the oil in a large skillet over medium heat. Test to see if the oil is warm by dipping a corner of the coated chicken into it: Does the oil bubble? If so, it's ready. Place 2 cutlets in the skillet and cook until golden brown, about 3 minutes per side. Transfer to a paper towel–lined plate or baking rack to drain. Repeat with remaining oil and chicken. Serve the cutlets warm with lemon wedges.

SKINNY TIP § Breading Is Not as Caloric as You Might Think
After I finished coating the cutlets, I measured the flour, eggs, and panko that were left over so that I could give this recipe an accurate calorie count. I couldn't believe what I learned! For coating all the cutlets in the recipe, I only used 1 tablespoon of flour, 1 egg, and just ¾ cup bread crumbs. The rest of the coating was still in the bowl where the chicken was able to roll around, indulgently, and take only what it needed to cover itself.

KITCHEN TIP § Panko?
For the bread crumbs, you want to use the crispiest crumb you can find. Panko is a crisp Japanese-style bread crumb that used to be considered a gourmet item and was sold in the fish department or in the Asian foods aisle. Now panko is mainstream; 4C brand makes seasoned and unseasoned versions, which my grocery store carries on the shelf next to the rest of the bread crumbs.

KITCHEN TIP § Lose Your Mittens
To avoid breading "mittens," use one hand to manage the flour and crumb coatings and another for the egg. That is, one hand manages the dry coatings while the other manages the wet coating, which keeps both hands mitten-free.

KITCHEN TIP § Don't Feel Like Pounding? No problem; have the butcher do it for you. Also, many grocery stores sell pre-pounded cutlets; feel free to buy them this way. If you leave them big and thick, the coating-to-chicken ratio won't be as high, so the cutlet won't be as delicious. Make the effort; it's worth it.

Plus, a pounded breast is easy to cook through properly—just a couple minutes per side. A thicker breast will take longer to cook. After you turn it, finish cooking it in a 400°F oven for 15 to 20 minutes.

SKINNY TIP § How Big Are Your Breasts? These days, chicken breast halves can range from less than ½ pound to 1 pound. Don't worry about the size of your breasts, just worry about the weight. If two breasts weight 1½ pounds, simply cut them in half so there's enough to go around. Each portion should be about 6 ounces.

quick chicken mole

PREP TIME: 15 minutes TOTAL TIME: 40 minutes MAKES 4 servings SERVING SIZE: 2 to 3 chicken thighs, with sauce

Mole is a flavorful Mexican sauce that feels slightly naughty because it's usually made with chocolate. Mole can be very time-consuming, so we're short-cutting the process with flavorful store-bought ingredients like salsa and pantry spices.

   This recipe might just become a regular in your rotation; it's almost too easy for how tasty it is. Serve with You Can Make White Rice (page 169) or corn tortillas.

1. Heat the oil in a large skillet over medium heat. Season the chicken with 1½ teaspoons of the salt and put the chicken, flesh side down, into the hot skillet. Cook until golden, 6 to 8 minutes. You may need to brown the chicken in batches; do not crowd the pan.

2. Turn the chicken over and add the chili powder, oregano, and cocoa to the pan. Stir the spices into the oil and cook until fragrant, about 30 seconds. Add the salsa and 1 cup water, and bring to a simmer.

Cook, partially covered, until the chicken has cooked through and the sauce has thickened, 20 to 25 minutes.

3. Cut the lime in half, and add the juice from one half to the sauce. Stir in up to ⅓ cup additional water to thin the sauce, if needed. Cut the remaining lime half into wedges; serve the warm chicken with the sauce and garnish with lime wedges.

NUTRITION INFORMATION
(PER SERVING):
CALORIES 368, CARBS 12G, FIBER 4G, PROTEIN 43G, TOTAL FAT 16G, SATURATED FAT 3G

   2   tablespoons vegetable oil
   3   pounds bone-in chicken thighs, skin removed (about 8 thighs)
   2   teaspoons kosher salt
1½   tablespoons chili powder
1½   tablespoons dried oregano
1½   tablespoons unsweetened cocoa powder
   1   16-ounce jar of your favorite salsa
   1   cup water, or more as needed
   1   lime

KITCHEN TIP § Slow-Cook It
To make Chicken Mole in the slow cooker, put all the ingredients (minus the oil) into the ceramic insert of the slow cooker. Since you're skipping the sauté step, you'll save 200 calories, about 50 calories per serving.

SKINNY TIP § Bone In, Skin Off?
Crisp chicken skin is snappy and delicious, but braised chicken skin is soft, flaccid, and just plain mediocre, which is why we remove it for this dish. Dark meat like chicken legs and thighs are the right choice for braising because they stay tender and moist, as they have more intramuscular fat. Remove the outer skin and enjoy the benefits of the fat within.

baked chicken murphy

PREP TIME: 30 minutes   TOTAL TIME: 35 minutes   MAKES 8 servings   SERVING SIZE: 2 cups chicken, vegetables, sausage & sauce

Do I hear New Jersey in the house? If so, then you know Chicken Murphy, and you probably love it. If you're (like me) not from Jersey, you've probably never heard of this dish unless you're a regular at Jersey diners, Italian restaurants, or the Bada Bing.

Italian restaurants? Murphy? *Wha?* That's exactly what confused me: Why is this "Italian" specialty called Murphy? Here's how the Jersey legend goes: It starts a lot like Chicken scarpiella, with garlic, peppers, sausage, and wine. Then someone stuck potatoes in it. Potatoes are associated with Irish cooking, so as soon as that happened, someone else started to call this dish "Murphy," and it stuck. So now Jersey has an Italian-American dish with an Irish name. You can't help but love a state with that much personality.

Traditionally made, this dish is a whole lot of fuss. It takes at least three skillets on the stovetop, so that the chef can bread and sauté the chicken, cook the onions and peppers, boil the potatoes, brown the sausage, and so on. But the home cooks I know love a one-dish, wham-bam, throw-it-in-the oven casserole, so that's how I remade The Murph for you.

That's right, Jersey, I'm making Murphy better. *You got a problem with that?*

1. Preheat the oven to 400°F.

2. In a large baking pan, layer the onion, peppers, garlic, mushrooms, sausage, potatoes, rosemary, and 1 teaspoon salt. Pour the wine over the vegetables and sausage, and lay the chicken on top. Season the chicken with the remaining teaspoon of salt and the oregano. Scatter the hot pepper slices over the top of the vegetables.

3. Cook until the chicken is cooked through and golden and the potatoes yield when pierced with a paring knife, about 1 hour and 15 minutes. Baste the chicken during cooking. Discard the rosemary before serving; serve warm.

NUTRITION INFORMATION (PER SERVING):

CALORIES 294, CARBS 22G, FIBER 3G, PROTEIN 27G, TOTAL FAT 9G, SATURATED FAT 2G

- 1 red onion, sliced
- 2 bell peppers (red and yellow), seeded and cut into 1-inch squares
- 4 garlic cloves, sliced
- 8 ounces white mushrooms, quartered
- 12 ounces sweet or spicy Italian chicken sausage, cut into 2-inch chunks
- 1 pound baby potatoes, cut into 1-inch pieces
- 5 sprigs fresh rosemary
- 2 teaspoons kosher salt
- 1 cup white wine or beer
- 1 3½-pound chicken, cut up, skin removed from legs and thighs, backbone discarded
- 1 teaspoon dried oregano
- ½ cup sliced pickled hot peppers, drained

KITCHEN TIP § Chicken Pieces

When I buy a cut-up chicken in the grocery store, it's usually in 4 pieces: 2 leg/thighs, and 2 breast halves/wings. But it's easy to double these numbers. Separating the legs from the thighs is simple; lay the piece skin side down, and follow the fat line that divides or runs between the leg and thigh. Cut through right there. You can also cut the breasts through the center (thanks to modern breeding they're often too big for one serving). Or, get 10 pieces by separating the wing from the breast, and cut the breast in half. I like to cut up the pieces before cooking because I dislike post-cooking fuss. But do what works for you.

KITCHEN TIP § Jersey Sauce

The sauce with my Murph is on the thin side, in part because you're not breading the chicken. To thicken this sauce, make something called a *beurre manié*: equal parts softened butter and flour combined to form a paste. For this recipe, start with 2 teaspoons of each. Separate the sauce from the chicken and vegetables (just the liquid), put it on the stovetop, and bring it to a simmer. Whisk in the butter-flour paste $\frac{1}{4}$ teaspoon at a time, and stop when the sauce reaches a thickness you like. Myself, I like a thin sauce because I like smashing the potatoes with the tines of my fork so that they can soak it up. *Mmmm.*

KITCHEN TIP § Cooking Potatoes

Potatoes are dense. In fact, in this dish, they are the ingredient that takes longest to cook. Help them do their thing by giving them some space; try not to put them directly under the big, bulky pieces of chicken or they'll take even longer to cook.

SKINNY TIP § Crank Up the Heat

If you want more heat, simply add more spicy pepper vinegar (the stuff you drained) to the sauce. This Murphy is designed for family eating, so I didn't go over the top with the heat.

SKINNY TIP § Calories: Don't Go Too Low You can play it Jersey style and serve your Murphy over pasta, or take a portion and a half. There's room to play in this recipe.

"If you're prone to drying out boneless, skinless chicken breasts, don't fret. It's not you, it's them."

chicken stir-fry with pineapples and cashews

PREP TIME: 20 minutes TOTAL TIME: 45 minutes MAKES 6 servings SERVING SIZE: 1 cup

In the summer of 2006, I traveled in Vietnam with my college roommate (see page 92 for more about her). When a food person and a doctor travel together, their expertise allows them to take culinary risks. We promised one another that we'd eat fearlessly, knowing (or maybe just hoping) that she could diagnose and cure whatever ailed us. As a result, we didn't turn down a single street vendor, no matter what he or she offered.

Vietnamese food was delicious, and no matter how much (or what) I ate, I lost weight. We started the day with dumplings and pho (soups) thick with herbs and had fresh fruits and vegetables at every meal. Fearless eating was rewarded. We were happy and satisfied eating all the local food we could find.

This recipe was inspired by that trip. And though the portions are big and the flavors are delicious, you're filling up on vegetables like mushrooms, red peppers, and scallions, which are mostly fiber and water. When you eat fruit and vegetable-centric stir-fries like this one, served over You Can Make White Rice (page 169), you'll be satisfied with fewer calories.

NUTRITION INFORMATION
(PER SERVING):

CALORIES 251, CARBS 21G, FIBER 2G, PROTEIN 18G, TOTAL FAT 11G, SATURATED FAT 2G

- 2 tablespoons oyster sauce
- 2 tablespoons Vietnamese or Thai fish sauce
- 1 tablespoon lower-sodium soy sauce
- 1 tablespoon sugar
- 2 tablespoons water
- 1 8-ounce can pineapple chunks in juice
- 1½ tablespoons vegetable oil
- 1 pound boneless, skinless chicken thighs, cut crosswise into 1½-inch strips
- 1 small red onion, cut into 1-inch cubes
- 2 garlic cloves, minced
- 1 teaspoon chili paste, or 1 large serrano chile, chopped, with seeds
- 1 large red bell pepper, seeded and cut into 1-inch squares
- 1 8-ounce can water chestnuts, drained
- 4 scallion greens, cut into 2-inch lengths
- ½ cup roasted cashews

1. Combine the oyster sauce, fish sauce, soy sauce, sugar, and water in a small bowl. Stir to combine and set aside. Drain the pineapple and reserve fruit and juice separately.

2. Heat the oil in a large skillet or wok over high heat. Add the chicken strips and cook, stirring occasionally, until browned, 3 to 5 minutes. Remove the chicken from the skillet and set aside on a plate or move the chicken up to the lip of the wok.

3. Add the onion to the skillet and cook, stirring, until it's just beginning to soften, about 1½ minutes. Add the garlic and chili paste and cook, stirring, until fragrant,

about 30 seconds. Stir in the oyster sauce mixture and continue to cook until slightly thickened. Add the bell pepper and pineapple, and cook over high heat, stirring, until the pineapple is nicely glazed, about 2 minutes. Pour the pineapple juice into the wok and use a wooden spoon to scrape the browned bits from the bottom of the pan.

4. Return the chicken to the wok, and add the water chestnuts. Stir the ingredients together until they are heated through, about 2 minutes. Remove from the heat, add the scallion greens and cashews, and stir to incorporate. Serve warm.

KITCHEN TIP § Oyster Sauce
Brands like Lee Kum Kee and Roland both carry oyster sauce, so it is easy to find in the Asian sections of mainstream grocery stores (you can also buy them online). Oyster sauce is a thick sweet sauce with a bit of oyster, and though you don't really taste oysters, you benefit from the flavor note. If you can't find oyster sauce, you can substitute hoisin sauce, which is also sweet but without oyster flavor.

sage-roasted turkey with apples and onions

PREP TIME: 25 minutes **TOTAL TIME:** 3 hours 15 minutes **MAKES** 10 servings **SERVING SIZE:** 5 slices of meat with ⅓ cup sauce

This recipe is inspired by my friend Lorraine. She has an Italian mother and a Jewish father who love cooking and eating; she grew up learning cooking techniques from relatives on both sides. To not cook would send all kinds of relatives into arm-waving fits.

Whenever I come over to eat, she introduces me to something new. One time, to accompany a pork roast, she made a simple side dish called "Apples and Onions." After the roast was in the oven, she cut an apple and an onion into wedges, tossed them with a little oil and seasoning, and put them in the oven to cook alongside her pork. The dish was simple and divine—my favorite kind. I'm including that side here with a simple roasted turkey breast.

1. Preheat the oven to 400°F.

2. Remove the turkey from the refrigerator and let it to come to room temperature. Prepare the turkey by separating the skin from the flesh with your fingers. Roll back the skin, and place the sage leaves on the breast meat. Season the meat with 1 teaspoon of the salt and roll the skin down again so that you can see the sage leaves through the turkey skin. Place the turkey in a large skillet or medium roasting pan and drizzle with 1 tablespoon of the olive oil. Place the turkey in the preheated oven and cook until lightly browned, about 30 minutes.

3. Meanwhile, toss the apple and onion wedges with the remaining ½ teaspoon salt and 1 tablespoon olive oil. Remove the skillet from the oven, and baste the turkey with pan juices. Add the apple and onion wedges to the pan, surrounding the turkey. Return the skillet to the oven and stir the apples and onions once during cooking. Cook the turkey until a thermometer inserted into the deepest part of the turkey breast registers 165°F, about 1 more hour.

4. Remove the turkey from oven, transfer to a platter, and cover with aluminum foil. Let the turkey rest for 30 minutes. Meanwhile, return the apples and onions to the oven and let them cook until soft and sweet, about 30 minutes. Remove the breasts from the bone, cut the turkey into ¼-inch-thick slices, and serve warm with the apples and onions.

NUTRITION INFORMATION
(PER SERVING):

CALORIES 328, CARBS 13G, FIBER 2G, PROTEIN 39G, TOTAL FAT 13G, SATURATED FAT 3G

- 1 5-pound bone-in turkey breast
- 12 to 15 fresh sage leaves
- 1½ teaspoons kosher salt
- 2 tablespoons olive oil
- 4 Golden Delicious apples, peeled and cut into ½-inch wedges
- 2 large onions, cut into ½-inch wedges

 **SKINNY TIP § That's a Lot of Turkey**
You're right, it is. This is the kind of item you can make on a Sunday afternoon and enjoy all week; what better ingredient for turkey sandwiches than fresh-roasted turkey? Enjoy it (with the apples and onions) on a sandwich for lunch. On its own, a 5-ounce serving of turkey is about 265 calories. That's enough for a big sandwich! Or enjoy it over greens.

seared duck breast with ginger bok choy

PREP TIME: 15 minutes TOTAL TIME: 30 minutes MAKES 4 servings SERVING SIZE: 5 to 7 slices duck with ¾ cup bok choy

Duck can be intimidating. When I show people how to make seared duck breast for the first time, they always look at me the same way.

Like: *No, you do it, I'm going to mess it up.*

I explain how to score and season the breast and put it in a cold pan. I turn to walk away and they cling to my leg: *Don't leave me. Not during duck. I'm going to mess it up.*

And then they do it, and it works, and I get a: *What's the big deal? There was nothing to it.* Happens every time.

If you're the slightest bit nervous about attempting duck, don't be. Remember, in less than 30 minutes you'll be a swaggering, crispy-duck-breast-searing pro.

NUTRITION INFORMATION
(PER SERVING):
CALORIES 419, CARBS 4G, FIBER 1G, PROTEIN 46G, TOTAL FAT 24G, SATURATED FAT 6G

2 14- to 16-ounce duck breasts
1½ teaspoons kosher salt
1 tablespoon vegetable oil
2 inch piece of fresh ginger, cut into matchsticks
2 scallion whites, sliced
1 large garlic clove, sliced
1 pound baby bok choy, trimmed, cleaned, and quartered (about 4 heads)
¼ cup water

1. Preheat the oven to 400°F.

2. Score the breasts on the fat side and season both sides of each with 1 teaspoon of the salt. Place the breasts fat side down in a cold skillet. Cook over medium-low heat until the fat renders. Continue cooking until much of the fat has rendered and you have a dark brown crust, 10 to 15 minutes total, increasing the heat to medium-high for the last 5 minutes.

3. Discard all but 1 tablespoon of the duck fat from the skillet. Turn the duck breasts in the skillet so that they are skin side up and place in the oven for 5 to 10 minutes, until a thermometer inserted into the thickest part of the duck registers 130°F. Remove the duck from the skillet and let it rest, covered with aluminum foil, for 10 minutes.

4. Meanwhile, in a large sauté pan over moderately high heat, heat the oil until hot but not smoking. Add the ginger, scallion whites, and garlic and sauté until fragrant, about 1 minute. Add the bok choy and water and steam until tips have wilted and stalks are crisp-tender, about 3 minutes. Season the bok choy with the remaining ½ teaspoon salt.

5. Cut the duck breasts into thin slices and serve warm with the ginger bok choy.

SKINNY TIP § One Breast Feeds Two A Moulard duck breast typically weighs between 12 and 16 ounces. The Moulard is a hybrid between a Pekin and a Muscovy duck and is bred for its big breasts and liver (foie gras). The breast itself is called a Magret, even though the duck is called Moulard. You can use either term; you'll get what you need.

I often buy D'Artagnan brand, which is carried in my supermarket. You can also find them online.

When you cook a 14-ounce duck breast, at least 3 to 4 ounces of fat will render off, which means you're left with two 5-ounce portions per breast, which is a perfectly appropriate portion. Do not serve one breast per person; that's too much meat (and can get expensive, quickly).

shrimp scampi

PREP TIME: 20 minutes TOTAL TIME: 30 minutes MAKES 4 servings SERVING SIZE: About 7 shrimp per person, with sauce

Shrimp scampi is shrimp sautéed in butter and oil, with a lot of garlic and parsley. You can find it at higher-end pizza places or on steakhouse menus, where the shrimp are served with copious amounts of garlicky butter sauce to whet your appetite for the steak that's on its way. Shrimp scampi isn't just good, it's crazy good.

Serve the scampi with bread or pasta for mopping up the sauce.

NUTRITION INFORMATION
(PER SERVING):
CALORIES 334, CARBS 4G, FIBER 0G, PROTEIN 36G, TOTAL FAT 14G, SATURATED FAT 5G

- 2 tablespoons olive oil
- 1½ pounds large raw shrimp, peeled and patted dry
- 1 teaspoon kosher salt
- 2 tablespoons unsalted butter
- 4 large garlic cloves, sliced
  Pinch of red pepper flakes
- 1 cup dry white wine
- ⅓ cup coarsely chopped fresh parsley
- 1 lemon, cut into wedges, for serving

1. Heat the oil in a large skillet over medium-high heat. Season the shrimp with the salt and add to the pan; be sure to leave space between the shrimp (you will need to cook them in batches). Cook until the shrimp have turned pink and just begun to curl, 1 to 2 minutes per side. Remove the shrimp with a slotted spoon, transfer to a plate, and cover with aluminum foil to keep warm.

2. Add the butter to the skillet with the oil and reduce the heat to medium. When the butter melts, add the garlic and red pepper flakes and tilt the pan so the garlic is submerged. Cook until the garlic has softened but not browned, 1 to 2 minutes.

3. Add the white wine to pan, increase the heat to medium-high, bring to a simmer, and cook until the liquid is reduced by half, 2 to 3 minutes. Reduce the heat to medium, return the shrimp to the pan, and bring to a simmer, about 1 minute more. Stir in the parsley. Transfer to a serving dish and serve warm with lemon wedges.

KITCHEN TIP § Frozen Shrimp
If you buy shrimp at the grocery store, there's only one way to go: frozen. I buy frozen shrimp that are peeled, deveined, and raw, so the hard work is done for me. The important thing is that the shrimp are frozen individually relatively soon after they're caught, so they are very fresh and you can defrost the amount you need, leaving the rest in the freezer for next time. While frozen they stay fresh, which is counterintuitive, so think of it as modern cryogenics, or Rip van Winkle

come true. Plus, frozen shrimp are less expensive than their fresh counterparts.

SKINNY TIP § But... But... Butter?
Many lower-calorie cookbooks ask you to sauté meat in a spritz of oil in a nonstick pan. That's a one-way ticket to disappointment; your recipes won't work. For this scampi recipe, you're sautéing the shrimp in 2 tablespoons of oil, which will contribute flavor to a delicious sauce. But what about that butter? Is it really necessary?

That's your call. Personally,

I like the butter because it rounds out the flavor in the sauce. But let's talk numbers: Butter, like all fats, is about 100 calories per tablespoon. If you leave out a tablespoon of butter, you'll save 25 calories per portion. Since large shrimp run about 25 calories each, you can swap out the butter, add 4 more shrimp, and end up with the same calorie count. Cook's choice!

sole piccata

PREP TIME: 10 minutes TOTAL TIME: 30 minutes MAKES 4 servings SERVING SIZE: 1 fillet with 3 tablespoons sauce

In some Italian restaurants, it is hard to get in and out without being overfed. As in Italy, you can't have an entrée without a pasta; it just isn't done. So when you order veal marsala, chicken piccata, or eggplant parmesan, you'll have your pasta, either first or on the side. The pasta, of course, could be a separate meal. As a high school student with a babysitter's budget, I loved these places. Who wouldn't love two meals for the price of one?

When I was in college and had my own kitchen, I tried to save money by cooking instead of over-ordering in Italian restaurants. In the grocery store, I found a recipe for veal marsala on the back of a bottle of marsala wine. I followed the recipes precisely and was rewarded with authentic-tasting marsala, *right there in my own kitchen!* It's always worth trying those back-of-the-bottle recipes; they're designed for the product you hold in your hand and built for success no matter how rudimentary your cooking skills.

Once I mastered marsala, I was motivated to try a piccata recipe I found in a book. Lemon sauces are bright and flavorful without weighing down the dish, so piccata made with lemons, wine, and capers tastes perfect to me.

This recipe is tangy and simple to prepare. It is also very low in calories. In fact, the calorie count is so low that you can opt for that side of pasta.

NUTRITION INFORMATION
(PER SERVING):
CALORIES 249, CARBS 5G, FIBER 0G, PROTEIN 33G, TOTAL FAT 8G, SATURATED FAT 3G

- 4 6-ounce fillets thin white fish, like sole, tilapia, fluke, or flounder
- 1¼ teaspoons kosher salt
- 1 cup plus 1 tablespoon all-purpose flour
- 1 tablespoon olive oil
- 1 tablespoon unsalted butter
- ⅓ cup dry white wine
- ⅓ cup lower-sodium chicken broth
- ¼ cup fresh lemon juice
- 2 tablespoons capers, rinsed and drained
- ¼ cup chopped fresh parsley

1. Season the fish on both sides with 1 teaspoon of the salt. Place 1 cup of the flour in a shallow baking dish. Dip the fish into the flour to coat; shake off excess.

2. Heat the oil and butter in a nonstick skillet. Add the coated pieces of fish and cook until golden, 2 to 3 minutes per side. You'll probably need to do this in batches; white fish fillets are thin and wide. Transfer the cooked fish to a platter and cover with foil to keep warm.

3. Add the remaining tablespoon of flour to the fat in the pan and whisk to form a paste. Cook the paste, stirring, until it turns light brown, 2 to 3 minutes. Whisk in the wine, chicken broth, and lemon juice; simmer over medium-high heat until the sauce thickens slightly, about 2 minutes.

4. Stir in the capers and parsley and season with the remaining ¼ teaspoon salt. Pour the sauce over the fish and serve warm.

KITCHEN TIP § How About Chicken Piccata? Go for it. Just use 1 pound of boneless, skinless chicken breasts that are pounded ⅓ inch thick (see tip for Chicken Milanese, page 190) in place of the fish.

KITCHEN TIP § Fish Spatula This is one of those tools that is totally worth the price. Fish spatulas are long and flexible and sort of look like a fin. They are designed to pick up fish fillets, which tend to be fragile and need a little extra TLC. Thin fillets like flounder and sole, and some thicker fillets like cod, tend to cleave when you pick them up. Forget tongs; even traditional spatulas can be a little rough. Fish spatulas are a kitchen tool that makes life easier.

halibut packets with tomatoes, olives, and basil

PREP TIME: 15 minutes TOTAL TIME: 25 minutes MAKES 4 servings SERVING SIZE: 1 fillet

I grew up fishing with my dad, and this is how we would prepare our catch when we actually caught something. Since we were fishing off Long Island, we fished for bluefish or flounder, but this preparation works for just about any fresh-caught fish. It's summery and light; if you don't feel like heating up the kitchen, cook the packets on the grill.

1. Preheat the oven to 425°F. Prepare four sheets of aluminum foil, each about 12 inches square.
2. On the first sheet of aluminum, layer 3 lemon slices and place a halibut fillet on top. Drizzle 1 teaspoon of olive oil on the fillet and season with a pinch of salt. Lay 3 tomato slices and 3 olives on top. Repeat using the remaining aluminum sheets and fillets, layering the ingredients as before.
3. Fold the foil over fish and seal each packet; be sure to leave space and do not wrap too tightly. Transfer packets to the oven and cook until the fish is opaque and cooked through, about 15 minutes (test one packet to confirm that the fish is cooked through, and be sure to check the part of the fish that is under the tomatoes).
4. Unwrap the foil packets and place the contents on serving plates. Garnish with basil and serve.

NUTRITION INFORMATION
(PER SERVING):

CALORIES 216, CARBS 4G, FIBER 2G, PROTEIN 30G, TOTAL FAT 9G, SATURATED FAT 1G

- 1 large lemon, very thinly sliced, seeds removed
- 4 5-ounce skinless halibut fillets
- 4 teaspoons olive oil
- 4 pinches of kosher salt
- 2 plum tomatoes, sliced
- 12 kalamata olives, pitted
- ¼ cup thinly sliced fresh basil

KITCHEN TIP § Foiled or Fancy?
Foil packets are a fun way to cook fish. It's a riff on a classic French technique called *en papillote*, a technique whereby you seal fish or chicken in a piece of parchment paper. As the ingredients cook, they release steam and cause the packet to puff. It's great ceremony to serve the parchment balloon on a plate, cut it open, and release a puff of delicious steam. I like foil because it's a bit less fussy and exactly the kind of thing a proud young fisherperson can help you prepare in the kitchen.

simplest salmon

PREP TIME: 10 minutes   TOTAL TIME: 25 minutes   MAKES 4 servings   SERVING SIZE: 1 fillet

My friend Michael, who introduced me to this recipe, is a monastic miracle. He lives in Brooklyn in a 300-square-foot apartment and rides a motorcycle in all seasons instead of driving a car. He grew up in Maine and is an exceptional gardener and cook. He's mastered the good life on a budget, and although he doesn't spend money on the small things (like a daily coffee you-know-where), he's always found money for big things, like taking vacations to Japan or Germany. By living modestly, he lives well.

This recipe is all Michael: Using three simple ingredients, he turns broiled salmon into something special. Equal parts mayonnaise and mustard give the sauce spice and body, becoming an enticing golden topping as the salmon cooks.

NUTRITION INFORMATION (PER SERVING):
CALORIES 344, CARBS 0G, FIBER 0G, PROTEIN 29G, TOTAL FAT 25G, SATURATED FAT 5G

- 2 tablespoons mayonnaise
- 2 tablespoons Dijon mustard
- 1 teaspoon kosher salt
- 4 5-ounce, 1-inch-thick skinless salmon fillets (see tip, page 206)

1. Preheat the broiler and place a rack about 6 inches from the broiler element.
2. In a small bowl, combine the mayo, mustard, and salt and stir to combine. Cover a broiler pan or baking sheet with aluminum foil. Place the salmon on the foil, pink side up, and brush 1 tablespoon of the mustard mixture on top of each fillet. Place under the broiler and cook until the top is brown and the salmon is firm when you squeeze it on the sides, about 8 minutes.

KITCHEN TIP § What Does 6 Inches Look Like? **Longer than you might think.** If you squat down and look at your broiler element, that's where you want to start your measurement. Though 6 inches doesn't seem like a lot, when you're thinking about a big oven, it's farther from your broiler element than you might think. The top rung is about 3 inches away—way too close to your broiler to get optimal coverage—and the next rung is 6 inches away, a better distance for broiling. Alternatively, if you want to bake the salmon, cook it in a 425°F oven until the salmon is cooked through, 12 to 15 minutes. The topping will not get as golden as it does under the broiler, but it will taste delicious.

KITCHEN TIP § Salmon Without the Scent **Lots of people love to eat seared salmon, but I've learned that my New York clients don't love the salmon scent that hangs around their not-so-well-ventilated apartments for days after they've made it. Every time I teach a fish class, someone asks me the best way to sear fish without having a fishy scent in the house.**

There are two options:
1. Clean up very well after searing the salmon so that all salmon splatters are gone. The aging salmon fat, splattered all over your stovetop, is what causes the smell. This is what those kitchen wipes were designed for; use them. Clean up, open the windows, turn on the fan, and light a candle.
2. Don't sear the salmon, *broil* the salmon. Broiling is the least fussy and most efficient way to prepare fish. It will cook perfectly, and the scent stays in the oven instead of splattering all over your stovetop.

salmon with teriyaki glaze

PREP TIME: 10 minutes TOTAL TIME: 25 minutes MAKES 4 servings SERVING SIZE: 1 steak brushed with 1 tablespoon teriyaki

Teriyaki sauce is easy to buy in a bottle, but it's also simple to make at home and a nice way to perfume your house with a sweet homemade sauce simmering on the stove.

This is a classic I-have-nothing-in-the-house sauce. You know you have brown sugar and soy sauce, and—yep, those are the ginger and scallions you bought a week ago (they've been in the crisper, they're fine). Make your teriyaki and voilà.

1. Preheat the broiler. Cover a broiler pan with aluminum foil and place a rack 6 inches beneath the broiler element.
2. Season the salmon with the salt, place in the prepared pan, and place under the broiler. Broil until cooked through, about 10 minutes; be sure to leave the oven door open.

3. While the salmon is cooking, combine the soy sauce, brown sugar, ginger, and scallion whites in a small saucepan. Bring to a simmer and cook until thickened, 3 to 5 minutes. Brush the glaze over the cooked salmon and garnish with the sliced scallion greens.

NUTRITION INFORMATION
(PER SERVING):

CALORIES 353, CARBS 15G, FIBER 0G, PROTEIN 30G, TOTAL FAT 19G, SATURATED FAT 4G

- 4 5-ounce, 1-inch-thick salmon steaks
- ½ teaspoon kosher salt
- ¼ cup lower-sodium soy sauce
- ¼ cup light brown sugar
- 2 coin-size slices fresh ginger
- 2 scallions, whites and greens divided and chopped

KITCHEN TIP § Rule of Thumb for Cooking Fish **When broiling fish or baking at a high temperature (more than 400°F), the rule of thumb is that it takes 8 to 10 minutes per inch of fish thickness. So, you can take your ruler and measure the inches, or you can look at the measuring stick you carry all the time: your thumb. The distance from your thumb knuckle to your thumb tip is approximately an inch.**

slow-roasted salmon with lemon-dill sauce

PREP TIME: 10 minutes TOTAL TIME: 30 minutes MAKES 4 servings SERVING SIZE: 1 fillet with 1¼ tablespoons sauce

One of the first cookbooks I ever owned contained a recipe for slow-roasted salmon, and it introduced me to the power of a cooking technique. Roasting, as you may know from many of the recipes in the Veg Out chapter (page 134), is the best way to get intense flavor without adding a lot of fat. And *slow* roasting makes a food rich yet tender and yielding, a more perfect perfection, like adding an extra hour to the most beautiful day of the year.

Unfortunately, slow roasting often calls for a lot of fat to keep fish from dehydrating. Instead, lay strips of orange zest over the fish; it will flavor the fillets and keep them moist.

1. Preheat the oven to 325°F.

2. Season the salmon with the salt. Place the salmon in a baking dish, drizzle with olive oil, and cover with the thyme sprigs and orange peel. Roast until the salmon is firm, 20 to 25 minutes.

3. Meanwhile, combine the sour cream, dill, chives, and lemon zest in a small bowl. Season with salt to taste and refrigerate until ready to use.

4. Remove thyme sprigs and zest from cooked salmon and serve the fish warm or at room temperature, with the sauce.

NUTRITION INFORMATION
(PER SERVING):
CALORIES 352, CARBS 1G, FIBER 0G, PROTEIN 29G, TOTAL FAT 25G, SATURATED FAT 7G

4   5-ounce, 1-inch-thick skinless salmon fillets (see tip below)
1   teaspoon kosher salt, plus more as needed
1   tablespoon olive oil
5   to 7 sprigs fresh thyme
    Long strips of orange zest from 1 orange (use a veggie peeler)
⅓   cup sour cream
2   tablespoons chopped fresh dill
1   tablespoon chopped fresh chives
    Grated zest of ½ lemon

SKINNY TIP § Salmon Skin
The easiest way to remove the skin from salmon is to ask your fishmonger to do it for you. If you've got a dog or a cat, be sure to bring it home and add it to the pet's dinner; your friend will be very glad you did. To skin salmon yourself, put the salmon fillet on a cutting board skin side down. Using a sharp knife, gently slide the knife blade under the skin and against the board, moving the skin from side to side as you push the knife along, blade facing the salmon skin.

If you haven't yet, try salmon skin. When seared properly, it's like salmon meets a potato chip. But if you're broiling salmon and it's sitting on its skin, it won't get crisp; it'll stay flaccid. Why waste your calories? (See chicken skin tip, page 188.)

KITCHEN TIP § Size Matters
For this recipe, your salmon fillets must be 1 inch thick, or you need to change the cooking time accordingly (see tip, opposite page). For a correct cooking time, thickness is more important than the weight.

mediterranean tuna salad

PREP TIME: 20 minutes TOTAL TIME: 20 minutes MAKES 4 servings SERVING SIZE: 1½ cups salad with crisp bread

Tuna salad is easy and delicious; it's the one dish almost everyone can make. In this version, instead of the predictable celery and mayo, mix it with fresh herbs, roasted peppers, and white beans. It's tuna salad gone sassy. This salad will keep refrigerated for up to 5 days and makes a delicious main course.

1. In a medium bowl, combine the white beans, tuna, parsley, red peppers, and capers and toss. Drizzle with the olive oil and lemon juice, toss, and season to taste with salt and black pepper. Serve with crisp bread.

NUTRITION INFORMATION
(PER SERVING):
CALORIES 410, CARBS 36G, FIBER 8G, PROTEIN 31G, TOTAL FAT 16G, SATURATED FAT 3G

- 1 15½-ounce can small white beans, rinsed and drained
- 2 5-ounce cans tuna in oil, drained
- 1 cup roughly chopped fresh parsley
- 1 cup roasted red peppers, rinsed, drained, and sliced
- 1 tablespoon capers, rinsed and drained
- 3 tablespoons olive oil
   Juice of ½ lemon
   Kosher salt and freshly ground black pepper
- 4 pieces crisp bread

 SKINNY TIP § Crazy for Crisp Bread Crisp bread comes in a range of flavors and runs about 50 calories per slice. Once you start playing with toppings, the options are as tasty as the ingredients in your kitchen. Here are a few of my favorites: a schmear of soft goat cheese with smoked salmon and chives (for those unfamiliar, a schmear is sort of "a scraping"—take ½ tablespoon of goat cheese or cream cheese, put it on a slice of bread, run a knife from one end to the other . . . you've just "schmeared"); hummus and roasted red peppers; ricotta, fresh tomatoes, salt, and pepper; or good old creamy peanut butter and strawberry jelly. They make a great snack, too. For a crisp bread breakfast recipe, see Crisp Bread with Egg and Avocado, page 29.

crispy fish sticks with tartar sauce

PREP TIME: 25 minutes TOTAL TIME: 40 minutes MAKES 4 servings SERVING SIZE: 5 sticks with 2 tablespoons sauce

My students often ask me to show them how to make dishes they enjoyed as kids. The ironic thing is that these weren't homemade dishes when they first had them; they were freezer-to-toaster (or microwave) meals.

So why make them from scratch if you don't have to? Because new cooks love to start with the comfy classics they love, remade with high-quality fresh ingredients. And when their version tastes better than the memory, that's an accomplishment.

1. Preheat the oven to 400°F. Cover a baking sheet with aluminum foil and coat with cooking spray.

2. Put the flour, eggs, and bread crumbs in three separate shallow bowls. Season the cod with the salt, then coat with flour (tap off any excess), beaten egg, and bread crumbs, and place on the prepared pan. When all the cod is coated, bake until cooked through, about 15 minutes. For even browning, turn once halfway through cooking.

3. While the cod is baking, combine the mayonnaise, cornichons, capers, chives, and lemon juice and mix well. Serve the fish sticks with the tartar sauce.

NUTRITION INFORMATION
(PER SERVING):

CALORIES 495, CARBS 46G, FIBER 3G, PROTEIN 31G, TOTAL FAT 20G, SATURATED FAT 4G

Cooking Spray
1 cup all-purpose flour
2 large eggs, lightly beaten
2 cups plain bread crumbs
1 pound cod fillet, cut into ½ by 4-inch strips
1 teaspoon kosher salt
⅓ cup mayonnaise
2 tablespoons chopped cornichons
1 tablespoons capers, rinsed, drained, and chopped
1 tablespoon chopped fresh chives or parsley
2 tablespoons fresh lemon juice

KITCHEN TIP § Make Ahead
You can make the sauce up to a week ahead of time; just keep it sealed in a refrigerator-safe container. This sauce is actually best about 20 minutes after it is made. Flavors can be like people on blind dates; they need some time to get comfortable with one another. Sometimes, if the flavors in a sauce or soup just aren't right, you can walk away, come back to it, and see how they've coalesced.

SKINNY TIP § Leftover Sauce?
I recently had an eight-year-old try these fish sticks, and she gobbled them down. Plus, she loved the sauce so much (and had extra), when she was done with the fish sticks, she asked for grape tomatoes to dip in the sauce. Tasty dipping sauces are one way to encourage kids to eat vegetables. Offer carrots, broccoli, sugar snap peas—whatever they like best!

KITCHEN TIP § Halve Your Fish in Thirty Minutes The most time-consuming part of this recipe is coating the fish. If you like, just cut the recipe in half and make enough for two people; it will take half the time.

KITCHEN TIP § Cornichons
Cornichons are a French term for "gherkin," a teeny tiny pickle that is often served with pâté. They are crisp, delicious, and cute, a key component of tartar sauce. No cornichons? Substitute pickle relish.

pot of mussels

PREP TIME: 15 minutes   TOTAL TIME: 30 minutes   MAKES 2 servings   SERVING SIZE: 25 to 30 mussels with broth and baguette

Based on informal polls that I've conducted, 19 out of 20 mussel lovers have never made mussels at home. And that used to be because they were hard to find in the grocery store. But now that you can buy big bags of mussels at Costco or Trader Joe's, the only thing standing between you and a homemade pot of mussels is the courage to put them in a pot.

1. 1. In a wide pot (braising pots are ideal) over medium heat, melt the butter. When it foams, add the shallot, garlic, fennel, and thyme to the pot; season with salt and cook, stirring, until softened, about 4 minutes. Add the wine and bring to a simmer. Add the mussels, cover, and cook until mussels have opened, 5 to 7 minutes.

2. Add the tomatoes to the pot and cook until warmed through, about 1 minute. Remove from the heat and stir in the parsley and basil (if desired). Discard unopened mussels, and ladle the warm broth into individual bowls or serve family-style. Be sure to include a big empty bowl for the discarded shells; serve with the baguette.

NUTRITION INFORMATION
(PER SERVING):

CALORIES 548, CARBS 65G, FIBER 6G, PROTEIN 37G, TOTAL FAT 11G, SATURATED FAT 5G

- 1 tablespoon unsalted butter
- 1 small shallot, minced
- 1 garlic clove, sliced
- 1 small bulb fennel, thinly sliced on a mandoline (see tip, page 55)
- 2 sprigs fresh thyme
- ¼ teaspoon kosher salt, plus more to taste
- ⅓ cup white wine
- 2 pounds mussels, rinsed and debearded (see tip below)
- ½ cup grape tomatoes, halved
- ¼ cup chopped fresh parsley
- ¼ cup torn fresh basil (optional)
- 1 8-inch baguette, warmed

KITCHEN TIP § Make Mussels Now that you can buy mussels at large grocery stores and even Costco, you can make them at home. All you really need is fat (butter, oil, bacon), aromatics (garlic, shallot, onion), liquid (beer, wine, clam broth), and herbs (parsley, basil, tarragon). Soften the aromatics in the fat, bring the liquid to a simmer, steam open the mussels, and refresh with some finishing herbs. That's all there is to it.

SKINNY TIP § What If I Skip the Bread? A baguette is perfect for soaking up that delicious broth. I wouldn't go without But if you choose to, you'll save 200 calories per serving.

KITCHEN TIP § How to Clean Mussels First, you want to see if the mussels are alive. Live mussels have tightly closed shells. If the shell is broken, toss it. If the shell is slightly open, tap it on the counter and see if it closes. If it does, it's a keeper.

Next, remove the beards and clear the barnacles. The beards are long stringy things that keep the mussels attached to ropes or jetties; it's how they keep from tumbling across the ocean. Those beards are strong, so pull hard.

Sometimes you'll find other little shells or barnacles on the mussels. To remove them, take the thin end of one mussel and use it to scrape the stuff of the other mussel, shoehorn style. Yep, that's fun too, possibly as cool as the tap test.

sausage and peppers

PREP TIME: 10 minutes TOTAL TIME: 1 hour MAKES 6 servings SERVING SIZE: 1½ cups

My friend Lorraine makes a killer sausage and peppers, "Italian Feast"–style. It's the same recipe her mother and grandmother made, and just like theirs, it is a little different every time she does it—and it's always good.

There's no written recipe, so here's how she explains it: "You slice onions and peppers—more onions than peppers because when they caramelize, they shrink to nothing. I don't like the taste of green bell peppers, so don't use those, but red peppers and Italian frying peppers work, plus they're the colors of the Italian flag.

"Brown your sausage in olive oil; I like a package of hot and a package of sweet; it's good diversity. Leave all that fat in the pan and cook your onions and peppers in it until the onions are caramelized. If the sauce gets thick, pour some chicken broth or water into it. Cook it another 15 minutes, or another 30, depending on when people are ready to eat it. It's really not that big of a deal. Just sausage and peppers."

Not a big deal? Maybe not for Lorraine, but this recipe is heaven. It combines my favorite kind of onion (caramelized) with spicy and sweet sausages. Sausage and peppers on a roll is enjoyed at New York City street festivals all summer long. It's sublime.

I've tweaked her version by using chicken sausage, which comes precooked. As a result, you save calories and cooking time. I kept it simple, but feel free to add oregano, basil, or red pepper flakes, and perk it up with a little red wine vinegar or white wine instead of water when deglazing the pan. The calories for this dish are nice and low, so get some Italian bread and serve this hoagie-style.

NUTRITION INFORMATION
(PER SERVING):

CALORIES 298, CARBS 21G, FIBER 4G, PROTEIN 23G, TOTAL FAT 14G, SATURATED FAT 3G

- 2 tablespoons olive oil
- 2 very large onions, halved and sliced (about 8 cups)
- 2 red bell peppers, seeded and sliced
- 2 cubanelle peppers, seeded and sliced
- 2 teaspoons kosher salt
- ⅓ cup water, or more as needed
- 1 12-ounce package sweet Italian-style chicken sausage
- 1 12-ounce package hot Italian-style chicken sausage

1. Heat the olive oil in a large skillet over medium heat. Add the onions and peppers, and season with 1 teaspoon of the salt. Cook, stirring occasionally, until the onions begin to brown, about 30 minutes. **2.** Add the water and use a wooden spoon to scrape the browned bits from the bottom of the pan. Slice the sausages in half crosswise (so you have two stout halves), and add to the onion mixture. Snuggle the sausages into the onions and be sure that the sausages are in contact with the bottom of the pan. Cook, stirring occasionally, until the sausages begin to brown and the onions are caramelized, about another 15 minutes. Add more water as needed to keep the onions golden, and scrape up any browned bits from the bottom of the pan to incorporate into the sauce. Add more water if you like a saucier sauce.

KITCHEN TIP § Italian Frying Peppers: Cubanelles Cubanelles are one of my favorite new ingredients. I grew up on brassy green bell peppers and always liked them. But many people and a large percentage of chefs can't stand them. Cubanelles, or Italian frying peppers, are long, light green peppers that have a lower water content than bell peppers, and as a result are perfect for frying. They are sweet and mild and can be enjoyed raw or cooked. Next time you reach for a green bell pepper, try a cubanelle.

KITCHEN TIP § How to Seed a Pepper To remove the seeds from peppers without creating a seedy mess, use the tip of your knife to cut around the stem of the pepper. Lift the entire stem and seed mass out in one piece and discard. Halve the pepper and flatten it. Use the tip of your knife to remove any remaining seeds and the white veins.

"She has an Italian mother and a Jewish father . . . to not cook would send all kinds of relatives into arm-waving fits."

herb-marinated pork tenderloin

PREP TIME: 20 minutes TOTAL TIME: 1 hour 15 minutes (or overnight for marinating) MAKES 4 servings SERVING SIZE: ¾ cup sliced pork

This recipe is the food equivalent of your little black dress: simple, versatile, and classic. For easy weekday meals, marinate a pork tenderloin in the morning, and the dish will take no more than 25 minutes to prepare at night. For a posh dinner party, double the marinade and use it to flavor a 2-pound roast pork loin. It will take about 50 minutes to cook in a 400°F oven, and it gives you a real Norman Rockwell moment when you set it on the table.

1. Add the rosemary, thyme, and garlic to a food processor. Pulse 8 to 10 times, until finely chopped; you may need to scrape down the sides of the bowl between pulses. (You can also chop by hand, if you prefer.)

2. Place the herb mixture in a large resealable plastic bag and add 1 tablespoon of the olive oil, the lemon zest, and the red pepper flakes. Squish the bag gently to combine the mixture. Add the pork to the bag and massage the marinade into the pork. Let the pork marinate at room temperature for 30 to 45 minutes, or refrigerate overnight for maximum flavor.

3. Heat a heavy skillet, preferably cast-iron, over medium heat and add the remaining tablespoon of oil. Remove the pork from the marinade and season well with salt. Place the pork in the skillet and sear on all four sides until golden brown and the internal temperature of pork is 140°F, 6 to 7 minutes per side, or 20 to 25 minutes total. Remove the pork from the skillet, cover with aluminum foil, and let rest for 10 minutes (the temperature will go up as it sits). Slice the pork and serve warm; you can keep the pork in a warm oven until ready to serve.

NUTRITION INFORMATION
(PER SERVING):

CALORIES 218, CARBS 2G, FIBER 1G, PRO-TEIN 29G, TOTAL FAT 10G, SATURATED FAT 2G

2	tablespoons fresh rosemary leaves
4	teaspoons fresh thyme leaves
2	garlic cloves, chopped
2	tablespoons extra-virgin olive oil
	Grated zest of 1 lemon
¼	teaspoon red pepper flakes
1¼	pound pork tenderloin, trimmed of excess fat
	Kosher salt

 SKINNY TIP § Divine Swine Please don't overcook the pork! Remember, trichinosis can be avoided if you cook your pork to 137°F and hold that temperature for a minute. Insert a meat thermometer into the center of the pork (the coolest part) to check the heat. For safety's sake, I always take my pork out of the pan at around 140°F, and let it rest to about least 145°F. A little bit of rosy color is a good thing and ensures that your pork stays moist. Properly cooking pork means you won't need to overcompensate with high-cal sauces to cover up the fact that it's dry.

 SKINNY TIP § Is That Calorie Count a Typo? Nope; those numbers don't lie. In this recipe, we're using 5 ounces of pork tenderloin per serving (which is more than enough protein for a meal). That's a very low-cal entrée, which means that you can increase the serving size, partner it with one of the higher-cal sides (polenta, Mashed Potatoes), enjoy a bigger serving of dessert, or opt for this dinner after you've had a big lunch. For an even lower-calorie option, grill the tenderloin and you'll save 25 fat calories per serving.

roast rack of lamb

PREP TIME: 30 minutes TOTAL TIME: 40 minutes MAKES 4 servings SERVING SIZE: Half a rack

Lamb is rich and delicious. It's more caloric than pork tenderloin or chicken breast, typically not what you pick when you want something lower in calories. But don't let the richness scare you; just get the best cut there is (the rack), and enjoy a smaller portion.

To serve, you can slice the individual ribs before and fan them on a plate. A rack has eight ribs; you cut it into eight individual ribs or four sets of two. I like to place two duos on a plate with the rib bones high in the air, as if they are crossing swords. After you've cut all the meat away with your knife and fork, pick that bone up and finish the job. The sweetest meat is closest to the bone, and Miss Manners gives you a full pass on this.

1. Preheat the oven to 400°F.

2. Heat the oil in large ovenproof skillet over medium-high heat until it shimmers. Season the lamb with salt and freshly ground black pepper and place the lamb fat-side down in the skillet and cook on all sides until golden, about 6 minutes total.

3. Place the lamb in the oven, fat-side up, and cook until the center of the lamb registers 125°F on a meat thermometer, approximately 10 minutes.

4. Place bread in a food processor and process until crumby. Add the herbs and pulse to just combine.

5. Remove the skillet from the oven, remove the lamb from the skillet, and smear the top and sides of the lamb with mustard. Cover the mustard with the breadcrumb mixture. Return the coated lamb to oven and cook until the crumbs are lightly toasted and the thickest part of the lamb registers 130° to 135°F on a meat thermometer for medium-rare, about 5 minutes.

6. Allow the lamb to rest for 10 minutes before carving. Carve and serve.

NUTRITION INFORMATION (PER SERVING):

CALORIES 338, CARBS 13G, FIBER 1G, PROTEIN 31G, TOTAL FAT 17G, SATURATED FAT 7G

- 1 tablespoon vegetable oil
- 2 1-pound racks of lamb
  Kosher salt and freshly ground black pepper
- 4 slices good quality stale white bread, torn into large pieces
- 2 tablespoons finely chopped fresh mint
- 2 tablespoons finely chopped fresh parsley
- 2 tablespoons finely chopped fresh chives
- 2 tablespoons Dijon mustard

KITCHEN TIP § To French or Not to French? To "French" a bone means to remove all the visible meat from the bone. We "French" a rack of lamb so that we can use the rib as a handle without dirtying our fingers. My friend Michael hates this tradition, knowing that the sweetest meat is closest to the bone. He feels that a Frenched rib robs him of the best part of the meal.

It's hard to find a rack of lamb in the grocery store these days that isn't Frenched, but you can always ask the butcher for a special favor.

baby back ribs with 30-minute barbeque sauce

PREP TIME: 25 minutes TOTAL TIME: 3 hours, or overnight MAKES 4 servings SERVING SIZE: ½ rack, plus sauce

Ribs are so fussed over these days; it's easy to forget how simple they are to make. But the truth is, you only need two things to make baby back ribs taste good: time and a spice rub. In fact, omit the sauce and save 106 calories per serving. Rib lovers will lure you into philosophical arguments about smoking, simmering, and saucing, but if you cook the ribs slow and long, you can't go wrong.

1. For the rub: Combine the salt, sugar, paprika, chili powder, onion powder, garlic powder, cayenne, and thyme in a medium bowl and whisk together.

2. For the sauce: Combine the ketchup, brown sugar, red wine vinegar, onion, garlic, chipotles, and sauce in a medium saucepan; bring to a simmer, and cook until onion is soft and the sauce is thick, 20 to 30 minutes. This is a chunky sauce. If you prefer a smooth sauce, puree it in the blender after it has cooked.

3. For the ribs: Generously cover each rack of ribs with ¼ cup of the rub. Let the ribs sit at room temperature for 1 hour, or wrap in plastic wrap and refrigerate overnight. Let ribs come to room temperature before cooking.

4. Preheat the oven to 325°F. Cover a baking sheet with aluminum foil.

5. Place the marinated ribs on top of the foil. Transfer to the oven and cook the ribs until the meat is tender and pulls away from the bones easily, 1½ to 2 hours. Remove the ribs from the oven.

6. Turn the broiler on and (if desired) brush each rack with ½ cup of sauce. Cook the naked or sauced ribs 6 inches from the broiler element for 5 minutes, until the naked ribs get a bit crispy or the sauce is bubbly and beginning to set. Or, finish cooking ribs on a medium-fire grill, turning until the sauce is set and the rib edges are crispy, 10 to 15 minutes.

NUTRITION INFORMATION (PER SERVING):

CALORIES 428, CARBS 37G, FIBER 3G, PROTEIN 32G, TOTAL FAT 18G, SATURATED FAT 6G

FOR RIB RUB:
- ½ cup kosher salt
- ½ cup packed light brown sugar
- ¼ cup hot paprika
- ¼ cup chili powder
- 2 tablespoons onion powder
- 2 tablespoons garlic powder
- 1 tablespoon cayenne
- 1 tablespoon dried thyme

FOR BARBEQUE SAUCE:
- 2 cups ketchup
- ½ cup light brown sugar, or more to taste
- ¼ cup red wine vinegar
- 1 small onion, grated or finely chopped
- 3 garlic cloves, minced
- 2 tablespoons chopped canned chipotles with sauce

FOR RIBS:
- 2 slabs baby back ribs, (about 4 pounds)
- ½ cup rib rub
- 1 cup barbecue sauce (optional)

SKINNY TIP § What to Do with the Leftovers? **Keep leftover rub and sauce on the table, for starters. Put it in little bowls and let the dipping begin. One tablespoon of sauce is 26 calories, and one teaspoon of rib rub is 15 calories.**

Although you'll need only ½ cup of rub for the ribs, this recipe makes enough for 2 cups. Save it; it's great with chicken or pork tenderloin.

You're making more than 2 cups of barbeque sauce, so you'll have leftovers of that, too. The rub will store in the pantry for up to 6 months, and the sauce will keep tightly sealed in the refrigerator for up to 1 month.
If you're looking for something new to do with that rub: Use it to flavor the rim of the glass (margarita style) next time you're making whiskey sours.

slow cooker pulled pork

PREP TIME: 15 minutes TOTAL TIME: 5 to 6 hours MAKES 12 servings SERVING SIZE: 1 bun with ½ cup pulled pork

Some things were born to work together: milk and cookies, Rocky and Adrian, *slow cookers and pulled pork*. A pork shoulder is a tough piece of meat, so you want to cook it for hours at very low heat. In fact, to make a Puerto Rican dish called *pernil*, some people recommend roasting pork shoulder for 8 to 10 hours. In a slow cooker, with the benefit of moist heat, you can cook it more quickly than that, but it still takes a good 5 or 6 hours to soften that big hunk of meat, all of which can happen while you're doing other things. Like going to the movies, taking a bike ride, or relaxing in a hammock. Slow is the way to go.

1. In the ceramic insert of a slow cooker, combine the onion, garlic, jalapeños, ½ cup of the vinegar, the ketchup, ¼ cup of the brown sugar, 1 tablespoon of the Worcestershire sauce, and 1 teaspoon of the salt; mix well. Add the pork and turn pork to coat with the sauce. Cook until the pork separates easily when pulled with a fork, on high for 5 hours or low for 6 hours.

2. Turn the slow cooker off, and use two forks to shred the entire pork shoulder. Remove and discard the bones.

3. Add the remaining tablespoon of cider vinegar, tablespoon of brown sugar, teaspoon of salt, the chili powder, cumin, and cocoa; stir to incorporate with the shredded pork. Serve the pulled pork on the buns.

NUTRITION INFORMATION
(PER SERVING):

CALORIES 276, CARBS 31G, FIBER 2G, PROTEIN 22G, TOTAL FAT 7G, SATURATED FAT 2G

- 1 medium onion, chopped
- 4 garlic cloves, peeled and smashed
- 2 tablespoons chopped pickled jalapeños
- ½ cup plus 1 tablespoon cider vinegar
- ½ cup ketchup
- ¼ cup plus 1 tablespoon light brown sugar
- 1 tablespoons Worcestershire sauce
- 2 teaspoons kosher salt
- 1 4- to 4½-pound bone-in pork shoulder butt, skin removed
- 1 tablespoon chili powder
- 1 teaspoon ground cumin
- 1 tablespoon unsweetened cocoa powder
- 12 hamburger buns, toasted

"Some things were born to work together: milk and cookies, Rocky and Adrian, *slow cookers and pulled pork.*"

KITCHEN TIP § Not Thin Skinned

Last summer, I lived near a farm and got into the habit of visiting a big momma pig and her piglets regularly. One day while I was there, the farmer's daughter hopped inside the pen, picked up the runt, and jumped back out of the pen so that she could give him some medicine. She did this in one quick motion to avoid Momma's wrath.

As soon as the runt was 50 yards clear of the pen, he let out a serious squeal. Momma perked up, locked eyes with the closest human (me), and charged: *800 pounds of fury, coming at me fast.*

I experienced several very long seconds of paralyzing fear. My feet couldn't move (running would have been useless anyway—pigs are fast!). Fortunately, Momma halted 1 foot shy of the electric "fence," a thin line of wire that surrounded the pen. Pigs are smart, and she knew she didn't want to tangle with that line, no matter how thick her skin. Luckily for me, she didn't know that the electric fence had been turned off for days.

If you pick up a pork butt, it will be covered in thick, leathery pig skin. If you slow-roast your pork, this skin will become crackly and delicious. But we're using a slow cooker, which doesn't do much for the skin, so you might as well get rid of it. Use a serrated knife and kitchen scissors to separate the skin from the flesh.

SKINNY TIP § No Buns, Hon?

No problem! Skip the bun in favor of corn tortillas. A standard bun has about 120 calories, and 6-inch corn tortillas have 40 calories each. You can have 3 tortillas or 1 bun.

KITCHEN TIP § Season Twice

When you prepare food in a slow cooker, you're cooking for a long period of time in a moist-heat environment. You aren't reducing the liquid, as you do with braising, or using intense dry heat, as you do with roasting. Long moist cooking without reduction is a great way to soften tough cuts, but it's not ideal for popping flavor. That's why in step 3, you add more flavor. Feel free to add more spice when reheating the pulled pork, too.

And speaking of reheating; I just reheated my pulled pork with some of Sue's Easy Cheesy Black Beans (page 176). Heaven.

seared pork chops with sautéed apples and leeks

PREP TIME: 15 minutes **TOTAL TIME:** 35 minutes **MAKES** 4 servings **SERVING SIZE:** 1 chop with ⅓ cup sauce

This recipe is the final project of one of my students, Carolyn. For the final, I asked her to make a meal that would highlight several of the techniques she learned and incorporate an ingredient that she had never used before. This is what she created, on the spot.

The only thing better than following a great recipe is having the skills to improvise your own. After creating a few of the recipes in this book, give yourself a challenge and see what you can come up with, Iron Chef–style. You've been eating all your life; you know the flavors that go well together. Once you've mastered some basic techniques, you can come up with dishes of your own. Pork, apples, leeks, and cream are natural partners; this simple dish has become an autumn meal I crave.

1. In a large skillet, melt the butter over medium-high heat. Add the apple slices and cook, gently tossing, until golden on each side, about 4 minutes total. Use a slotted spoon to transfer the apples to a plate and cover with aluminum foil to keep warm.

2. Add the oil to the same skillet over medium-high heat. Season the chops with ½ teaspoon of the salt and add the chops to the hot oil. Cook until golden, about 4 minutes per side. Transfer the chops to a plate.

3. Add the flour to the fat remaining in the skillet and whisk together to make a paste. Whisk in the wine and cook until the wine has almost evaporated, about a minute. Whisk in the chicken broth and bring to a simmer. Add the leeks and cook, stirring occasionally, until they have softened but are still bright green, 3 to 4 minutes. Whisk the half-and-half and mustard into the sauce. Return the chops to the sauce and simmer until warmed through, about 2 minutes. Add the parsley and season with the remaining ½ teaspoon salt.

4. Serve the pork chops with the leek sauce and apples.

NUTRITION INFORMATION (PER SERVING):

CALORIES 314, CARBS 14G, FIBER 2G, PROTEIN 29G, TOTAL FAT 14G, SATURATED FAT 5G

- 1 tablespoon unsalted butter
- 1 Golden Delicious apple, peeled and cut into ¼-inch-thick slices
- 1 tablespoon vegetable oil
- 4 1-inch bone-in pork chops (about 2½ pounds)
- 1 teaspoon kosher salt
- 1½ teaspoons all-purpose flour
- ⅓ cup white wine
- 1 cup lower-sodium chicken broth
- 2 leeks, trimmed, halved, cut into 1-inch pieces, and washed
- ¼ cup half-and-half
- 2 teaspoons Dijon mustard
- ⅓ cup roughly chopped or whole parsley leaves

 KITCHEN TIP § Avoid Premature Flipping If the chop doesn't want to leave the comfort of the hot pan after it's been cooking for 4 minutes, don't pry it from the skillet. While the chops cook, they stick to the skillet. When they're done, they'll release. Trust the chop.

 SKINNY TIP § Thick or Thin? For a thicker sauce, remove the cooked chops and simmer the sauce until it reaches a consistency you like. For a thinner sauce, slowly whisk in a little more chicken broth.

The same logic works for the chops. If you have thin, boneless chops, they tend to cook quickly, so reduce the sauté time and let your chops tell you when they want to flip (see Avoid Premature Flipping tip on this page).

sloppy joe

PREP TIME: 15 minutes TOTAL TIME: 35 minutes MAKES 10 servings SERVING SIZE: 1 bun with ½ cup Joe

A Sloppy Joe is somewhere between a Bolognese sauce (page 128) and a hamburger. And since there's no way a soft bun can contain a sauce the way it holds a burger, Sloppy Joes are messy; there's no getting around it.

My mom would not make Sloppy Joes for me when I was a kid (due to the mess factor), which makes them twice as much fun for me to eat now. I've been thinking about Joe for decades; this recipe is worth the wait.

1. Heat the oil in a large skillet over medium heat. Add the ground beef and cook, stirring and breaking it up, until it begins to brown, about 6 minutes. Stir in the tomato paste and cumin and cook until all the pinkness from the meat is gone, another 2 minutes. Remove the meat with a slotted spoon and reserve; leave the remaining fat in the pan.

2. Add the onion, chile, and garlic to the fat in the skillet and cook, stirring, until the vegetables are soft but not browned, about 5 minutes.

3. Return the ground beef to the skillet with the vegetables. Stir in the tomato sauce, ketchup, Worcestershire sauce, brown sugar, red wine vinegar, and chipotles and sauce, and simmer over low heat until the sauce is thickened and the flavors are blended, 5 to 10 minutes.

4. Divide the meat sauce among the toasted buns and serve with pickle spears.

NUTRITION INFORMATION
(PER SERVING):

CALORIES 305, CARBS 31G, FIBER 2G, PROTEIN 19G, TOTAL FAT 12G, SATURATED FAT 3G

- 2 tablespoons vegetable oil
- 1½ pounds 90% lean ground beef
- 2 tablespoons tomato paste
- 1 teaspoon ground cumin
- 1 medium onion, chopped
- 1 poblano chile, seeded and chopped (see tip, page 213)
- 3 garlic cloves, sliced
- 1 8-ounce can tomato sauce
- ½ cup ketchup
- 1 tablespoon Worcestershire sauce
- 1 tablespoon light brown sugar
- 1 tablespoon red wine vinegar
- 2 canned chipotle chiles, chopped, plus 1 tablespoon chipotle sauce
- 10 hamburger buns, toasted
  Pickle spears, for serving

SKINNY TIP § Chipotle World!
Just ten years ago, I had no idea what a chipotle was. Now you see chipotles everywhere. In salsas, in salad dressings, it's even the name of a restaurant chain. Chipotles are smoked jalapeños simmered in a vinegary tomato sauce. They are rich and spicy and come packaged in small 7-ounce cans.

If you open a fresh can to make this recipe, you'll have left over chipotles. Don't toss them. Instead, freeze the leftovers in small containers or in plastic ice cube trays. They'll keep frozen for up to 3 months.

Try using chipotles the next time you want to make a spicy homemade dip, or put a few teaspoons into the Lemony Hummus with Parsley (page 108) or Smoky Babaghanouj (page 111). It's a terrific skinny ingredient because a little goes a long way: 2 tablespoons have only 25 calories.

KITCHEN TIP § The Legend Lives
This recipe makes a lot of Joe. Good! Give your friends Joe to go, or keep him in the freezer for up to 6 months. Freeze Joe in small containers and defrost when you want to make nachos or beef up a sauce.

classic roast beef

PREP TIME: 15 minutes TOTAL TIME: 1 hour 15 minutes MAKES 8 servings SERVING SIZE: 5 to 7 slices of beef

This is your Sunday roast, the one you want to have with Popovers (page 172), peas, and Fluffy Mashed Potatoes (page 160). When cooking a roast, you want to buy the best-quality meat you can (prime), season it simply, and roast it to the right temperature. For that, you need a good butcher and a meat thermometer.

My first meat cookbook was *The Complete Meat Cookbook* by Bruce Aidells and Denis Kelly. If you want a meat bible, this is the one. This recipe is inspired by theirs. If you recognize the Aidells name, you may have seen it in the grocery store. Bruce Aidells makes a line of serious sausages. The man knows his meat.

1. Place a roasting pan fitted with a rack in the oven and preheat the oven to 450°F.
2. Combine the oil, garlic, thyme, salt, and pepper in a small bowl. Trim the excess fat from the roast but leave a thin layer of fat, which will baste the meat as it cooks. Brush the marinade all over the meat.

3. Roast the meat until it reaches 125°F in the center for medium-rare, 30 to 40 minutes. Remove the meat from the oven, cover with foil, and let it rest for an additional 15 to 20 minutes before carving. Cut into thin slices and serve warm.

NUTRITION INFORMATION
(PER SERVING):
CALORIES 293, CARBS 0G, FIBER 0G, PROTEIN 22G, TOTAL FAT 22G, SATURATED FAT 8G

- 2 tablespoons olive oil
- 2 garlic cloves, minced
- 1 teaspoon chopped fresh thyme, or ½ teaspoon dried thyme
- 1 tablespoon kosher salt
- 1 2-pound piece beef filet, at room temperature

 KITCHEN TIP § If You're Out of the Oven, Why Are You Still Cooking? When you remove roasts or other cooked meats from the oven, they will continue to cook as they sit (see tip for Herb-Marinated Pork Tenderloin, page 214). In fact, the temperature on this roast will increase another 5 to 10 degrees as it rests. Worry not: A rested roast is a juicier roast.

 KITCHEN TIP § Taking Temperature Since you can't tell your roast to open up and say "aaah," you want to be sure to insert the thermometer into the coolest part of the roast, which is deep in its center.

According to *The Complete Meat Cookbook*, you want to remove the meat from the oven at the following temperatures so that it can rest "up" to the proper doneness:
Rare: 115° to 120°F
Medium-rare: 125° to 130°F
Medium: 130° to 140°F

fuss-free meatballs in marinara

PREP TIME: 30 minutes TOTAL TIME: 1 hour MAKES 6 servings SERVING SIZE: 1 cup meatballs and sauce (5 meatballs, ¼ cup sauce)

As a kid, I hated making my bed. The sheet, the blanket, the pillows, running back and forth from one side of the bed to the other. *What a pain in the neck.* And then I got a duvet: sheet and comforter in one. A flick of the wrist and the bed is made.

This recipe is like that. Meatballs are traditionally fried in oil before they are simmered in the sauce, which can be kind of a pain in the neck, absurdly caloric, and definitely messy.

In this recipe, we "duvet" that approach by simmering the meatballs in marinara sauce (that we also make from scratch, though you can use your favorite jarred sauce). The meatballs flavor the sauce, the sauce flavors the meatballs, and the whole thing is done more efficiently and less calorically than if you'd fried the meatballs first. Sever with 2 ounces of spaghetti (per person) for an additional 200 calories per serving.

NUTRITION INFORMATION (PER SERVING):
CALORIES 345, CARBS 13G, FIBER 3G, PROTEIN 28G, TOTAL FAT 20G, SATURATED FAT 8G

- 1 tablespoon olive oil
- 2 garlic cloves, sliced
- 1 28-ounce can crushed tomatoes
- 2 teaspoons kosher salt
- 1 slice bread
- ½ pound 90% lean ground beef
- ½ pound ground veal
- ½ pound ground pork
- ½ cup grated Parmesan cheese (about 2 ounces)
- 1 large egg
- ½ small onion, finely minced
- ⅓ cup chopped fresh parsley
- ⅓ cup plus 2 tablespoons chopped fresh basil
- 1 teaspoon dried oregano
- ¼ teaspoon red pepper flakes

1. Heat the oil in a large pot over medium heat. Add the garlic and cook, stirring, until golden, about 2 minutes. Add the crushed tomatoes and 1 teaspoon of the salt and bring to a simmer. Simmer the sauce over low heat as you prepare the meatballs.

2. Place the bread in a medium bowl and cover with water. Let the bread soak for 5 minutes, then gently squeeze out excess liquid. Tear into small pieces.

3. Combine the ground beef, veal, pork, cheese, egg, onion, parsley, 2 tablespoons of the basil, oregano, the remaining teaspoon salt, and red pepper flakes in a large bowl. Add the bread pieces. Use your hands to combine the mixture, keeping lightness in your hand and air in the meatballs (don't squish the meat, or you'll end up with tough balls). Roll the meat mixture in your hands to create meatballs about the size of a golf ball (you should have about 30 balls).

4. Add the meatballs to the sauce as you shape them. Once you've added all the meatballs, cook, covered, until the meatballs are firm and have cooked through, about 30 minutes, turning about halfway through since the sauce will not cover the balls. Remove from the heat and stir the remaining ⅓ cup basil into the sauce. Serve warm.

KITCHEN TIP § What About Turkey Balls? Ground turkey and 90 percent lean ground beef have the same amount of fat and calories. Ground veal also has the same amount of calories as ground turkey and half the fat. Ground pork is about 30 percent more caloric than ground turkey, though I think it's worth the flavor. This combination of ground pork, veal, and beef is easy to find in grocery stores; it's often packaged as "meatloaf blend."

If you want to use turkey instead of the pork, go for it; you'll save 40 calories per serving and 5 grams of fat.

skirt steak with chimichurri sauce

PREP TIME: 20 minutes TOTAL TIME: 30 minutes MAKES 6 servings SERVING SIZE: 6-inch piece of steak with 1½ tablespoons sauce

Chimichurri sauce, sometimes called the "salsa of Argentina," is a terrific complement to a well-marbled piece of steak. Herby and garlicky, this sauce is bright, which means it's acidic and tangy. It refreshes your palate the same way pickled ginger refreshes your palate between bites of sushi. If you love the pickle on your hamburger, or tangy coleslaw with pulled pork, this recipe is for you.

NUTRITION INFORMATION
(PER SERVING):

CALORIES 403, CARBS 1G, FIBER 0G, PROTEIN 38G, TOTAL FAT 26G, SATURATED FAT 7G

1 small garlic clove, peeled
1 cup gently packed fresh parsley
¾ cup gently packed cilantro leaves
⅓ cup olive oil
¼ cup red wine vinegar
Grated zest of 1 lemon
¼ teaspoon red pepper flakes
¼ teaspoon kosher salt, plus more for steak
2 pounds skirt steak, trimmed of fat
1 tablespoon vegetable oil (as needed)

1. Place the garlic in a food processor and pulse until finely chopped (you may need to scrape the sides of the bowl). Add the parsley and cilantro and pulse until roughly chopped. Transfer the mixture to a bowl and whisk in the olive oil, red wine vinegar, lemon zest, red pepper flakes, and salt. Use immediately or refrigerate for up to 2 days.

2. Heat a grill or a large heavy skillet, preferably cast iron, over medium-high heat until very hot. Season the steaks with salt and place them on the grill. If using a skillet, add the oil to the skillet before cooking (you may need to cook in batches). Cook until the first side is golden brown, about 3 minutes. Turn the steaks and cook on the other side for 2 to 3 minutes more. Before serving, let the steaks rest for 10 minutes, covered with aluminum foil. Serve with the chimichurri sauce.

KITCHEN TIP § Get Grilling
Skirt steak is well marbled, which is a food euphemism for fatty. As they say in culinary school, "fat equals flavor," which is part of the reason we love well-marbled cuts like skirt steak and ribeye. If I could, I'd always cook skirt steak on the grill, since the fat cooks out of the meat and spatters on the stovetop. Happily, all that spattering means you end up with less fat (and calories) in the meat. Don't worry; you'll never miss them.

SKINNY TIP § Eye Games
If you follow this recipe, you'll end up with 5 ounces of steak per person, which is a 5- to 6-inch piece of meat. Now, that's more than enough protein, but for those of you who took the 64-ounce challenge at your local steakhouse, it seems like not very much meat. But by enjoying the foods you love with an eye to portion control, you'll get to have your steak and skinny jeans, too. Fill that plate with delicious sides like Steakhouse Sweet Potato Wedges (page 166) or Fluffy Mashed Potatoes (page 160), and enjoy every bite.

SKINNY TIP § Extra Sauce?
Stir leftover chimichurri into Asparagus Soup with Toasted Almonds (page 76), use a dipping sauce for grilled polenta (see tip, page 165), or enjoy it with a piece of grilled pork or rotisserie chicken. One tablespoons of chimichurri is about 60 calories. Though the color will be brightest just after you make it, the tangy flavor will live on for days.

thai beef

PREP TIME: 25 minutes TOTAL TIME: 40 minutes MAKES 6 servings SERVING SIZE: 1 cup

I am fascinated with global home cooking, but it can be a challenge to stay true to those recipes using American grocery store ingredients. My friend Andrew shared this recipe with me to show me how easy it can be to replicate Thai flavors using ingredients we can easily find in the States.

This recipe is all about the sauce, which is tangy, sweet, and slightly spicy, finished with handfuls of fresh basil and cilantro. Because the sauce is so vivid, I'm calling for London broil because it's a less fatty (ergo, less flavorful and less caloric) cut of meat. Try this sauce with chicken, pork, or tofu in place of the beef; the sauce is the thing.

Serve Thai Beef over You Can Make White Rice (page 169). Garnish with scallions, mung beans, some chopped roasted peanuts, and a wedge of lime.

NUTRITION INFORMATION (PER SERVING):

CALORIES 262, CARBS 20G, FIBER 1G, PROTEIN 29G, TOTAL FAT 7G, SATURATED FAT 2G

- 1½ pounds flank steak, top round, or London broil
- 1 teaspoon kosher salt
- 1 tablespoon vegetable oil
- 2 large onions, halved and sliced into ⅓-inch-thick half-moons
- ½ cup lower-sodium soy sauce
- ½ cup light brown sugar
- ⅓ cup fresh lime juice
- 2 tablespoons Vietnamese or Thai fish sauce
- 3 serrano chiles or 2 jalapeños, thinly sliced (depending on desired heat)
- 2 large garlic cloves, minced
- 1 cup fresh coarsely chopped basil leaves, lightly packed
- 1 cup fresh coarsely chopped cilantro leaves, lightly packed

1. Turn the broiler on and place a heavy ovenproof skillet, preferably cast iron, 6 inches from the broiler element. Heat the skillet for at least 10 minutes.

2. Season the flank steak with the salt, rubbing it into the meat. Carefully remove the skillet from the oven (it's hot), place on the stovetop, and place the meat in the skillet (it will sizzle). Return the skillet to its spot under the broiler, and cook until the meat is medium-rare, about 10 minutes. Remove the skillet from broiler, transfer the meat to a plate, and cover with aluminum foil. Let rest for at least 10 minutes before slicing.

3. Heat the oil in a large skillet over medium-high heat. Add the onions and sweat until they are soft and beginning to caramelize, about 20 minutes. Stir in the soy sauce, brown sugar, lime juice, fish sauce, chiles, and garlic. Bring to a simmer and cook gently over medium heat until reduced by half, about 7 minutes.

4. Remove the sauce from heat and stir in the basil and cilantro. Taste to ensure that the sauce is sweet, sour, salty, and spicy. Adjust the seasonings as needed to ensure that each flavor is present.

5. Cut the steak into thin slices against the grain and toss with sauce. Serve warm.

"You'll get to have your steak and skinny jeans too."

 SKINNY TIP § London Calling
Don't go looking for London broil in London, as there is no cut of meat that goes by that name on the other side of the pond. London broil is a tough, lean cut of meat—the kind of steak you'll want to marinate, cook, and serve sliced. It's the steak my mom served so that we could have steak without breaking the bank.

You can use skirt steak if you like, but you'll end up with a smaller portion of steak for the same number of calories. An ounce of trimmed, broiled skirt steak has 62 calories, while an ounce of London broil has 51 calories.

 KITCHEN TIP § Method to the Madness I absolutely love this technique for cooking London broil. By preheating the pan in the oven, the meat is cooked from below by the heat of the pan at the same time as it's cooked from above by the heat of the broiler. When you slice the meat, it will be evenly browned outside and perfectly medium-rare inside. Try this cooking method whenever cooking meat under the broiler.

 SKINNY TIP § More Caramelized?
I've had this recipe two ways, with just-caramelized onions and with deeper, richer more caramelized onions (this takes 30 to 40 minutes). Both are delicious. The more caramelized version is slightly more time-consuming, and it gives you less volume because those onions shrink as they cook. Try it both ways and see what you like; the calories are the same.

risotto with shrimp and peas

PREP TIME: 5 minutes TOTAL TIME: 35 minutes MAKES 4 servings SERVING SIZE: 1¾ cups

Risotto isn't difficult to make; it's just a dish that's filled with superstition. If you stop stirring the risotto, *you will lose your job*. If you stir in the wrong direction, your *heart will break*. If you use a cold broth, *you'll suffer a life of loneliness*, or—gasp!—*a bad risotto*.

Though I usually don't mess with superstitions, there's no truth to these if's, chemically speaking. I've made risottos by cooking them in the oven without stirring—utter blasphemy—and they're still creamy. I've tried them with cold broth, and they still work (they just take a bit longer). That creaminess is the nature of the short-grained arborio or carnaroli rice. If you try to make a risotto with basmati, you can stir until the end of time and you still won't have a creamy risotto. (Yep, I've done that too. *And I'm still stirring*.)

When you do stir the risotto, keep those grains of rice submerged or your risotto will cook unevenly. Personally, I think the Italian grandmas made up the superstitions because they wanted some company in the kitchen, and what better chore for an unskilled son or daughter than stirring? Busy hands are happy hands, and crowded kitchens make grandmas smile.

NUTRITION INFORMATION
(PER SERVING):
CALORIES 549, CARBS 63G, FIBER 1G, PROTEIN 39G, TOTAL FAT 15G, SATURATED FAT 7G

- 4 cups lower-sodium chicken broth
- 1 cup water
- 1 tablespoon olive oil
- 2 tablespoons unsalted butter
- 1 small onion, chopped
- 2 garlic cloves, chopped
- 1 tablespoon kosher salt, or more to taste
- 1½ cups arborio or carnaroli rice
- ½ cup dry white wine
- 1 pound frozen jumbo shrimp, defrosted, peeled, and sliced in half lengthwise
- ½ cup frozen peas
- ½ cup chopped fresh parsley
- ½ cup grated Parmesan cheese (about 2 ounces)
- ¼ cup sliced fresh basil
  Freshly ground black pepper

1. Bring the chicken broth and water to a gentle simmer in a small saucepan. Heat the olive oil and 1 tablespoon of the butter in a large, wide saucepan over medium heat. When the butter has melted, add the onion, garlic, and 1 teaspoon of the salt and cook, stirring, until the onion is translucent, about 4 minutes. Add the rice and stir for 1 minute. Add the wine and cook until it is absorbed, about 1 minute.

2. Add another teaspoon of salt and 1 cup of warm chicken broth to the rice. Cook, stirring, until the broth is absorbed by the rice and your spoon leaves a trail when moving through the rice. Repeat, adding 1 cup of broth at a time and stirring until the rice is tender yet firm and the mixture is creamy, 25 to 30 minutes.

3. When you add the last cup of liquid and it is simmering, add the shrimp, peas, and remaining teaspoon of salt to the pot. Continue to cook and stir. When the rice is cooked through and still firm and the shrimp are pink, remove the risotto from heat. Add the parsley, Parmesan, basil, and remaining tablespoon of butter and stir together until the butter has melted. Serve with pepper.

SKINNY TIP § Salt Strategy I was taught to make a good ragù sauce by Anna Klinger, the chef of Al Di La in Park Slope, Brooklyn. When she makes her ragù, she adds small pinches of salt through the hour-long cooking process. Frequent salting helps the flavor bloom every step of the way.

When I made this risotto, I tried salting at the end (to save you the steps), and it just wasn't right. I let it sit, came back to it and it came alive. The salt needed time to do it's thing; season early and often.

scratch pizza

PREP TIME: 30 minutes TOTAL TIME: 2 hours MAKES 6 servings SERVING SIZE: Half a pizza

Don't flip that page! Pizza is something I used to shy away from until I developed this recipe. First, it was all that *dough*, and second, it seemed like a lot of work for something I could get down the street for two bucks. It required a pizza stone and a peel (that long paddle you use to "gently slide" the pizza onto the stone) and a bit of gymnastics to get the two to work together without tossing my toppings all over the oven.

   This is a very easy way to make pizza. Yes, you're going to knead the dough, but it's gratifying, so go with it. Your taking part in the magical, historical, biblical (and I'll say it, sexy) process of making bread. It's primal.

1. Combine the yeast with the water and let it sit until it foams, about 10 minutes.
2. Mound the flour on the counter or in a large, wide bowl and make a well in the center. Slowly pour 1 cup of the yeast mixture into the well, mixing it into the flour with a fork until you've got a shaggy dough. Add 2 tablespoons of the olive oil and the salt; begin kneading. You want the dough to have the stickiness of a lint roller. If needed, add the remaining water and even out with flour.
3. Knead until the dough becomes smooth as a baby's head, about 5 minutes. Drizzle the remaining teaspoon of olive oil into a medium bowl and work it around the bowl with your hand. Put the dough in the bowl and cover the bowl with plastic wrap, leaving space so that it has

enough room to rise. Let it rest in a warm spot until it doubles in size, about 1½ hours.
4. Place a turned-over baking sheet in the oven and preheat the oven to 500°F.
5. Divide the dough into three parts and use your fingers to press one of the dough pieces into a large circle ¼ inch thick. If needed, use a rolling pin to roll the dough.
6. Remove the baking sheet from the oven and place the prepared dough on top of it. Working quickly, place the dough on the inverted baking sheet and top with ½ cup of the sauce and ½ cup of the cheese, leaving a ¾-inch uncovered ring around the dough for the crust. Return the baking pan to the center of the oven and cook until cheese is bubbling and the crust is browned, 8 to 10 minutes. Repeat with the remaining dough, cheese, and sauce.

NUTRITION INFORMATION
(PER SERVING):
CALORIES 378, CARBS 53G, FIBER 3G, PROTEIN 15G, TOTAL FAT 12G, SATURATED FAT 4G

1 ¾-ounce package active dry yeast
1¼ cups warm water
3 cups all-purpose flour
2 tablespoons plus 1 teaspoon olive oil
1 teaspoon kosher salt
1½ cups tomato sauce
1½ cups part-skim shredded mozzarella cheese (about 6 ounces)
1 cup fresh basil leaves

SKINNY TIP § Less Is More
Less is more when topping thin-crust pizzas, so go easy and remember to leave a ¾-inch untopped ring of dough around the outer edge.

KITCHEN TIP § Bench Scraper
The bench scraper is a tool that pastry cooks reach for as often as savory cooks reach for their knives. It's helpful to have around if your dough is sticky and you want to manipulate

it without adding too much flour. Since it has a clean edge (the "scrape" part), the bench scraper can separate the dough from a flat surface more effectively than, say, the side of your hand.

herbed omelet with goat cheese

PREP TIME: 10 minutes TOTAL TIME: 10 minutes MAKES 1 serving SERVING SIZE: 1 omelet

This is the meal to make if you want to have a simple, special dinner for yourself or if a friend has stopped by and is in need of some home cooking. Even if you think you've got nothing in the house, I bet you have eggs. And with eggs, you have an omelet.

The right equipment is three-quarters of the omelet battle, so invest in an 8-inch ovenproof nonstick skillet and a small silicone spatula. Serve the omelet with an Arugula Salad with Parmesan and Truffle Oil (page 42) and you'll have a full meal in 20 minutes.

NUTRITION INFORMATION
(PER SERVING):
CALORIES 242, CARBS 1G, FIBER 0G, PROTEIN 15G, TOTAL FAT 20G, SATURATED FAT 9G

- 2 teaspoons unsalted butter
- 2 large eggs
  Kosher salt and small grind of black pepper (optional)
- 1 tablespoon coarsely chopped fresh herbs, including parsley, chives, chervil, and/or tarragon
- ½ ounce soft, fresh goat cheese, crumbled

1. Melt the butter in an 8-inch ovenproof nonstick skillet over medium heat. Crack the eggs directly into the skillet and, working quickly, use a heatproof spatula to beat the eggs in the skillet. Season with a pinch of salt, pepper (if desired), and half of the herbs. Let the eggs cook over medium-low heat until the bottom is set, about 1 minute. (If you don't think you can mix the eggs and add herbs and spices in under a minute, gently beat the eggs in a small bowl before adding to the skillet. I'm trying to save you a dish to wash, but not at the expense of your omelet!)

2. Sprinkle the cheese onto the omelet, pop the skillet under the broiler to soften the cheese, and cook until the eggs are almost completely set, about 1 minute.

3. Remove the skillet from under the broiler and fold the omelet into thirds (letter-in-an-envelope style). Make the first fold in the skillet and the second fold as you slide the omelet out of the pan and onto a plate.

4. Sprinkle with another small pinch of salt and the remaining herbs on top. Serve warm.

 KITCHEN TIP § PSST . . . The Secret Is PCCT Parsley, chives, chervil, and tarragon are the components of a French herb blend called *fines herbes*. These four are like the Beatles; though they give great individual performances, they are at their best when combined.

You're familiar with parsley (grassy, refreshing) and chives (gentle onion flavor), but how about George and Ringo? Chervil and tarragon have the flavor of black licorice. Tarragon is aggressive, and chervil is subtle. If you want to use dried *fines herbes* in this recipe, use 1 teaspoon instead of a tablespoon, and use it all in the egg mixture, as dried herbs work best when cooked. And don't worry about finding all these herbs for this dish. If you have them, terrific; if not, use what you have.

 KITCHEN TIP § Warm Your Plates Eggs get cold quickly. Help them stay warm by preheating the serving plate in a warm oven for a few minutes or the microwave for 30 seconds. The microwave approach works for cold coffee mugs, too.

save room for
dessert

"I shouldn't. I love it, but I shouldn't.

OK, a sliver.

That's too much!

Oh this is good. I hate how good this is."

Sound familiar? Desserts are bittersweet. On the one hand, we want to eat them. Of course we do, they're delicious. But on the other hand, we can't help but think: *Should I have them? Do I need them?*

Desserts are high in calories and they're not exactly packed with vitamins. From an analytical perspective, they're the world's least-necessary food.
So, should you?

Of course, you should. Dessert is a pleasure. Everyone from the pickiest eaters to omnivores can agree on that. The question is not whether you should have dessert, it's how best to have it. In the United States, we like cake, pie, or a bowl of ice cream for dessert. Other cultures do dessert differently.

In Morocco, for example, there may be date cakes or phyllo stuffed with pistachios and honey on special occasions. You're not expected to eat an entire dessert course on a nightly basis, and a fruit bowl is always offered after dinner. It's a small kiss of sweet, and it's enough. Plus, Moroccan dinners tend to have more sweet flavors throughout the meal than American dinners do, which explains why we're left with that sweet craving.

A piece of fruit is always a good option for dessert, and you can take it to the next level by making Apple Crumble (page 238), Grilled Pineapple with Ice Cream (page 256), or Chocolate-Covered Strawberries (page 253). These fruit desserts are under 200 calories each, which is more indulgent than a plain piece of fruit but way less caloric than a piece of cake.

And speaking of pieces of cake, have you ever made Flan (page 242)? It's custard cooked with homemade caramel on top. It's surprisingly easy to make (just four ingredients), looks impressive, and feeds a crowd gracefully. One serving, including caramel sauce, is 200 calories.

In this chapter you'll find *no-way-is-that-low-cal* favorites like Flourless Chocolate Cake (page 266) and Rice Pudding (page 245). And, of course, you need cookies, so try Cherry Chocolate Chip Oatmeal Cookies (page 259), Pecan Snowballs (page 262), or Double-Chocolate Biscotti (page 261).

I've cut out the unnecessary calories, *but I haven't cut corners*. You'll still be using butter, sugar, and eggs; and no, the ice cream isn't low-fat. You'll have your favorites, which will taste real good, and the portions will be right, too. I'm never going to give you a sliver and expect you to be satisfied. A 9 inch cake feeds 12. That makes sense; that's what it's supposed to do. A 9x13-inch cake feeds 16; everyone gets a 2x3-inch portion. That, too, is enough.

No more sneaking spoonfuls of dessert in the dark, over the sink. No more *I love it but I shouldn't*. It's not enough that you have your cake. You should enjoy it, too.

apple crumble

PREP TIME: 25 minutes **TOTAL TIME:** 1 hour 10 minutes **MAKES** 9 servings **SERVING SIZE:** 2-inch square

Apples are an affable fruit, but it's the topping that makes a crumble taste divine. When you prepare this recipe, make a double batch of the topping and keep the extra half in your freezer. You'll find a reason to use it.

A single serving of crumble is 2 heaping tablespoons and has 110 calories. For a single-serving crumble, put your favorite fruits, like peaches and blueberries in a small ramekin, top with the mixture, and bake at 375°F until the fruit is bubbly and the crumble is golden brown, 25 to 30 minutes.

1. Preheat the oven to 375°F.

2. For the topping: In a food processor, combine the flour, oats, sugars, cinnamon, and salt. Pulse to combine. Add the butter and pulse until mixture has pea-size pieces of butter mixed in with the flour and oats. Transfer the topping to a bowl and refrigerate for at least 15 minutes.

3. For the filling: In a large bowl, combine the apples, sugar, flour, cinnamon, lemon juice, and salt and toss ingredients together.

Transfer the filling to an 8-inch square baking dish.

4. After the topping has chilled, scatter it over the top of the filling in the baking dish. Be sure the topping is crumbly; keep working it with your fingertips to be sure there are lots of pebble-size bits. Bake in oven until the fruit is bubbly and the top is golden brown, about 45 minutes. Cool for at least 15 minutes before serving.

NUTRITION INFORMATION
(PER SERVING):
CALORIES 198, CARBS 36G, FIBER 3G, PROTEIN 1G, TOTAL FAT 7G, SATURATED FAT 4G

FOR THE TOPPING:
- ¼ cup all-purpose flour
- ¼ cup old-fashioned rolled oats
- ¼ cup packed light brown sugar
- ¼ cup granulated sugar
- ¼ teaspoon ground cinnamon
- ¼ teaspoon kosher salt
- 5 tablespoons unsalted butter, cut into small bits and chilled

FOR THE APPLE FILLING:
- 5 apples, your choice or a combination (Rome and Golden Delicious for firmness, McIntosh for sauciness, Granny Smith for tartness), peeled, cored, and thinly sliced
- ¼ cup granulated sugar
- 1 tablespoon all-purpose flour
- ½ teaspoon ground cinnamon
  Juice from ½ lemon
  Pinch of kosher salt

KITCHEN TIP § Apple Crumble **Anytime** Serve this dish warm or at room temperature, for breakfast or dessert. Store at room temperature, covered with plastic wrap, for up to 2 days, or refrigerated for up to 5. Reheat, uncovered, in a 350°F oven for 10 to 15 minutes.

KITCHEN TIP § A Surprise Visit from Grandma When testing this recipe, I purchased Granny Smith apples by mistake. They're a terrific tart eating apple, but not something I typically choose when cooking. Well, that's about to change. These tart apples are a terrific counterpart to the

sweet crumble topping. I've made this recipe dozens of times, and this apple variety is my new favorite.

carrot cake

PREP TIME: 25 minutes **TOTAL TIME:** 2 hours (includes cooling time) **MAKES** 16 servings **SERVING SIZE:** 2 by 3-inch piece of cake with frosting

If we're going to talk carrot cake, let's be real: You and I both know a big part of the carrot cake experience is the cream cheese frosting. It's only two ingredients: cream cheese and confectioner's sugar, and it's good.

It would be easy to reduce the calories in carrot cake by getting rid of that frosting, but that wouldn't be right. Did you know that most carrot cake recipes call for at least ½ cup of oil? It's true. And you definitely *don't taste that.* Let's lose those calories.

To keep the cake moist, I've added more carrots. Carrot cake + extra carrots – unnecessary oil = moist carrot cake with cream cheese frosting – extra calories. Now there's a balanced dessert.

1. Preheat the oven to 350°F. Coat a 9x13-inch baking pan with cooking spray and dust with flour.
2. Combine the flour, cinnamon, baking powder, baking soda, salt, and allspice in a bowl and whisk together. Add the carrots, raisins, and nuts to the flour mixture and toss to coat. Set aside.
3. Whisk the eggs together in a medium bowl, add the orange zest and juice and the brown and granulated sugars, and mix well. Pour the egg mixture into the carrot mixture and stir with a wooden spoon until just combined. Pour the batter into

the prepared pan and bake until firm, 35 to 40 minutes.
4. Meanwhile, as the cake is baking, put the cream cheese in a medium bowl or the bowl of a standing mixer. Add half the confectioner's sugar and, using handheld beaters or the paddle attachment on low speed, combine the sugar and cream cheese. Beat to incorporate remaining sugar.
5. Remove the cake from the oven and let it cool completely in the pan on a cooling rack. Remove the cake from the pan and spread the cream cheese frosting on the cake. Cut into 16 pieces and serve.

NUTRITION INFORMATION
(PER SERVING):

CALORIES 264, CARBS 46G, FIBER 2G, PROTEIN 3G, TOTAL FAT 5G, SATURATED FAT 2G

Cooking Spray
1½ cups all-purpose flour
1 teaspoon ground cinnamon
¾ teaspoon baking powder
¾ teaspoon baking soda
½ teaspoon salt
¼ teaspoon ground allspice
1 pound carrots, peeled and grated (about 3 cups)
½ cup raisins, soaked in warm water for 10 minutes and drained
½ cup walnut or pecan pieces, roughly chopped
4 large eggs
Grated zest and juice from 1 navel orange (⅓ cup juice)
1¼ cups packed light brown sugar
¼ cup granulated sugar
4 ounces (½ brick) cream cheese, at room temperature
1 cup confectioner's sugar

SKINNY TIP § Not a Fan of Nuts or Raisins? I tested this cake with nuts and raisins and without. You know I cut the unnecessary calories wherever possible, but I really liked the texture of the raisins and nuts in this cake, caloric though these ingredients may be. If you choose to leave out the

nuts, you'll save 24 calories per portion. If you skip the raisins, you'll save 22 calories per portion.

KITCHEN TIP § Want More Frosting? Too much frosting on a cake can make my teeth hurt. This recipe has my ideal frosting-to-cake ratio, but you

might like more. Go for it. For every ounce of cream cheese (96 calories), you want to use ¼ cup confectioners' sugar (117 calories). To figure out the per-portion additional calories, divide by 16.

berry cobbler with buttermilk biscuits

PREP TIME: 20 minutes **TOTAL TIME:** 1 hour 10 minutes **MAKES** 9 servings **SERVING SIZE:** 1 biscuit with ¼ cup fruit and ¼ cup yogurt

Here's what it's like when you have homemade buttermilk biscuits in the oven: The house starts smelling really good. Buttery, biscuity, baking good. Then the timer goes off, you take them from the oven, and out they come, golden, earnest, homey. You pick one up. It's hot, so you toss it hand to hand to cool it. The bottom is perfectly browned, so you know it's cooked right and you pull it apart, respectfully. It's tender, barely held together, and out comes a little puff of steam . . . and then . . . into your mouth, and . . . you can't help but close your eyes and take a moment.

Ahem. And that's just the biscuits. Imagine what it's like when you combine them with warm fresh berries, all bubbly and sweet? Words fail me. Try it for breakfast; it's a total treat.

1. Preheat the oven to 400°F.

2. Whisk the cinnamon, sugar, and cornstarch together in a bowl. Add the berries; toss gently to coat. Transfer the mixture to a 9-inch square baking dish.

3. Add the flour, baking powder, baking soda, and salt to a food processor and pulse until combined. Add the butter and process until mixture resembles coarse meal. Transfer the mixture to a large bowl and add the buttermilk slowly, mixing with a wooden spoon until the dough just comes together. The batter will be sticky.

4. Transfer the dough to a lightly floured work surface. Working quickly and handling dough at a minimum to keep the butter cold, use floured fingers to pat the dough to a 1-inch thickness. Use a 2-inch round biscuit cutter or cookie cutter to cut 9 biscuits. Cut the biscuits as close together as possible to minimize scraps. If needed, gather the scraps together to cut additional biscuits until you have 9.

5. Top the berries in the baking dish with the biscuit dough, spacing evenly. Place dish in the oven and bake until berries are bubbling and biscuits are golden brown, about 35 minutes. Transfer the dish to a wire rack and let cool for 10 minutes.

6. Combine the yogurt and almond extract in a small bowl. Serve the biscuits and fruit with a dollop of flavored yogurt.

NUTRITION INFORMATION
(PER SERVING):
CALORIES 318, CARBS 45G, FIBER 6G, PROTEIN 9G, TOTAL FAT 12G, SATURATED FAT 7G

¼ teaspoon ground cinnamon
½ cup granulated sugar
3 tablespoons cornstarch
6 cups (3 pints) fresh blackberries, blueberries, and/or raspberries, or frozen, defrosted
1¾ cups all-purpose flour, plus more for work surface
1 teaspoon baking powder
1 teaspoon baking soda
1 teaspoon kosher salt
8 tablespoons (1 stick) unsalted butter, very cold and cut into pieces
1 cup buttermilk
2¼ cups 2% Greek yogurt
½ teaspoon almond extract

KITCHEN TIP § No Biscuit Cutter? No worries! Grab a tall glass and cut away. For this cobbler, you can also use a 2-ounce ice cream scoop or form dough balls in well-floured hands. If you're making biscuits, the dough-ball method doesn't work well; it will stunt their growth. But for a cobbler, it works just fine. Work quickly. You want that butter to stay cold. But don't let me stress you out; if you're moving slowly, just pop everything back into the fridge and let it chill before transferring it to the oven.

KITCHEN TIP § Homemade Biscuits For homemade biscuits, follow steps 1, 3, and 4. Place cut biscuits on a cookie sheet and bake for 18 minutes at 425° F, until golden. Each biscuit is less than 200 calories.

flan

PREP TIME: 30 minutes TOTAL TIME: 1 hour 15 minutes, plus chilling time MAKES 12 servings SERVING SIZE: 1 slice with sauce

Look at this ingredient list! Can you believe that to make flan, all you need is sugar, milk, eggs, and vanilla? That's it.

Maybe I'm overstating it. In addition to the ingredients, you're also going to learn a few new cooking techniques: how to make caramel and how to use a water bath.

These are the sort of things that seem hard (like cooking duck; see page 198), but once you learn to do them, it's a breeze. And when you give birth to that flan (there's a sound effect and everything), it's impressive.

So get in that kitchen and give it a try. Chances are you already have the ingredients.

NUTRITION INFORMATION (PER SERVING):

CALORIES 200, CARBS 30G, FIBER 0G, PROTEIN 7G, TOTAL FAT 7G, SATURATED FAT 3G

1½ cups granulated sugar
¼ cup water
4 cups milk
6 large eggs
4 large egg yolks
1 teaspoon vanilla extract
Generous pinch of salt
Hot tap water

1. Preheat the oven to 325°F. Prepare a water bath by placing a 9-inch cake pan inside a larger ovenproof pan, like a large flat-bottomed skillet. Be sure that there is enough room between the two containers so that you can add water between them.

2. In a small saucepan, combine ¾ cup of the sugar and the water. Place over medium heat, cover, and cook for 5 minutes. When the mixture comes to a simmer, remove the lid. Do not stir or place any implements in the caramel; just let it be. After 5 to 7 minutes, the caramel will begin to turn brown. Keep an eye on it, as it can go from light brown to deep caramel to bitter and burnt rather quickly. Wait until the bubbles slow down and you see a lot of steam. Remove the pan from the heat and watch it (it will keep cooking). As soon as it's a dark, deep caramel, pour it into the 9-inch cake pan. Tilt the pan so that the bottom is completely covered in caramel. The caramel will harden as it cools, so be sure to work quickly.

3. Bring the milk to a simmer on the stovetop. Meanwhile, whisk together the eggs, yolks, remaining ¾ cup sugar, the vanilla, and salt in a medium bowl. When the milk comes to a simmer (don't let it boil over), slowly whisk it into the egg mixture. Pour this into the cake pan on top of the hardened caramel.

4. Place the filled cake pan into the larger pan, and fill the space between the two pans with hot tap water about ⅔ of the way up the cake pan. Place the nested pans in the oven. Cook until the custard has set (jiggle it carefully so that the water doesn't splash, or test it with the tip of a knife), about 45 minutes.

5. Remove the flan from the water bath and let it sit at room temperature until it is cool enough to touch, about 15 minutes. Transfer the flan to the refrigerator and let it chill for at least 30 minutes (warmer flan) or a few hours (cold flan). Run the tip of a knife around the sides of the plate and invert the pan onto a large rimmed platter (over the sink, as you may have spillage). Serve wedges with spoonfuls of caramel.

"I'll take healthy and happy over cranky and scrawny any day."

KITCHEN TIP § Why a Water Bath?
A water bath insulates your custard so that it cooks gently. If the heat is too high, the eggs will curdle. If you don't like the idea of carrying those nested pans plus water to the stove, you can add the water while the pans are in the oven, using a liquid measuring cup or a coffee pot.

If you do it right, you'll be rewarded with a luxurious, smooth wedge of flan, plus lots of caramel. All for 200 calories.

KITCHEN TIP § Getting Highlights: Honey or Caramel? I have brown hair. And the few times I've splurged on highlights, the colorist always asks: honey or caramel? I hate to be a food dork, but this has always bothered me. There are about as many shades of honey as there are of caramel.

While you make this dessert, you're going to see at least a dozen different caramel colors. Go to the edge of darkness because that bittersweet dark caramel will balance the sweet creamy flan interior. In this recipe, you want contrast. As for my hair, I avoid the semantic debate and let my colorist choose. She's the pro.

KITCHEN TIP § Is Your Flan Stuck?
If the flan has chilled for a while, the caramel may stick to the bottom of the pan. To warm the caramel, run your warm hands over the bottom of the cake pan, or submerge the pan in hot water briefly before inverting.

cherry clafouti

PREP TIME: 10 minutes **TOTAL TIME:** 1 hour **MAKES** 12 servings **SERVING SIZE:** 1 slice

Clafouti is a French dessert that is made in the spring, when cherries appear. The batter is between cake and custard; it's most like a thick crepe.

It takes no more than 10 minutes to prepare the batter in a blender and pour it over the cherries. The clafouti gets puffy and golden as it cooks; it can be made, baked, and cooled in an hour.

This is a good option if friends come by for a snack in the afternoon. I like to make it in a 9-inch cast-iron skillet, which leads to ooohs and aaahs when you present it at the table.

1. Preheat the oven to 400°F. Generously coat a 9-inch round cake pan or cast-iron skillet with cooking spray and set aside.

2. In a blender, combine the eggs, milk, sugar, vanilla, and salt. Blend to combine. Add the flour and pulse to incorporate.

3. Put the cherries in the prepared skillet and pour the batter over the cherries. Place the skillet in the oven and cook until puffed, golden brown, and firm in the center, 30 to 40 minutes. Dust with confectioners' sugar before serving.

NUTRITION INFORMATION
(PER SERVING):
CALORIES 129, CARBS 20G FIBER 1G,
PROTEIN 5G, TOTAL FAT 3G,
SATURATED FAT 1G

Cooking Spray
6 large eggs
1¼ cups whole milk
½ cup granulated sugar
1 tablespoon vanilla extract
¼ teaspoon kosher salt
⅔ cup all-purpose flour
1 12-ounce bag frozen sweet cherries, defrosted and at room temperature, or 1 heaping pint fresh black cherries, stems removed
2 teaspoons confectioner's sugar (see tip, page 251)

KITCHEN TIP § Choosing Cherries
Since this is a recipe that celebrates cherry season, until recently I had only ever made it in the spring, with fresh cherries. I tested my recipe for the cookbook in the winter, so I had to use frozen cherries; I was blown away. It was fantastic, perhaps even better? Now I can eat clafouti year-round.

If you use frozen cherries, just be sure to defrost them and let them come to room temperature before cooking. If you cook them frozen, they will let out a lot of liquid as they cook, which will alter the texture of the batter.

KITCHEN TIP § The Pits
Traditionally, pits are kept inside the cherries when making clafouti. When you cut the cherries to remove the pits, they have a tendency to bleed into the batter. My perspective was: Be authentic! And warn your guests.

Now that I've used frozen (pitted) cherries, I've changed my mind. I was claiming authenticity, but in truth I was being lazy. Pitted cherries make for easier eating, and frozen pitted cherries add no additional work for the cook. Unless you live in cherry country, frozen pitted cherries are the way to go.

rice pudding

PREP TIME: 5 minutes **TOTAL TIME:** About 3 hours **MAKES** 6 servings **SERVING SIZE:** ½ cup

Put away your favorite scented candles; you're about to enjoy three hours of aromatherapy for free. The scent of cinnamon and sweet rice will permeate your home as this pudding cooks—a side benefit to this recipe (and no extra calories!).

1. Preheat the oven to 300°F.

2. In an 8-inch square baking dish, combine the milk, sugar, rice, salt, and cinnamon and whisk to combine. Place in the oven and cook, whisking every 30 minutes or so, until thickened, 2½ to 3 hours. Let cool at room temperature for 20 minutes and refrigerate and serve chilled.

NUTRITION INFORMATION
(PER SERVING):
CALORIES 166, CARBS 25G, FIBER 0G, PROTEIN 6G, TOTAL FAT 5G, SATURATED FAT 3G

4 cups whole milk
⅓ cup granulated sugar
¼ cup uncooked arborio or short-grain rice
½ teaspoon kosher salt
¼ teaspoon ground cinnamon

KITCHEN TIP § Fannie Farmer
I found a version of this recipe in Marion Cunningham's famous *The Fannie Farmer Cookbook*. I've made rice puddings with eggs, cream, and leftover cooked rice, but I was intrigued by a recipe that calls for such a small amount of rice and is baked in the oven. It seemed too good to be true, and when I tried it, I found that the sugars in the milk actually caramelized, and as the rice puffed and expanded, it thickened the milk naturally with its starch.

This rice pudding rocks, and not just because it's delicious. It hits all three of my lower-calorie cooking requirements: it's simple, smart,

and real. This rice pudding is easier to make than stovetop rice puddings, optimizes intelligent cooking techniques, and uses ingredients that Grandma would recognize.

KITCHEN TIP § Stovetop Pudding
Sure, you can cook this on the stovetop. In fact, it takes less time (about 1 hour 15 minutes). But because you've got heat coming from the bottom, you'll have to stir it more frequently—that is, you'll have to babysit it more. Also, more liquid tends to evaporate when cooking on the stove top you'll have a smaller yield.

KITCHEN TIP § Pudding Skin?
When you whisk the rice pudding while it cooks, you're doing three things: First, by moving the rice, you help distribute the starch. Second, you're avoiding the "pudding skin" that tends to form on top of cooked milk dishes. And third, as the pudding cooks, about 1 cup of the milk evaporates, which adds to the rich caramel flavor of the pudding. When you whisk, you ensure that your pudding does not have a "water line" from the pre-evaporation liquid levels and is ready for oven-to-table presentation.

tres leches cake

PREP TIME: 30 minutes **TOTAL TIME:** 1 hour 15 minutes, plus overnight **MAKES** 16 servings **SERVING SIZE:** 2 by 3-inch piece

When I hire a new instructor for The Wooden Spoon, instead of a formal interview, I ask the chef to show me how to prepare a meal that he or she loves. After all, what better way to get to know a person than cook together?

I ask the chef to dig past training and restaurant experience to the foods his or her mother and father and—better yet—grandmothers and grandfathers made. The home kitchen is where a love of food starts—almost every pro chef I know will tell you that.

J.P. Chavez is a personal chef and an instructor at The Wooden Spoon. He is from Mexico City, and so he gave me a Mexican home-cooking class. We started with shrimp ceviche and tortilla soup, moved on to chiles rellenos with pork and tomato sauce, rice and beans, and finished with this outrageous Tres Leches Cake.

Tres Leches is a Mexican celebration cake, and the name means "three milks." It is always made with condensed and evaporated milks, plus another milk or cream. This Tres Leches has all that for under 260 calories per serving.

NUTRITION INFORMATION
(PER SERVING):
CALORIES 257, CARBS 40G, FIBER 1G, PROTEIN 8G, TOTAL FAT 8G, SATURATED FAT 4G

- 5 large eggs, yolks and whites separated
- 1½ teaspoons fresh lemon juice
- 1 cup granulated sugar
- 1 teaspoon kosher salt
- 1 cup all-purpose flour
- 1½ teaspoons baking powder
- ¼ cup whole milk
- 2 teaspoons vanilla extract
- 1 14-ounce can sweetened condensed milk
- 1 12-ounce can evaporated milk
- ½ cup sliced almonds, toasted (see toasting tip, page 110)

1. Preheat the oven to 350°F. Coat a 9x13-inch baking dish with nonstick spray.
2. With electric beaters or a standing mixer with a whisk attachment, beat the egg whites at medium speed until bubbly and frothy, then add the lemon juice. Gradually add ½ cup of the sugar (in a couple of stages) until you have stiff peaks. Set the stiff egg whites aside.
3. Prepare a clean bowl and switch to the paddle attachment (if using a standing mixer). In the bowl, combine the egg yolks, salt, and remaining ½ cup of sugar. Beat until light yellow and able to hold a figure 8 (see tip right), about 3 minutes.
4. Whisk the flour and baking pow-der together in another medium bowl. Add half of the flour mixture to the yolk mixture and mix to incorporate. Add the milk and 1 teaspoon vanilla to the yolk mixture and mix to incorporate. Add the remaining flour mixture and mix again. Stop and scrape down the sides of the bowl as needed to be sure all ingredients are incorporated.
5. Using a flexible spatula, take about ½ cup of the egg whites and squiggle them into the yolk mixture to lighten the yolks. Fold the remaining whites into the yolks in three stages. Pour the batter into the prepared baking dish and place in the oven. Cook until the cake is golden and set and a knife inserted in the center comes out clean, about 40 minutes. Remove the cake from oven, place the pan on a baking rack, and let cool completely.
6. Pierce the cooled cake all over with a knife or fork. In a small bowl, whisk the condensed and evaporated milks and the remaining teaspoon of vanilla in a bowl and pour all over the cake. Cover the cake with plastic wrap and refrigerate overnight. When ready to serve, top with toasted almonds.

"The home kitchen is where a love of food starts—almost every pro chef I know will tell you that."

KITCHEN TIP § Separating Eggs

To separate eggs, you'll need three bowls. Use one bowl as your separating bowl, over which you will divide egg white and yolk. A second bowl is for the reserved yolks, the third for the reserved whites. You want a unique separating bowl because, should you do a less than perfect separating job, you'll have one egg casualty at the most. If you separate the eggs over the bowl of reserved whites, and on the last egg you get a little yolk in the whites, you'll have to start all over again. Ugh.

Though you can get a little white in the yolk, you want to do everything you can to avoid getting yolk in the whites. In order for the whites to whip (and grow to four times their size), they need to be in an environment completely devoid of fat. Yolks are fatty. Keep 'em separate or those whites won't rise to the occasion.

KITCHEN TIP § Ribbon Stage

I love the first part of making a batter, when the sugar and the egg yolks get thick and foamy. It's called the "ribbon" or "figure 8" stage because that's how you know you've got the right texture. You're at optimum foaminess when you can lift your beaters and draw a figure 8 with the batter that drips from your beaters. If you can see that ribbony 8 for a moment, you're all set to proceed with the next phase.

"NO MORE SNEAKING SPOONFULS OF DESSERT IN THE DARK, OVER THE SINK. IT'S NOT ENOUGH THAT YOU HAVE YOUR CAKE. YOU SHOULD enjoy it, too."

lemon curd tartlets

PREP TIME: 25 minutes TOTAL TIME: 25 minutes MAKES 6 servings SERVING SIZE: 1 tartlet

Poor lemon curd. It's an unfortunate name for something so delicious. But lemon curd lovers know this sour-and-sweet sauce is something special and that it partners well with a graham cracker crust and blueberries. It's as easy as it looks, so start squeezing. When life hands you lemons . . .

1. In a medium saucepan, combine the sugar, lemon juice and zest, eggs, cornstarch, and salt. Place over medium heat and whisk constantly, until it's the texture of vanilla pudding, about 6 minutes. Be sure to get into the corners of the pan when you're whisking.

2. Remove the lemon curd from the heat, spoon it into tartlet shells, and top with blueberries. Before serving, dust tartlets with the confectioner's sugar.

NUTRITION INFORMATION
(PER SERVING):
CALORIES 289, CARBS 53G, FIBER 3G, PROTEIN 5G, TOTAL FAT 8G, SATURATED FAT 2G

¾ cup granulated sugar
   Juice and grated zest of 3 lemons
3 large eggs
1½ tablespoons cornstarch
   Pinch of kosher salt
6 mini graham cracker crusts
1 pint (2 cups) fresh blueberries
1 teaspoon confectioner's sugar

SKINNY TIP § Fairy Dust
A dusting of confectioner's sugar adds a nice little something to finish a dessert. A light dusting can be less than a calorie, as a full teaspoon is only 10 calories. You can put the sugar in a sifter, or put it in a fine-mesh strainer and tap-tap-tap, tambourine-style, against your hand. A little sprinkling will fall onto your dessert. A teeny amount of effort makes the dessert a lot more lovely.

pavlova with berries

PREP TIME: 30 minutes **TOTAL TIME:** 1 hour 30 minutes **MAKES** 10 servings **SERVING SIZE:** 1 filled cup

This is a girly dessert. It's a light meringue filled with whipped cream and berries. Have it at a shower, a Mother's Day celebration, a divorce party, or any other time you get the girls together. It's very low in calories, but it has the fun stuff: real whipped cream. There's no sugar added to the whipped cream because there's plenty in the meringues and let's face it: You're sweet enough.

1. For the meringues: Preheat the oven to 300°F. Line two baking sheets with parchment paper.

2. Combine the egg whites and salt in a large bowl and beat with electric beaters or in a standing mixer on medium speed until foamy, about 3 minutes. Add the vanilla, then add the sugar gradually as you continue beating the egg whites until the mixture holds stiff peaks and is foamy and glossy, like marshmallow-scented shaving cream, about 5 more minutes.

3. Dollop the beaten egg whites by the ¼ cupful onto the prepared baking sheets (approximately 10 per sheet). Use the bottom of a tablespoon to "hollow out" the meringues; they should look like puffy nests that are 3 to 4 inches in diameter. Place in the oven and bake for 1 hour.

4. For the topping: Meanwhile, combine the berries, fresh herbs, sugar, lemon zest, and water. Stir to dissolve the sugar and let the berries macerate for at least 30 minutes while the meringues are cooking. Beat the cream using electric beaters or a standing mixer until it can hold its shape and has doubled in size.

5. Just before serving, top each meringue with whipped cream and berries. Garnish with additional herbs.

NUTRITION INFORMATION
(PER SERVING):

CALORIES 209, CARBS 27G, FIBER 1G, PROTEIN 2G, TOTAL FAT 11G, SATURATED FAT 7G

FOR THE MERINGUES:
- 4 large egg whites
- ¼ teaspoon kosher salt
- ½ teaspoon vanilla extract
- 1 cup granulated sugar

FOR THE TOPPING:
- 1 pint (2 cups) fresh berries (blueberries, raspberries, or blackberries)
- 2 tablespoons loosely packed sliced fresh cilantro, basil, or mint, loosely packed, plus small leaves as garnish
- 1 tablespoon granulated sugar
  Grated zest of 1 lemon
- 2 tablespoons water
- 1¼ cups heavy cream

 KITCHEN TIP § Storing Meringues If you don't plan to use the meringues immediately, keep them in the turned-off oven as long as overnight (this will help them dry out). Thereafter, keep them in a sealed plastic bag (with all the air pushed out) in the refrigerator for up to 5 days before using.

KITCHEN TIP § The Daredevil Test This test is not for the fearful. If you're not sure if your egg whites are beaten enough, invert their bowl. If they stay in the bowl, defying gravity, you're good to go. If they fall on the floor, start over.

KITCHEN TIP § Heavy vs. Whipping Cream Heavy cream and whipping cream have the same number of calories. Whipping cream has stabilizers that help the cream stay puffy after it has been whipped. I am not partial to either; I buy whichever is on sale.

 KITCHEN TIP § Savory Herbs in Dessert? Although mint is the herb that appears most frequently in desserts, others work well, too. Both tarragon and rosemary pair well with strawberries, cilantro enhances pineapple, and basil works well with blueberries and raspberries. Try a small amount of these fresh herbs next time you're making a fruit salad.

chocolate-covered strawberries

PREP TIME: 20 minutes **TOTAL TIME:** 1 hour 20 minutes **MAKES** 8 servings **SERVING SIZE:** 3 to 4 berries

Come Valentine's Day, you'll find stemmed chocolate-dipped strawberries everywhere, and they cost as much as $5 per berry! With this recipe, you can make a whole box of strawberries for less than $10. It's fun, simple to do, and your strawberries will look totally professional when done. Try this one with the kids.

1. Melt the semisweet chocolate chips in a double boiler or in the microwave (see tip below). Add the vegetable shortening or oil and stir to make a chocolate sauce.
2. Cover a pan or plate with parchment or wax paper. Dip the strawberries in the chocolate sauce and let cool on prepared pan. If it is a hot or humid day, let cool in

the refrigerator to help the coating set.
3. When chocolate coating has set, melt the white chocolate chips (see tip below). Using the tines of a fork, drizzle melted white chocolate onto the coated strawberries. Cool until hardened; refrigerate again if necessary.

NUTRITION INFORMATION
(PER SERVING):
CALORIES 144, CARBS 17G, FIBER 3G, PROTEIN 2G, TOTAL FAT 10G, SATURATED FAT 5G

- 1 cup semisweet chocolate chips
- ½ teaspoon vegetable shortening or oil
- 1 pound whole strawberries, with stems if possible
- ¼ cup white chocolate chips

KITCHEN TIP § How to Melt Chocolate According to my bag of Ghirardelli chocolate chips, this is how it's done.

Stovetop: Place the chips in a double boiler over gently simmering (not boiling) water. Stir the chips constantly until melted.

Microwave: Heat the chocolate in a microwave-safe container at medium power for 1 to 1½ minutes. Stir until bowl no longer feels warm. Continue heating at 15- to 30-second intervals, stirring until smooth.

KITCHEN TIP § Keep Your Chocolate Dry Chocolate-covered strawberries are a breeze to make. The only thing that might muck up the works is

if your chocolate seizes and becomes grainy while you're dipping the strawberries. This will happen if water gets into the chocolate. To avoid that, do not wash your strawberries before dipping, and avoid any water droplets from the double boiler setup. Be sure to keep the chocolate dry. Whatever you do, don't slice those berries before dipping (no matter how large they are), or the chocolate will seize up instantly. I learned that one the hard way.

KITCHEN TIP § Extra Chocolate for No Additional Calories! As you get toward the end of your strawberry dipping, you might find yourself low on chocolate.

You can "brush" the chocolate onto the strawberries with a pastry brush, or use more chocolate chips. However much you melt, you'll use only 1 cup of the chips to cover these strawberries. So, put the leftover melted chocolate in a sealed container, and keep until you have a need for chocolate.

Also, I've included far more white chocolate than you will use to coat the berries so that you can have Jackson Pollack–style splatter paint fun. Go at it; it's playtime. Chop up the cooled leftovers and use them for The 100-Calorie Cookie (page 259).

profiteroles

PREP TIME: 15 minutes **TOTAL TIME:** 1 hour **MAKES** 6 servings **SERVING SIZE:** 3 filled profiteroles

Profiteroles are adorable pastries that can be filled with anything you like. The dough is simple to make, and the oven "pops" the pastries for you, providing a nice, empty space in the center just waiting for a filling. Classically, they're filled with ice cream, but you can also try lemon curd (page 251), almond-flavored yogurt (page 240), whipped cream, or skillet blueberries (page 263).

1. Preheat the oven to 400°F. Cover a baking sheet with parchment or wax paper.
2. In a medium saucepan over medium heat, combine the milk, butter, sugar, and salt and bring to a simmer. Add the flour to the mixture and cook, stirring vigorously with a wooden spoon, until it pulls away from sides of the pan and forms a ball, about 1 minute.
3. Remove the pan from the heat and allow the pan to cool a bit (just a minute or so, enough so that the eggs don't scramble; see tip, page 123). Add the eggs one at a time, beating well with a wooden spoon after each addition. Continue to beat until the mixture is smooth and glossy, about 2 minutes.
4. Transfer the mixture to a resealable plastic bag. Press the batter toward one of the corners of the bag and snip the corner to create a small hole, about ⅓ inch wide. Pipe the batter into eighteen 1½-inch mounds on a parchment-lined baking sheet; each mound should be about 1 tablespoonful of batter.
5. Bake the profiteroles for 10 minutes, then reduce the heat to 350°F. Continue baking until the puffs are crisp and golden, about 15 minutes more. Turn the oven off and keep the profiteroles in the oven for another 15 minutes. Remove the profiteroles from the oven and place on a cooling rack.
6. When the profiteroles are cool, use a serrated knife to slice each in half horizontally. Fill each profiterole with a small scoop of ice cream, and top with the reserved lid. Serve 3 profiteroles per person, drizzled with 2 teaspoons of chocolate sauce.

NUTRITION INFORMATION
(PER SERVING):

CALORIES 249, CARBS 24, FIBER 2G, PROTEIN 6G, TOTAL FAT 17G, SATURATED FAT 9G

- ½ cup whole milk
- 4 tablespoons (½ stick) unsalted butter
- 1 tablespoon granulated sugar
  Pinch of kosher salt
- ½ cup all-purpose flour
- 2 large eggs
- 1½ cups your favorite ice cream
- ¼ cup chocolate sauce, for serving (see tip below)

KTICHEN TIP § Piping Profiteroles
To get the most pop from your profiteroles, pipe them as tall as they are wide, like little balls. If you pipe the batter wide (like flattened cookies), they won't stand as tall on the plate. Pipe tall.

SKINNY TIP § Chocolate Sauce
If you want to cut calories, skip the chocolate sauce. A serving of profiteroles without chocolate sauce is just 217 calories.
   To make your own chocolate sauce, melt 1 cup of chips in ⅔ cup warm whole milk, whisking until blended. The calories are the same as store-bought.

KTICHEN TIP § Ice Cream Prep
Remove your ice cream from the freezer and let it sit in the fridge for 20 minutes before serving. That will help soften the ice cream for optimal scoopability.

grilled pineapple with ice cream

PREP TIME: 15 minutes **TOTAL TIME:** 30 minutes **MAKES** 8 servings **SERVING SIZE:** 2 pieces pineapple with ice cream

Hot pineapple tastes good, whether it's stir fried as part of a savory dish (page 196) or for dessert. Pineapple is a natural combination of sweet and sour, and when you add heat, it amplifies both flavors.

1. Preheat the grill or a grill pan to medium heat.

2. Cut the top and bottom from the pineapple. Use a serrated knife to peel the pineapple, cutting from top to bottom. Quarter the pineapple lengthwise, remove the core, cut each quarter in half lengthwise, and repeat so that you have sixteen 6-inch-long pieces of pineapple that are about ¾ inch thick.

3. Brush the pineapple with the oil and place the slices on the grill (or in the grill pan). Cook for 3 to 4 minutes per side, or until you can see grill marks. Serve with ice cream.

NUTRITION INFORMATION
(PER SERVING):
CALORIES 156, CARBS 23G, FIBER 2G, PROTEIN 2G, TOTAL FAT 7G, SATURATED FAT 3G

- 1   fresh pineapple
- 2   tablespoons vegetable oil
- 1   pint vanilla ice cream

 SKINNY TIP § Real Ice Cream? Absolutely! You're having grilled fruit for dessert, so there's plenty of room, calorically speaking, to enjoy a little ice cream. Instead of splitting a pint among four people (per the ½-cup serving size), we're dividing it among eight people. When restaurants serve a dessert à la mode, they rarely serve ½ cup of ice cream per serving. We're doing the same thing here. And when you enjoy a small amount, you can afford to make it count.

 KITCHEN TIP § Pineapple Swizzle I like to slice the pineapple into long planks for this recipe because of the way they look; chunks or rounds are familiar, but planks are unexpected. And with this method, you're removing the tough core, but don't throw it away; it makes a terrific swizzle stick in a drink.

 KITCHEN TIP § Savory Grilled Pineapple If you like this recipe, try grilled pineapple as a side dish with dinner or lunch. Sprinkle it with cinnamon or cumin, grill it, and serve with pork, chicken, or fish. Or, turn your leftover grilled pineapple into a salsa with jalapeños, cilantro, and red onion. Once you've mastered grilled pineapple, you'll find lots of ways to use it.

cinnamon baked apples

PREP TIME: 15 minutes TOTAL TIME: 1 hour 10 minutes MAKES 6 servings SERVING SIZE: 1 apple

The key to this recipe is to use small apples. After all, baked apples are really about the tasty brown sugar and butter sauce that sits in the apple cavity. Therefore, your goal is to maximize the filling-to-apple ratio without adding tons of additional butter and sugar. Don't waste calories on a whole, honkin' piece of fruit—optimize the ratio.

This dessert makes a magnificent breakfast, especially with a dollop of almond yogurt (page 240).

1. Preheat the oven to 375°F. Using a melon baller, scoop out the stem, core, and seeds of the apples, leaving the bottom intact. Using a vegetable peeler, remove the skin from the top third of each apple. Put the apples in an 8-inch square baking dish or another dish where they fit snugly.
2. In a small bowl, stir together the sugar, raisins, pecans, and cinnamon. Divide the mixture among the apples, filling the cavity. Pour the cider over and around the apples. Dot each of the apples with butter.
3. Bake the apples until tender, about 50 minutes, basting with cider every 15 minutes or so. Remove from the oven and let the apples stand until cool enough to eat. Baste as needed. Serve the apples warm with the pan juices.

NUTRITION INFORMATION
(PER SERVING):
CALORIES 219, CARBS 41G, FIBER 4, PROTEIN 1G, TOTAL FAT 7G, SATURATED FAT 3G

6 small (4- to 6-ounce) baking apples (such as Golden Delicious or Rome)
⅓ cup packed light brown sugar
¼ cup raisins
¼ cup chopped pecans
½ teaspoon ground cinnamon
1 cup apple cider
2 tablespoons unsalted butter, cut into 6 pieces

KITCHEN TIP § Three Apples to Know My farmers market offers at least 30 varieties of apples, and that's too many for me to keep straight. Plus, if I'm curious I can speak with the farmer, or my grocery store has those little placards that tell me what to do with the apples. Add Google, Wikipedia, and Applepedia (really), and there are lots of ways to learn about apples. That said, here are three apples worth memorizing: a baking apple, a sauce apple, and an eating apple:

1. Rome apples are a baking apple, which means they don't dissolve into sauce when they cook. They get really big, which means less peeling per pound when you're making a pie (or an Apple Crumble, page 238).

2. McIntoshes are for apple sauce (see next tip). Plus, they're nice and sweet to eat.

3. Golden Delicious look like a blushing Granny Smith. Goldens are my apple of choice for all around; they are sweet-tart, and they keep their shape while they cook. They're available year-round at the grocery store.

So, Romes are for baking, Macs are for sauce, GDs are for all around. Class dismissed.

KITCHEN TIP § Applesauce: Yes, You Can Here's a quick apple-sauce recipe: Grab some McIntosh apples. Do not peel them. Remove the cores with a corer or by cutting around the cores. Put the apple chunks in a pot with ¼ cup water. Cook over medium-low heat until the apples break down, about 10 minutes. Stir. Cook over medium heat for another 15 to 20 minutes, until you have a sauce. Stir again. Depending on the sweetness or tartness of your apples, add sugar or lemon juice. Add cinnamon if you like. Remove the skins before serving. (We left them in because they make the sauce a gorgeous pink color.) Pretty easy, right?

pomegranate poached pears

PREP TIME: 10 minutes **TOTAL TIME:** 1 hour **MAKES** 6 servings **SERVING SIZE:** ⅓ pear

Deck the halls! You're simmering pears, allspice, and cinnamon sticks in pomegranate juice; the kitchen is about to smell like holiday potpourri. Don't be surprised if you find a few new friends in the kitchen, noses a-wiggling.

As the pears simmer, they will become crimson on the outside yet stay white on the inside. Slice the pears when you present the dessert, and garnish with cinnamon sticks.

1. Place the pears in a medium pot and cover with the pomegranate juice. Add the cinnamon and allspice to the pot and bring to a simmer. Simmer, partially covered, until you can insert the tip of a knife into the pear, 45 minutes to 1 hour. Carefully turn the pears once while poaching and baste during cooking to ensure even color.

2. Keep the pears in the pomegranate liquid until ready to serve. Serve the individual pear halves on plates, or slice them and fan them out on plates to enjoy the contrast of the pretty red edges.

NUTRITION INFORMATION (PER SERVING):
CALORIES 58, CARBS 15G, FIBER 3G, PROTEIN 0G, TOTAL FAT 0G, SATURATED FAT 0G

- 3 firm Bosc pears, peeled, halved lengthwise, seeds removed (see tip below)
- 1 16-ounce bottle pomegranate juice
- 3 cinnamon sticks, or ¼ teaspoon ground cinnamon
- ¼ teaspoon ground allspice

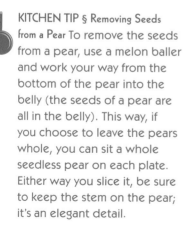

KITCHEN TIP § Removing Seeds from a Pear To remove the seeds from a pear, use a melon baller and work your way from the bottom of the pear into the belly (the seeds of a pear are all in the belly). This way, if you choose to leave the pears whole, you can sit a whole seedless pear on each plate. Either way you slice it, be sure to keep the stem on the pear; it's an elegant detail.

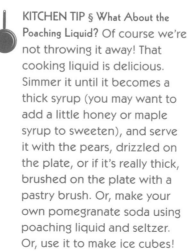

KITCHEN TIP § What About the Poaching Liquid? Of course we're not throwing it away! That cooking liquid is delicious. Simmer it until it becomes a thick syrup (you may want to add a little honey or maple syrup to sweeten), and serve it with the pears, drizzled on the plate, or if it's really thick, brushed on the plate with a pastry brush. Or, make your own pomegranate soda using poaching liquid and seltzer. Or, use it to make ice cubes!

They're especially delicious (and beautiful) in lemonade. Or, add a few tablespoons of salt and sugar to the liquid and use it as a holiday spiced brine for pork.

SKINNY TIP § Gild the Pear The calorie count on this dish is crazy low, so if you like, serve it with toasted hazelnuts and a small wedge of creamy Gorgonzola.

cherry chocolate chip oatmeal cookies (the 100-calorie cookie)

PREP TIME: 25 minutes **TOTAL TIME:** 1 hour **MAKES** 30 servings **SERVING SIZE:** 1 cookie

It's totally counterintuitive to put this recipe in a skinny cookbook. It's actually a riff on the classic "Vanishing Oatmeal" cookie recipe from the lid of the Quaker Oats container, with all the good stuff. You know it, you love it; there's a reason it's been on the lid of the container for decades.

But then, to improve upon perfection, I add two high-calorie ingredients: chocolate chips and dried cherries. Have I lost it? Nope. My goal with this recipe is to satisfy you so completely that one of these cookies, all by itself, is enough.

1. Preheat the oven to 350°F. Line baking sheets with parchment paper.

2. In a medium bowl, whisk the flour, cinnamon, baking soda, and salt together and set aside.

3. Using a hand mixer or a standing mixer with a paddle attachment, beat the butter and sugars until light and fluffy, 1 to 2 minutes. Add the egg and vanilla and beat to incorporate. Add the flour mixture to the butter mixture, beating on low speed to combine. Stir in the oats, chocolate chips, and dried cherries.

4. Drop the dough onto prepared baking sheets by the rounded tablespoonful, leaving 2 inches between cookies. Flatten the cookies with the palm of your hand and bake until the edges are just turning brown, about 20 minutes. Cool for 2 minutes on the baking sheet, then cool completely on baking racks.

NUTRITION INFORMATION
(PER SERVING):

CALORIES 101, CARBS 15G, FIBER 1G, PROTEIN 1G, TOTAL FAT 5G, SATURATED FAT 3G

- ¾ cup all-purpose flour
- ½ teaspoon ground cinnamon
- ½ teaspoon baking soda
- ¼ teaspoon kosher salt
- ½ cup (1 stick) unsalted butter, at room temperature
- ½ cup light brown sugar
- ¼ cup granulated sugar
- 1 large egg
- ½ teaspoon vanilla extract
- 1 cup old-fashioned rolled oats
- ¾ cup semisweet chocolate chips
- ¾ cup dried cherries

SKINNY TIP § The Dayenu Cookie On Passover, there is this song that Jewish people (like me) sing, called "Dayenu." It's about being thankful. *Dayenu* is a Hebrew word that means "it would have been enough for us." Whenever I have this cookie, I can't help but think about that song. "If I could have had the oatmeal cookie with the real butter . . . *it would have been enough for me.*" "If I didn't have the butter, but I had the chocolate chips . . . *it would have been enough for me.*" "If I didn't have the chips, but I had the dried cherries. . . . " You get the drift. And to think this cookie, with all that good stuff, is only a hundred calories, which means that you could have two *and a cup of skim milk* as a guilt-free mid-afternoon snack that's under 300 calories! *Dayenu.*

double-chocolate biscotti

PREP TIME: 15 minutes **TOTAL TIME:** 1 hour 30 minutes **MAKES** 12 servings **SERVING SIZE:** 2 biscotti

My biscotti habit knows no limits. I enjoy them with coffee as a pre-breakfast treat, as a snack with tea in the afternoon, or as dessert. They're not exactly healthy, as they're a combination of flour, sugar, eggs, and two kinds of chocolate. But, if you need chocolate, feed the need. Don't wait until it gets out of hand and you're scarfing down a chocolate-frosted deep-fried donut. Eat defensively: Have a biscotti.

If you prefer bigger biscotti, slice on a sharp diagonal for 12 long cookies.

1. Preheat the oven to 300°F.

2. Combine the flour, cocoa, sugar, baking soda, and salt in a medium bowl and whisk together. In a separate bowl, lightly beat the eggs and almond extract; add the egg mixture to the dry ingredients and stir to combine. Stir in the chocolate chips.

3. Coat a baking sheet with cooking spray. Use your hands to shape the dough into a log about 11 inches long by 3 inches wide.

4. Bake for 30 minutes, remove the pan from the oven, and cool for 10 minutes. Place the cooled log on a cutting surface and use a serrated knife to slice the biscotti into ½-inch slices. Place these slices on the baking sheet, return to the oven, and cook until firm, 25 to 30 minutes. Cool and store in an airtight container.

NUTRITION INFORMATION
(PER SERVING):
CALORIES 89, CARBS 16G, FIBER 2G, PROTEIN 3G, TOTAL FAT 3G, SATURATED FAT 1G

- ⅔ cup all-purpose flour
- ½ cup unsweetened cocoa powder
- ⅓ cup granulated sugar
- ½ teaspoon baking soda
  Pinch of kosher salt
- 2 large eggs
- ½ teaspoon almond extract
- ⅓ cup chocolate chips
  Cooking Spray

KITCHEN TIP § **Wet Hands** This is a stiff, sticky dough, so moisten your hands before shaping it into a log and it will be much easier to manipulate.

SKINNY TIP § **Sweet Restraint** I don't have a sweet tooth. My guilty pleasures are more along the lines of crispy bacon than cake and cookies. If you take your coffee without sugar, this recipe is perfect for you: chocolaty yet not too sweet. If you live for sweets, use ½ cup chips instead of ⅓ cup, for an additional 11 calories per serving.

KITCHEN TIP § **Better Baking?** Well, Well . . . Many baking recipes ask you to "make a well" before you combine the wet and dry ingredients. This means you make a little indentation in the center of the dry ingredients, pour the wet ingredients into it, and then stir to incorporate.

This is the best way to incorporate wet and dry ingredients; you're less likely to get flour clumps or overmix.

pecan snowballs

PREP TIME: 40 minutes **TOTAL TIME:** 1 hour 15 minutes **MAKES** 16 servings **SERVING SIZE:** 3 cookies

These cookies are tender like shortbread, with a gentle, rich pecan flavor. Though I call these little guys Pecan Snowballs, you may know them as Mexican wedding cookies or Russian tea cookies. Call them what you like; a cookie by any other name would taste as sweet.

NUTRITION INFORMATION
(PER SERVING):
CALORIES 107, CARBS 13G, FIBER 0G, PROTEIN 1G, TOTAL FAT 6G, SATURATED FAT 3G

1. Preheat the oven to 350°F. Line two cookie sheets with parchment paper.

2. In a medium bowl, combine the butter and ¼ cup of the sugar. Using an electric beater at medium speed, beat until fluffy, about 4 minutes. Add the vanilla and beat to combine.

3. Put the pecans and 1 tablespoon sugar in the bowl of a food processor. Chop until nuts are very fine, about 30 seconds. Add the flour, cinnamon, and salt and pulse to combine.

4. Add the flour mixture to the butter mixture. Using electric beaters at low speed, beat until combined. The dough will be crumbly (don't overwork it; see tip below).

5. To form cookies, press the dough into the bowl of a teaspoon, packing it firmly. To get the dough out of the spoon, tap the spoon on the baking sheet. Place the shaped dough on the prepared sheets, flat side down, at 1-inch intervals. Bake until golden on the bottom, about 15 minutes.

6. Place the remaining ½ cup sugar in a shallow bowl. Toss the warm cookies with the sugar, no more than 5 cookies at a time. Remove the coated cookies to a plate and let cool.

- 6 tablespoons (¾ stick) unsalted butter, at room temperature
- ¾ cup plus 1 tablespoon confectioner's sugar
- ½ teaspoon vanilla extract
- ⅓ cup chopped pecans, toasted (see tip below)
- 1 cup all-purpose flour
- ⅛ teaspoon ground cinnamon
  Pinch of kosher salt

KITCHEN TIP § **How to Toast Pecans** Toasting nuts makes them more flavorful. To toast pecans, put them in a single layer in a small skillet, place in a 350°F oven (or toaster oven), and cook until fragrant, about 8 minutes. Remove the nuts from the skillet and let cool before using. You can also toast them over medium-low heat on the stovetop in 3 to 5 minutes, but keep an eye on them, as they can go from brown to burned quickly. Oven cooking is more moderate.

KITCHEN TIP § **How Crumbly Is "Crumbly"?** Pretty darn crumbly, as it turns out. This is a short dough, the same as used in shortbread cookies. A "short" dough means there's a lot of butter and no egg, so the flour is working extra hard to hold everything together. On the pro side, it's tender; on the con side, the dough doesn't hold together all that well, which is why I've got the workaround in step 5 of pressing the dough into a teaspoon. If you had to shape the cookies in your hands, the dough would never hold together. But by using a teaspoon as a mold, it does. If you have shaped teaspoons (I've seen hearts, shells, stars), this is the time to use them!

skillet blueberry flambé

PREP TIME: 10 minutes **TOTAL TIME:** 10 minutes **MAKES** 6 servings **SERVING SIZE:** ¼ cup blueberries

A hot buttered skillet and fresh blueberries are a little bit of magic. And as magicians know, putting on a show is just as important as the magic itself. Amplify this simple dish by setting it on fire, and no one need know how simple it really is.

I like to use these berries as a topping over ice cream or Greek frozen yogurt, but try it with pavlova (page 252) and lemon curd (page 251) or angel food cake.

1. Melt the butter in a medium skillet over medium-high heat. Add the blueberries to the skillet and cook to warm the berries through, about 1 minute. Either turn off the heat, tilt the pan, and carefully use a lit match to light the gin; or, if you have a gas stove, carefully tip the skillet just enough so that the flames come in contact with the gin; they will ignite immediately. In either case, the gin will quickly ignite and flambé; be ready for it. The flames will die out on their own in 10 seconds or less.

2. Season the berries with salt and serve warm over whatever you like.

NUTRITION INFORMATION (PER SERVING):
CALORIES 72, CARBS 7G. FIBER 1G, PROTEIN 0G, TOTAL FAT 4G, SATURATED FAT 2G

- 2 tablespoons unsalted butter
- 1 pint (2 cups) fresh blueberries
- 1 shot (1 fluid ounce/2 tablespoons) gin or 80-proof booze of your choice (see tip below)
- Pinch of kosher salt

KITCHEN TIP § Does It Have to Be Gin? This recipe was inspired by The Spotted Pig gastropub in Manhattan, and they use gin to flambé their berries. You can use rum, vodka, Grand Marnier, or any 80-proof (or higher) booze you like.

lace cookies (florentines)

PREP TIME: 20 minutes   **TOTAL TIME:** 35 minutes   **MAKES** 15 servings   **SERVING SIZE:** 2 cookies

I used to love going into Italian bakeries when I was young, in part because the baker would always toss a free cookie to a well-behaved kid. I'd always ask for a florentine. Those flat lacy cookies were sometimes chocolate dipped (double yum), and had a texture unlike the other cookies—brittle yet buttery, thin and full of little bumps and holes. My mom and I could make regular cookies, muffins, banana bread, but how did they make that thin brittle cookie?

I kept this mystery in the back of my mind until I went to culinary school and learned that it's uneven crushed nuts that create the lacy texture. Now I think of this dessert as very adult, something to enjoy with espresso.

1. Preheat the oven to 350°F. Line two baking sheets with parchment paper.

2. Put the almonds in the bowl of a food processor. Pulse three or four times, until nuts are coarsely chopped.

3. In a medium saucepan, combine the sugar, corn syrup, and butter over medium heat and bring to a simmer, stirring. Remove from the heat and stir in the flour, vanilla, salt, and chopped almonds until combined.

4. Drop the batter by the teaspoonful onto the prepared sheets. The cookies will spread (a lot) during baking, so allow for no more than 8 cookies per sheet. Bake the cookies until they have spread and are golden, 8 to 10 minutes.

5. Remove the baking sheets from the oven, and remove the cookies and parchment from the baking sheet. Let the cookies cool on the parchment on cooling racks until crisp, about 10 minutes.

NUTRITION INFORMATION (PER SERVING):
CALORIES 98, CARBS 14G, FIBER 1G, PROTEIN 1G, TOTAL FAT 5G, SATURATED FAT 2G

½ cup almonds, toasted (see toasting tip, page 110)

½ cup packed dark or light brown sugar

¼ cup light corn syrup (see tip right)

3 tablespoons unsalted butter

3 tablespoons all-purpose flour

½ teaspoon vanilla extract

Pinch of kosher salt

"If an ingredient isn't spelled right, it's not going to taste right. Lite ain't rite."

 KITCHEN TIP § Kitchen Efficiency Since this recipe makes 30 cookies, and you're limited to 8 cookies per baking sheet, you're going to be making four sheets of cookies. Since the batter is sticky and gets harder as it sits, here's how to do it most efficiently: Portion out 8 spoonfuls of batter on each of your two prepared sheets. While they're cooking, prepare another two sheets of parchment with cookie dough. As soon as the cooked cookies come out of the oven, remove the parchment and cookies and let them cool. You can immediately put the new parchment with cookie dough on those hot sheets and put them back in the oven.

 SKINNY TIP § Beware Lite Corn Syrup Light corn syrup is what you need for this recipe. "Light" here refers to color (there is also dark corn syrup, thus the need to be explicit). Do not confuse it with "lite" corn syrup. Lite has ⅓ fewer calories than regular corn syrup and is a whole lot less effective for this recipe; it will leave these cookies greasy and soft. I know, sometimes the grocery store feels like one big skinny booby trap. As a general rule, if an ingredient isn't spelled right, it's not going to taste right. Lite ain't rite.

KITCHEN TIP § Dessert or Accessory? When warm, florentines are malleable, so you can roll them into tubes or make them into small cups to hold ice cream. Use a thin spatula or dull knife to pick up the warm cookies, and drape them over a small bowl or wooden dowel to create the shapes you like.

flourless chocolate cake

PREP TIME: 15 minutes TOTAL TIME: 1 hour and 15 minutes MAKES 12 servings SERVING SIZE: 1 slice

When you serve this cake to friends and family, everyone will want the recipe. It has a crunchy, glossy top crust like the best brownies and a soft interior. Since it's flourless, it's thick with chocolate and has a truffle texture on the inside.

This cake is rustic, which is a euphemism for rough around the edges. I find crumbly cakes and free-form pies more inviting than prissy tartlets and fussy seven-layer cakes. When you make this cake, there will be crumbs and little bits that you can steal off the plate with your fingertip. This cake is perfectly imperfect, which is exactly what makes it so inviting.

1. Preheat the oven to 350°F. Coat a 9-inch cake pan with cooking spray, cover with parchment paper, and coat parchment with cooking spray.

2. Melt the butter in a small saucepan over medium heat, add the chips, and remove from heat. Let sit until chips have melted (about 1 minute) and whisk together.

3. Meanwhile, whisk together the sugar and cocoa in a medium bowl. Make a well (see tip, page 261) in the cocoa mixture, add eggs, vanilla, and salt, and whisk to combine. Add the melted chocolate to the dry mixture and whisk to incorporate. Pour the mixture into the prepared pan and place in oven. Cook until set, about 1 hour. Remove the cake and place on a cooling rack.

4. To serve, first allow cake to cool completely—at least 1 hour. Invert the cake pan onto a large plate or baking sheet and tap pan gently so that the cake falls out (it will be upside down). Remove parchment from cake and invert again onto a large serving plate (the cake will be right side up). Cut into 12 slices and serve, dusted with cocoa powder.

NUTRITION INFORMATION
(PER SERVING):
CALORIES 217, CARBS 24G, FIBER 2G, PROTEIN 4G, TOTAL FAT 14G, SATURATED FAT 8G

Cooking Spray
½ cup (1 stick) unsalted butter
1 cup semisweet chocolate chips
¾ cup granulated sugar
⅔ cup unsweetened cocoa powder, plus 1 teaspoon for garnish
4 large eggs
¼ teaspoon vanilla extract
Generous pinch of kosher salt
Cocoa powder, for garnish

KITCHEN TIP § The Magic of "Rustic" Culinary school students are asked to choose one of two paths: culinary (savory) or baking (pastry). But it's not really a choice—the two tracks demand totally different personality types—so it is more about your proclivity. The bakers tend to be more precise, weighing and measuring, while the savory cooks are more likely to throw their ingredients in a pan, taste, and adjust. Bakers are bakers and cooks are cooks. You can't be as casual with baking as you are with cooking because you can't add this and that to a cake once it's baked. With savory cooking, you can season to taste and respond to your ingredients and the seasons; it's an improvisation.

Because of this, a culinary student in a baking class is like a fish riding a Vespa. As one of these fish, my pastry always tasted good, but the i's weren't dotted and the t's weren't crossed. My pastry instructor didn't want to knock my confidence, so she'd tell me that I had a real skill for "rustic" desserts. If your baking is delicious but a little lopsided, remember: you're not doing it wrong, you're doing it rustic.

INDEX

A